ALEXIS DE TOCQUEVILLE was born in 1805 at Verneuil of an aristocratic Norman family. After being called to the Bar in 1825 he became assistant magistrate at Versailles. In 1831 a government mission to the United States, ostensibly to study the penal system, resulted in a book, *Democracy in America* (1835), which gave him a European reputation and became one of the classics of liberal literature. In 1833 he had visited England and married an Englishwoman, keeping an extensive diary of his *Journeys to England and Ireland* (translated in 1958). In 1839 he was returned to the Chamber of Deputies by the Norman farmers, and after the Revolution of 1848 he was the most formidable opponent of the Socialists and extreme Republicans. In 1849 he was vice-president of the Assembly, and from June to October was minister of Foreign Affairs. After the coup d'état, he retired to agricultural pursuits on his Norman estate, and there wrote the first volume of his most important work, *L'Ancien Régime et la Révolution* (1856). He died in 1859.

_Julie_

# ALEXIS DE TOCQUEVILLE

---

# THE ANCIEN REGIME
# AND THE FRENCH
# REVOLUTION

TRANSLATED BY
STUART GILBERT

WITH AN INTRODUCTION
BY HUGH BROGAN

COLLINS/FONTANA

First published in Fontana 1966
Fourth impression September 1974

© in the translation Doubleday & Company Inc. 1955
© in Introduction Hugh Brogan

Made and Printed in Great Britain by
C. Nicholls & Company Ltd.
The Philips Park Press
Manchester 11

This translation by Stuart Gilbert first published
under the title 'The Old Régime and the French
Revolution' by Anchor Books 1955

# CONTENTS

INTRODUCTION *by Hugh Brogan* 7

FOREWORD 23

PART ONE

1 Conflicting opinions of the Revolution at its outbreak  33
2 How the chief and ultimate aim of the Revolution was not, as used to be thought, to overthrow religious and to weaken political authority in France  37
3 How, though its objectives were political, the French Revolution followed the lines of a religious revolution and why that was so  41
4 How almost all European nations had had the same institutions and how these were breaking down everywhere  45
5 What did the French Revolution accomplish?  49

PART TWO

1 Why feudalism had come to be more detested in France than in any other country  52
2 How administrative centralization was an institution of the old régime and not, as is often thought, a creation of the Revolution or the Napoleonic period  61
3 How paternal government, as it is called today, had been practised under the old régime  70
4 How administrative justice and the immunity of public servants were institutions of the old régime  80
5 How the idea of centralized administration was established among the ancient powers, which it supplanted, without, however, destroying them  84
6 Of the methods of administration under the old régime  88
7 How in France, more than in any other European country, the provinces had come under the thrall of the metropolis, which attracted to itself all that was most vital in the nation  98
8 How France had become the country in which men were most like each other  103

9 How, though in many respects so similar, the French were split up more than ever before into small, isolated, self-regarding groups 107

10 How the suppression of political freedom and the barriers set up between classes brought on most of the diseases to which the old régime succumbed 121

11 Of the nature of the freedom prevailing under the old régime and of its influence on the Revolution 132

12 How, despite the *progress of civilization*, the lot of the French peasant was sometimes worse in the eighteenth century than it had been in the thirteenth 143

PART THREE

1 How towards the middle of the eighteenth century men of letters took the lead in politics and the consequences of this new development 160

2 How vehement and widespread anti-religious feeling had become in eighteenth-century France and its influence on the nature of the Revolution 170

3 How the desire for reforms took precedence of the desire for freedom 178

4 How, though the reign of Louis XVI was the most prosperous period of the monarchy, this very prosperity hastened the outbreak of the Revolution 189

5 How the spirit of revolt was promoted by well-intentioned efforts to improve the people's lot 199

6 How certain practices of the central power completed the revolutionary education of the masses 206

7 How revolutionary changes in the administrative system preceded the political revolution and their consequences 211

8 How, given the facts set forth in the preceding chapters, the Revolution was a foregone conclusion 221

APPENDIX

The *pays d'états*, with special reference to Languedoc 229

NOTES 240

GENERAL NOTES 306

SUGGESTIONS FOR FURTHER READING 319

# INTRODUCTION BY HUGH BROGAN

Except for Americans, crossing the Channel has always been a more epochal experience than crossing the Atlantic. Any veteran traveller will agree to this, as a proposition on the purely physical plane, at once; but I am not sure that it is nearly so true there as it is at the cultural level. The Americans and the English can understand each other pretty well, intellectually, even when their tastes differ; and often their tastes are the same. But the French and the English have always communicated in terms of mingled fascination and incredulity. Alexis de Tocqueville, who knew a great deal about both sides of the Channel and both sides of the Atlantic, was particularly conscious of the immense difference between the political institutions of the countries lying to North and South of the smaller body of water, and the immense similarities between the institutions of those lying East and West of the larger. But a man with a different set of references might have been equally struck, as so many have been, by the same phenomena in the realms of literature, music, painting, and, nowadays, films (*Les Cahiers du Cinéma* is the latest illustration of the sort of madness that descends when the French try to understand *les Anglo-Saxons*). And the Channel stretches, with its usual effect, between the two nations' conceptions of history.

I am not here referring to academic history, which invariably tends to be a matter of technique (like so much other modern art) and must be appreciated as such. Since the Second World War, as a matter of fact, there has been a remarkable efflorescence of French historiography, building on the work of such men as Marc Bloch and Georges Lefebvre, which English historians have regarded with admiration and awe, to which they have, indeed, made their own notable contributions. But the sad fact is that whatever happens in the long run, a nation's view of its past is not likely to be substantially affected, at any given moment, by what the academics of the day are doing or saying. What it thinks of as its history is shaped much

more by such things as the love of picturesque incident and
narrative, or the need for political myths. Apply this truth to
England and France, and it instantly becomes apparent that,
on the whole, the English see their past as something complete,
something irrelevant, a source, maybe, of entertainment and in-
struction, but never dangerous as living things are dangerous;
whereas for the French the past is an arsenal of weapons for
use in the battle of life: a source of slogans, myths, ideas, values
and examples with which to maintain party, class, or national
solidarity; with which to threaten the ideological foe; with
which, in short, to understand and master the present.

The English, it is true, have a few myths of their own in
contemporary use—the fast-fading poppies of Flanders fields;
Jarrow; Munich; Suez. But what are these to the powers con-
jured up by the innumerable symbolic dates of French history,
whether years—1789, 1830, 1848, 1958—or days—IX Ther-
midor, XVIII Brumaire, 4 September, 18 June? Friendly
critics will perhaps put this down to the superior intellectual
imagination of the French (and to their better educational
system); unfriendly ones may trace it to the deep divisions of
French society that seem to endure through every régime,
every war and every peace—divisions that are perhaps exacerbated by time, not healed. But the fact cannot be overlooked,
however it is to be explained. And a modern country in which
such a matter as the process for the canonisation of Joan of Arc
could have strong political overtones is one that will always
seem particularly foreign to English eyes.

Nevertheless, the effort to understand it must be made. This
is not only so that in future the Foreign Office may have the
sense to avoid such gaffes as the Queen's allusion, during her
State visit to Germany, to the Waterloo victory as a striking
instance of traditional Anglo-German friendship. The French,
mindful of all that has happened since Blucher rescued
Wellington, were outraged. But, though there really is no
excuse for such insular oafishness at this time of day, there is
a much more important reason for our continuing to attempt
to understand the French, the French past, and the French attitude to history. It is, that that past, that history, is so largely
our own; that our neighbours, different though they are, and

wide though the ditch of the Channel has proved to be, have in fact influenced English history and stamped the English character more than any other people whatever. To understand them is to understand ourselves; and we must also learn, or attempt to learn, the lesson that their view of their history teaches: the lesson that the past is not dead, but determines our lives more than we necessarily realise.

The great Revolution instils this lesson more thoroughly than any other part of the French saga.

After all, its challenge directly provoked one of Britain's heroic periods; yet we do a good number of our ancestors a stupid injustice if we succumb to the glamour of that heroism too thoughtlessly. In our taste for the picturesque, we love to remember Pitt trusting that England would save Europe by her example; Nelson refusing to see the signal; Wellington and the thin red line. But we forget Fox hailing the fall of the Bastille; the ideological panic that led us to postpone essential reforms for more than thirty years; the elimination of the last traces of Irish autonomy; and the fact that what Byron called "the crowning carnage, Waterloo" ensured the triumph of re-action throughout Europe—for the Germans, Italians, Belgians and Poles the triumph of liberty *à l'anglaise* meant the destruction of the first real freedom that, thanks to the Revolution and Napoleon, they had ever known. Furthermore, the peaceful transition from the old order to the new that has characterised English history ever since 1688 has blinded us, too often, to two important facts: first, that this transition owed less to the instinctive wisdom of the race, than to the salutary fright we gave ourselves in the seventeenth century, which the French kindly renewed in the eighteenth; second, that not all countries have been free to choose, as we have been. Perhaps the English of today need the lesson that there are circumstances in which revolution is not only inescapable, but right, less than the Americans do; but there have been times, in the not-remote past, as when Churchill tried to stamp out Bolshevism by armed intervention in Russia, when our self-satisfaction has seriously impaired our perception of moral and political reality. Ever since Burke pitied the plumage, but forgot the dying bird, this has been a weakness of the British attitude to the Revolution; we have condescended to the French, with their strange passion for killing each other, too much; and in recent times we have tended to make the same mistake *vis-à-vis* revolutions in other parts of the world. If the open-minded study of the French affair will correct this attitude—and it is hard to think of a better way—then it is clearly important that we begin that study. And we cannot begin it better than with Alexis de Tocqueville's *Ancien Régime*, which, in its author's opinion, showed that the Revolution was both inevitable and just.

## II

There are few historical monographs which can be recommended in such terms; and almost none which deserve them after more than a hundred years. Yet it is generally agreed that the *Ancien Régime* does. It has been preserved against time partly, of course, of those salty virtues for lack of which so many no less conscientious studies fall dead from the press: by its lucidity, brevity, wit, masculine intelligence and highly personal style. But, valuable though they are, these qualities do not explain why Professor Geyl calls it "one of the world's great masterpieces of historical interpretation"; why the great Lefebvre owned that it awakened his respect and admiration; why Lord Acton felt that he could, without seeming ridiculous, say of its author: "He is always wise, always right, and as just as Aristides."* And these distinguished critics have had their judgments endorsed by countless ordinary readers. Yet to understand the justice of these encomia, and the vitality of the book that provoked them, it is necessary to do more than read it and succumb to its fascination. Some work of reflection and analysis must be attempted before it will yield up all its greatness. Well, at least it is not disagreeable work.

*There is, perhaps, a sting in the tail here. Aristides, it will be remembered, was exiled from Athens because his fellow-citizens were tired of hearing him called "the Just". Indeed, Acton goes on to say: "His intellect is without a flaw, but it is limited and constrained. He knows political literature and history less well than political life; his originality is not creative, and he does not stimulate with gleams of new light or unfathomed suggestiveness."

But before the task is undertaken, it may be sensible to consider the life and character of the author. For (to anticipate the argument) the most cursory reading of the *Ancien Régime* shows that it has the usual twin aspects of French historical writing: it is both an account of time past, and a challenge to the present. Tocqueville, of course, wrote for a present, that of Napoleon III, which is now itself remote (if less remote, General de Gaulle being the master of France, than it seemed ten years ago). But, as we shall see, his challenge is still real. He expresses convictions that are by no means irrelevant to our concerns today; and to understand how this can be, and how he came to express them through an historical work, it is necessary to rely not only on such generalisations about the French as I began this essay with; not only on such analysis of the text as that with which I shall end it; it is also essential to know something of Tocqueville himself. For *The Ancien Régime and the Revolution* is in some ways a unique, because very personal, synthesis of study and experience. To catch its full flavour we must look at the man who achieved it.

### III

His gifts and his background equipped him ideally to be an historian of the Revolution. On his mother's side he was descended from the great Malesherbes, protector of the Encyclopaedists, President of the Cour des Aides, defender of the *parlements*, under Louis XV: would-be reformer of the Court and administration under Louis XVI; defender of the ex-King at his trial under the Revolution. For this last heroic step Malesherbes was eventually sent to the scaffold on the usual trumped-up charges of the Reign of Terror. Most of his family perished with him; but his younger grand-daughter and her husband, Hervé de Tocqueville, who were left alive in the Conciergerie prison for a time after Malesherbes' execution, escaped death through the fall of Robespierre. They lived in comfortable obscurity under the Directory and Napoleon, confining themselves to the circles of those aristocrats who had neither emigrated nor reconciled themselves to the new order.

But the memory of Malesherbes ensured that from the beginning the Tocquevilles' youngest son, Alexis—born in 1805—was aware of his share in the great tradition of the *parlementaire* nobility, and of the possibility of doing great service to France. It was perhaps the consciousness of his descent that enabled him to defy the prejudices of his father's family and embark, as a young man, on a legal career, although, as was pointed out to him, the Tocquevilles had always been *noblesse d'épée*.

The paternal heritage was indeed markedly different from that of Malesherbes. Where the *noblesse de robe* had been engaged in a more or less continuous dispute with the monarchy ever since the Fronde, a dispute that became more and more heated as the eighteenth century wore on, the Tocquevilles, country nobility of the Cherbourg peninsula, had a tradition of personal loyalty to the King, which usually expressed itself as a readiness to help fight his wars for him. The Revolution did not change this tradition; rather, the House of Bourbon became the object of a sort of cult for the nobility that had fallen with it; and when in 1814 the Kings returned, Hervé de Tocqueville entered the Royal service, and was employed as Prefect in various departments from then until the July Revolution of 1830, when, refusing to take the oath to the usurping Louis Philippe, he retired once more, and this time permanently, into private life. But, as with Malesherbes, so with Hervé: another's life-work gave Alexis de Tocqueville every opportunity of gaining valuable insights into some of the most salient features of French society both before and after the Revolution. Thus it was wholly natural that, the son of a Prefect, he was the first to discover that the Prefecture was but the Intendancy of the old order under another name.

It must not, however, be supposed that it was easy for Tocqueville to reconcile his family traditions with his own experience. On the contrary, as he saw the restored Bourbon monarchy drifting with steady imbecility towards reaction and ruin, he grew less and less capable of giving it the unquestioning loyalty of his class. It became impossible for him to accept the ancient dogmas of divine right and aristocracy in which he had been reared. Long before the Revolution of July he perceived that a new age of democracy was dawning, with which it was essential to come to terms; and when Charles X was overthrown, and was succeeded by a seemingly more adaptable King, Tocqueville, with a heavy heart, recognised the necessity of the change, and as a junior magistrate took the oath of allegiance that his father refused.

The gulf that opened up between him and his family as a result of this action was painful enough; but he soon discovered that his legitimist connexions made him unacceptable to his Orleanist superiors also. Plainly, a fresh departure was needed, if his lively ambition was to be satisfied; so he crossed the Atlantic to study the only working model of a democracy then known to the world. He would write a book, he planned, which should be an anatomy of the United States and the coming democratic order. By its excellence it would vindicate his opinions, bring him fame, and launch his political career.

This is not the place to attempt a description of *Democracy in America*. It is enough to say that with the publication of the first two volumes, in 1835, its author achieved his goal. The book was immediately recognised as destined to be a classic of both politics and sociology; and doors opened to him everywhere. Soon he was a member of the Institut, and had the *entrée* of all the best drawing-rooms of London and Paris, in an age when genius was to be found there more frequently than nowadays (if indeed there are any drawing-rooms left); and in 1839 was elected to the Chamber of Deputies.

He was not very successful there. He sat on the left of the Chamber, and considered himself a liberal, supporting the monarchy of July, but not the narrow, timid, shortsighted government of Louis Philippe's most famous minister, Guizot. The new monarchy, Tocqueville quickly saw, and said, was as incapable of reforming itself as the Bourbon kingship had been; and at length he publicly predicted that it would meet a similar end. But no attention was paid to Cassandra, and in 1848 Louis Philippe went the way of Charles X.

Tocqueville was no longer the somewhat romantic idealist of 1830. His study of democracy had convinced him that it had potentials for tyranny quite as dangerous as those associated with monarchy or oligarchy; and he feared that the February Revolution, like that of 1789, had let the genie out of the bottle.

Political and social equality, he saw, were things just in themselves, and inevitable, given the circumstances of the age; but
they tended to lead on, as they had under the Jacobins, to what
he regarded as visionary and dangerous demands for economic
equality too. The clamour of the people of Paris for food, work,
and shelter he pitied and scorned as proceeding from their
ignorance of the immutable laws of political economy; and he
applauded the willingness of the bourgeoisie and rural con-
servatives to unite to shoot the workers down in the ferocious
June Days. But, striking though this departure from the gentle
principles of liberalism was, Tocqueville did not cease to believe
in liberty and equality, and to work, according to his lights,
for a socio-political structure in which the interests of the various
classes of France would be harmoniously and freely reconciled,
as they had not been since 1789. Alas, his last and bitterest
disappointment was at hand. He and his friends entered the
first ministry of the Presidency of Louis Napoleon Bonaparte in
the spring of 1849; but they were too independent for the President, who was already plotting to make himself Emperor, and
in the autumn they were dismissed. Thereafter there was nothing
Tocqueville could do but watch helplessly as Louis Napoleon
moved towards the destruction of parliamentary institutions in
France. In December, 1851, the blow fell: in a *coup d'état* the
President, with the aid of the army, eliminated the liberals from
politics, and made himself sole master of France. Then Tocqueville at last followed his father into the internal exile which had
swallowed up so many Frenchmen in the previous half-century.

It will be proper to expound Tocqueville's political ideas
when we reach the appropriate passages of the *Ancien Régime*;
suffice it to say, here, that he never ceased to cherish the ideals
of what, today, we would call Western Democracy; and that
he held liberty to be the most important of those ideals. He had
seen it extinguished by Louis Napoleon in an instant more
completely than it had been since the fall of the first Napoleon.
He had seen the ruler of France use the governmental apparatus
and exploit the timidity of the masses to overwhelm his opponents. How had it been possible? Was there some evil
fatality at work in French history forbidding the achievement
and maintenance of liberty? With these questions in mind

Tocqueville resumed his writing trade, ambition's last hope, and turned, as a Frenchman would, to the past to explain the present.

As he saw it, the clue to the problem was centralisation. Long ago, in America, he had been impressed by the connexion between local self-government and political liberty. Now, in France, Napoleon III, like his predecessors, disposed of administrative machinery which ensured that all initiative and decision should come from Paris. Local government in France had been slightly decentralised under the July Monarchy; but the system of Prefects remained intact, and was the chief means by which whoever commanded Paris could be sure that his will would make itself felt in the provinces. The efficiency and docility of the Prefects, joined to the long-instilled inertia of the people, made the tyrant's task simple. How had this over-powerful machine come into existence?

At first Tocqueville, like all his contemporaries, assumed that, essentially, centralisation was the work of Napoleon I. The answer to the question therefore lay in the annals of the Consulate and Empire. With this in mind he began to plan a book on the subject (the great Napoleon had always fascinated him, anyway) and he even got so far as to write two chapters of it, on the *coup d'état* of Brumaire, in which he traced French submission to the first Bonaparte (and, readers might infer, to the second) to weariness and fear. But the more he studied, the clearer it became that it was not Napoleon, nor even the Revolutionary assemblies, who had instituted the centralisation from which France suffered. It had been an invention of the old order. With the old order, therefore, he would begin.

As it happened, Tocqueville's early death (in 1859) meant that his grand projected history of the Revolution and Empire was never finished. He had always been a slow worker, writing, re-writing, and agonizing over his books: it had taken him eight years to produce *Democracy in America,* and his history was planned on an even larger scale. But in 1856 its first volume was brought out, under the title *The Ancien Régime and the Revolution*. In its pages we can today discover as much as Tocqueville himself ever did of the ideals that animated him and the character of the nation that he loved, and of which he was so intimately a part (he could trace his ancestry back to the time of the Norman Conquest). We can also admire the book as the earliest truly dispassionate account of the catastrophe with which it deals. Inevitable mistakes and prejudices have been detected, of course, by modern historians. But it still stands up as a model of historical writing. It is time to examine it in detail.

IV

It is not always easy to tell the wood from the trees when reading Tocqueville. This difficulty arises from his method of setting to work. He builds up his effects by countless small touches: short sentences, short paragraphs, short chapters. He does this, paradoxically enough, in the cause of lucidity, stating every point in his argument as simply and tersely as possible, so as to avoid confusion in his own mind, and the reader's, as to what he is really saying and thinking. Occasionally, indeed, he makes the mistake of under-statement—for example, the argument in the last paragraph of Part II, chapter 5, should have been stated at greater length. But such blemishes are rare. On the whole, both *Democracy in America* and the *Ancien Régime* resemble fine-wrought steel chains, each link being strong and round. Such weaknesses as they contain are not usually ones of logic, but of information or vision. Still, it is also true that they are like *pointilliste* paintings: best judged at a slight distance, if best savoured close at hand. Let us stand back a little from the *Ancien Régime*.

Apart from the Foreword, which was written in its present form as an afterthought to clarify his views, at the suggestion of friends, the *Ancien Régime* is divided into three Parts. This arrangement was another afterthought, for in the first edition there were only two Parts. Subsequent reflection induced Tocqueville to split the second in two; but the decision was not altogether a happy one. It is true that the present Part Two contains a more or less static account of monarchical centralisation and its effect on French society, while Part Three traces chronologically the developments that touched off the explosion of 1789; but this difference cannot compare in importance with that between Part One and Part Two.

For in his opening Part Tocqueville is concerned with nothing less than the problem of what the Revolution essentially was. A true historian, he goes about his task in straightforward fashion, leaving its importance to be discovered as he proceeds. He makes many bold assertions about the nature of the Revolution; but does not, at this stage, present much evidence for them. The subject is too big. All he can do, in this preliminary exposition, is suggest that the Revolution was primarily a socio-political, not an anti-religious movement; that indeed it had much in common with earlier religious movements, such as the rise of Islam and the Reformation; that it was only the explosive phase of movement that had been gathering strength for six generations, as the feudal system decayed; and that it was common to all Europe, as feudalism had been. Tocqueville, in fact, is here stressing the *universality* of the Revolution: it would not be going too far to borrow a useful phrase of Mr. John Lukacs', and sub-title Part I "The European Revolution". In it are many big ideas to which Tocqueville would certainly have returned had he lived to complete his history (one might instance his remarks on the reception of the Revolution in England and Germany). However, since death intervened, they received no further discussion, from him at least.

But if the Revolution ended as a European phenomenon, it began as a French one. If its causes were universal, its occasion was not. Tocqueville was well aware of this, and of the problem that it posed; so in Part II he sets out to explain why it was in France, rather than elsewhere, that the Revolution first erupted. The allusions to other countries change in character: he makes them in order to show what was unique about France. Too strict an insistence on French peculiarity, however, might defeat its own purpose by making the reader feel that the Revolution was not a European movement after all. So Tocqueville is also careful to present France as a *particular* instance of the *universal* phenomenon. His success in thus explaining the occasion of the Revolution while at the same time illuminating, and convincing us of, his general theory of its cause, and thus fully enlightening us as to its nature, is one of his most notable intellectual triumphs.

His achievement in Parts II and III does not stop there. For one thing, the effort to make the actions of the revolutionaries comprehensible and to show that "the Revolution was a foregone conclusion" forces him to paint a huge, detailed portrait of the régime that they attacked. The result is a remarkable depiction of civil society in decay: men at odds, institutions crumbling, subversive ideas springing up like weeds in a fertile garden run wild. With characteristic irony he shows that the monarchy fell, not because it was backward, but because it was one of the most modern European governments; and it is with an almost Machiavellian relish that he paints the selfishness of the nobility and the other privileged classes; shows the universal meddlesomeness of the central administration and the short-sightedness of its views, not to mention its frequent inefficiencies*; and how all the various impulses to reform, however well-intentioned, on whoever's part (and everybody was a reformer in late eighteenth-century France) tended inexorably to a conclusion far beyond anything the reformers desired or dreamed of. At times the reader is reminded of the ironical world of Chekhov's dramas, in which, regardless of their doom, the little victims play, or at least mope, while we, with the benefit of hindsight, see doom bearing down all too clearly.

Even this does not exhaust the interest of Parts II and III. For in them the sociologist of *Democracy in America* is at work again, displaying, inferentially, the manner in which societies hold together, as well as that in which they collapse. Lefebvre, a veteran Marxist, was much struck by the discussion of the class struggle in the *Ancien Régime*, especially as it was conducted without benefit of the *Communist Manifesto*, which Tocqueville never read; and even those who are not Marxists may agree that Tocqueville shows, again and again, explicitly and implicitly, by positive and negative example, how a society works. Human motivation is a more complex thing for him than it seems to have been for Marx; but his discussion of the

---

* This point is happily illustrated by the passage on the Press under the old order – see Part II, chapter 6.

degradation of the French peasantry in the eighteenth century shows as lively an awareness of the operation of economic conditions on human behaviour as anything else that the nineteenth century produced. Nor ought we to respect him less because, son of a Prefect that he was, he distinguished the operations of bureaucracy as an autonomous force in shaping the destinies of men, nations and classes. It is an insight which even today, in the age of the Pentagon, the Welfare State, the decay of Parliament and the rise of the organisation man, progressive thought has not really assimilated; perhaps because it is too depressing.

Not that this would have surprised Tocqueville. His genius for doing several things at once with unfailing grace and clarity did not rest content with simultaneous historical and sociological exploration. His whole life had bred in him a passionate concern with the subjects he was discussing. So under his hand the issues that confronted the eighteenth century live again. For, as he said, "when studying our old social system under its infinitely various aspects I have never quite lost sight of present-day France ... I have tried not merely to diagnose the malady of which the sick man died but also to discover how he might have been saved." Now, according to Tocqueville the malady that destroyed the old order was double. Under that order the French were not equal, politically, socially, economically or legally; and they were not free. The first ill was the consequence of feudalism, the second of centralisation. But whereas to undo the work of feudalism—the more ancient grievance— was relatively easy, to undo the work of the monarchy and establish liberty in France proved extremely difficult. Again and again (but particularly towards the end of the book) Tocqueville wrestles with the problem of making Frenchmen love liberty and loathe Bonapartism as much as he does himself. But by the last page he still has not found any solution better than exhortation.

Mr. Richard Herr, author of a most interesting study of the *Ancien Régime*, believes that he never would have found a more effective solution; that the book is an unanswerable demonstration that a régime of liberty is impossible in France because the French cling tenaciously to equality but always weary of trying to combine it with freedom. He admits, however, that Tocqueville himself did not take this view. On the contrary, he was incapable of despairing permanently either of France of or liberty; and he regarded his work as a call to his countrymen to set to work to complete the task of the great men of '89, the men who coined the slogan, *Liberty, Equality, Fraternity*. He saw that the labour would be, as it has proved, long and hard, marred with defeats, frustrations and uncertainties; but he was certain that it could and should be undertaken, and rejoiced in every event which, like the enormously favourable reception of the *Ancien Régime* on its publication, suggested that his words were being taken to heart; words such as these, from Part III, chapter 3 : —

" ... In the long run freedom always brings to those who know how to retain it comfort and well-being, and often great prosperity. Nevertheless, for the moment it sometimes tells against amenities of this nature, and there are times, indeed, when despotism can best ensure a brief enjoyment of them. In fact, those who prize freedom only for the material benefits it offers have never kept it long.

"What has made so many men, since untold ages, stake their all on liberty is its intrinsic glamour, a fascination it has in itself, apart from all 'practical' considerations. For only in countries where it reigns can a man speak, live, and breathe freely, owing obedience to no authority save God and the laws of the land. The man who asks of freedom anything other than itself is born to be a slave."

v

Permanently excellent though it is, the *Ancien Régime* has imperfections, which must be mentioned by any candid friend.

On a number of minor factual points* Tocqueville has been corrected. Lefebvre has pointed out that, contrary to what is

*Most of the errors listed here can be found in Lefebvre's introduction to the *Ancien Régime* in the Mayer edition of Tocqueville's *Oeuvres Complètes*, or in Richard Herr's *Tocqueville and the Old Régime*.

said in Part I, chapter 4, the *terriers* of the *seigneuries* did not necessarily deteriorate in the post-medieval period: some even improved. The men of letters were by no means all of them such inexperienced political dilettanti as Tocqueville makes them. By 1789 many of the Intendants were noblemen; the administration was not so exclusively staffed by men of low birth as Tocqueville seems to think (see Part II, chapter 11). Nor was the nobility so easy to enter as he imagines: it had been closing its ranks against interlopers throughout the century. And feudal hardships were not the only ones that the peasantry as a class had to bear: many of them had a contractual relationship with the landowners, being tenant farmers, share-croppers, or agricultural labourers.

The rest of his sins are mainly ones of omission. He says nothing about the huge debt arising out of France's participation in the War of American Independence, which contributed so largely to the government's financial difficulties, and hence to its downfall. Lefebvre is severe with him for devoting too much space to the nobility and too little to the Third Estate: the peasantry is the only section of the Third to get a chapter to itself, the upper bourgeoisie makes only sporadic appearances, and the petty bourgeoisie and artisan class are scarcely mentioned. Yet this was the Estate, after all, which dominated the Revolution—by whom and for whom it was made.

Even more serious is the mistake about centralisation on which all the critics pounce. Tocqueville's account of its origins and development is far too simple. It was not simply the result of royal ambition and greed, as he seems to think; nor were the nobles the simple defenders of public liberty that at times he almost strays into calling them (mostly he knew better—probably he was misled by his own aristocratic instincts). The common people for long supported the growth of royal power because it put a stop to nobles' cynical and tyrannous exploitation of their feudal rights, and to their incessant fighting among themselves. Tocqueville sees the support, but not the reason. Nor does he see that centralisation was essential, in some form or other, as a protection of France against invasion. Indeed, as Lefebvre remarks drily, "it is a surprising lapse on

the part of a sociologist and historian not to take the part of
war in the life of the French sufficiently into account." Yet
it is certainly Tocqueville's lapse.

And it leads him into a further mistake, for he says almost
nothing about the determined attempt at de-centralisation by the
Constituent Assembly. He knows that the centralised administration collapsed between 1787 and 1789; but he seems to assume
that it was Napoleon who rescued France from anarchy by
resurrecting the old monarchy. In fact, it had been the outbreak
and necessities of war that had driven the revolutionaries to
restore centralisation. But Tocqueville, who seems to have made
no study of the Jacobin period, never perceived this. Had he
done so, he might have had second thoughts about the origins
of the monarchial centralisation too.

But these are, in the aggregate, small blots. Substantially
the *Ancien Régime and the Revolution* remains what it
was: one of the most honest, most profound, and most eloquent
of histories. There are no signs yet of its outliving its use-
fulness. As long as history is read, France loved, or liberty
cherished, Tocqueville's masterpiece will keep its place.

*October, 1968.* The events of May in Paris this year led M.
Raymond Aron to recommend the study of Tocqueville. He
was thinking of Tocqueville's *Recollections*, which contain a
depressing picture of the 1848 Revolution; but readers of the
*Ancien Régime* may feel that it, too, has something to say to us
in the wake of the Revolution in 1968. For once more the
English have grown interested in the way the French go about
their civil convulsions. And Tocqueville's remarks about the
Frenchman once more vindicate his book's claim to be taken
seriously: "So long as no one thinks of resisting, you can lead
him on a thread, but once a revolutionary movement is afoot,
nothing can restrain him from taking part in it. That is why our
rulers are so often taken by surprise; they fear the nation either
too much or not enough, for though it is never so free that the
possibility of enslaving it is ruled out, its spirit can never be
broken so completely as to prevent its shaking off the yoke of an
oppressive government." At this moment of her history, no
better interpreter of France can be found.            Hugh Brogan

# FOREWORD

It is not my purpose here to write a history of the French Revolution; that has been done already, and so ably that it would be folly on my part to think of covering the ground again. In this book I shall study, rather, the background and nature of the Revolution.

No nation had ever before embarked on so resolute an attempt as that of the French in 1789 to break with the past, to make, as it were, a scission in their life line and to create an unbridgeable gulf between all they had hitherto been and all they now aspired to be. With this in mind they took a host of precautions so as to make sure of importing nothing from the past into the new order, and saddled themselves with all sorts of restrictions in order to differentiate themselves in every possible way from the previous generation; in a word, they spared no pains in their endeavour to obliterate their former selves.

I have always felt that they were far less successful in this curious attempt than is generally supposed in other countries and than they themselves at first believed. For I am convinced that though they had no inkling of this, they took over from the old order not only most of its customs, conventions, and modes of thought, but even those very ideas which prompted our revolutionaries to destroy it; that, in fact, though nothing was further from their intentions, they used the debris of the old order for building up the new. Thus if we wish to get a true understanding of the French Revolution and its achievement, it is well to disregard for the moment the France of today and to look back to the France that is no more. This is what I have aimed at doing in the present book, and I must admit that it proved to be a far less easy task than I had expected when I first embarked on it.

The early monarchy, the Middle Ages, and the Renaissance have been the subject of exhaustive treatises and painstaking research work; thus we are well acquainted not only with the historical events but also with the legislative systems, customs, and ideologies of the French government and people in these periods. But nobody so far has thought fit to study the eighteenth century with the same meticulous care. True, we imagine we know all about the French social order of that period, for the good reason that its surface glitter holds our gaze and we are familiar not only with the life stories of its outstanding figures but also, thanks to the many brilliant critical studies now available, with the works of the great writers who adorned that age. But we have only vague, often quite wrong conceptions of the manner in which public business was transacted and institutions functioned; of the exact relations between the various classes in the social hierarchy; of the situation and sentiments of that section of the population which as yet could neither make itself heard nor seen; and, by the same token, of the ideas and mores basic to the social structure of eighteenth-century France.

I have tried to strike to the heart of this phase of the *ancien régime,* so near to us in time, but overshadowed so completely by the Revolution. With this in view I have not merely reread those well-known books which made literary history in the eighteenth century, but given much time to studying records that, while less known and rightly regarded as of minor importance, throw perhaps more light on the true spirit of the age. I have given special attention to the public documents in which Frenchmen voiced their opinions and aspirations on the eve of the Revolution. The minutes of the meetings of the "Estates" and, later, of the provincial assemblies were particularly enlightening. Above all, I have made use of the *cahiers* (written instructions given to the deputies by their constituents) drawn up in 1789 by the three Orders of the State. This long series of manuscript volumes constitutes, as it were, the swan song of the old régime, the ultimate expression of its ambitions, its last will and testament.

But I have also had recourse to other, no less rewarding sources of information. In a country where a strong central administration has gained control of all the national activities there are few trends of thought, desires or grievances, few interests or propensities that do not sooner or later make themselves known to it, and in studying its records we can get a good idea not only of the way in which it functioned but of the mental climate of the country as a whole. Were a foreigner given free access to the confidential files of the Ministry of the Interior and those of our prefectures, he would soon come to know more about present-day France than we know ourselves. In the eighteenth century, as readers of this book will not fail to note, the government of France was already highly central-ised and all-powerful; indeed, the range of its activities was prodigious. We find it constantly coming to the rescue of indi-viduals in difficulties, issuing permits or vetoes, as the case might be; lavish of promises and subsidies. Its influence made itself felt at every turn, not only in the management of public affairs but also in the private lives of citizens and families. Moreover, as there was no danger of publicity, no one felt any qualms about informing it of his personal troubles, even when these reflected no credit on himself. I have devoted much time to studying such records of this order as have survived in Paris and in several provinces.*

In their archives I found (as indeed I had expected) a living memorial of the spirit of the old régime, the ways men thought and felt, their habits and their prejudices. For in them every-one expressed his views with total frankness and voiced his inmost thoughts. Thus I had access to a mine of information which was not available to contemporaries, since these archives were kept rigorously secret.

The more closely I studied these documents, the more I was struck by the innumerable resemblances between the France of that period and nineteenth-century France. Men had, it seemed, already many of the sentiments and opinions which I had al-ways regarded as products of the Revolution, and in the same way many of the customs commonly thought to stem from it

*I have made considerable use of the records of several great "intendan-cies," particularly those of Tours, which are exceptionally revealing and concern a very large *généralité*, with a population of a million, situated in the heart of France. I take this opportunity of expressing my gratitude to M. Grandmaison, the young but highly expert Keeper of the Record Room at Tours. My study of the records of other *généralités* (including those of the Ile-de-France) has convinced me that public business was conducted on the same lines in most parts of the kingdom.

exclusively had already entered into our mores. It would seem, in fact, that the peculiarities of our modern social system are deeply rooted in the ancient soil of France. The nearer my researches brought me to that fateful year 1789, the more clearly did I see the spirit which sponsored the conception, birth, and fruition of the Revolution gaining ground, and little by little all its salient features taking form under my eyes. For it was not merely foreshadowed in the years preceding it; it was an immanent reality, a presence on the threshold. These records disclose not only the reasons of the events accompanying its outbreak but also, and perhaps even more clearly, those of its after-effects on the destinies of France. The Revolution had, indeed, two distinct phases: one in which the sole aim of the French nation seemed to be to make a clean sweep of the past; and a second, in which attempts were made to salvage fragments from the wreckage of the old order. For many of the laws and administrative methods which were suppressed in 1789 reappeared a few years later, much as some rivers after going underground re-emerge at another point, in new surroundings.

In the work I now present to the public my aim is, firstly, to indicate the reasons why it was in France rather than elsewhere that the Great Revolution, stirrings of which were perceptible in almost all European countries, came to a head; secondly, why it presented itself as an almost natural outcome of the very social order it made such haste to destroy; and, lastly, why the monarchy which had weathered so many storms in the past collapsed so suddenly and catastrophically.

This book, in my opinion, calls for a sequel and I propose, if my health permits and I have the leisure, to follow it up with another, which will describe the reactions of these same Frenchmen—with whom, thanks to my research work, I have consorted on such familiar terms under the old régime—to the vicissitudes of the long, eventful years of the revolutionary period. They were men who had been shaped by the old order, and I shall show how they remained the same essentially and, in fact, despite superficial alterations due to the march of events, never changed out of recognition.

I shall begin by depicting them as they were in the heyday
of the Revolution; when the love of equality and the urge to
freedom went hand in hand; when they wished to set up not
merely a truly democratic government but free institutions, not
only to do away with privileges but also to make good and
stabilise the rights of man, the individual. Youth was at the
helm in that age of fervid enthusiasm, of proud and generous
aspirations, whose memory, despite its extravagances, men will
forever cherish: a phase of history that for many years to come
will trouble the sleep of all who seek to demoralise the nation
and reduce it to a servile state.

In tracing the course of the Revolution I shall draw attention to the events, mistakes, misjudgments which led these self-
same Frenchmen to abandon their original ideal and, turning
their backs on freedom, to acquiesce in an equality of servitude
under the master of all Europe. I shall show how a government,
both stronger and far more autocratic than the one which the
Revolution had overthrown, centralised once more the entire
administration, made itself all-powerful, suppressed our dearly
bought liberties, and replaced them by a mere pretence of
freedom; how the so-called "sovereignty of the people" came to
be based on the votes of an electorate that was neither given
adequate information nor an opportunity of getting together
and deciding on one policy rather than another; and how the
much vaunted "free vote" in matters of taxation came to signify
no more than the meaningless assent of assemblies tamed to
servility and silence. Thus the nation was deprived both of the
means of self-government and of the chief guarantee of its
rights, that is to say the freedom of speech, thought, and literature which ranked among the most valuable and noblest
achievements of the Revolution—though the then government
professed to be acting under its auspices and invoked its august
name.

I shall stop at the point at which the Revolution appears
to be to have, to all intents and purposes, achieved its aim and
given birth to the new social order, and then proceed to examine
the nature of this social order in some detail. I shall try to
make clear in what respects it resembles and in what it differs

from the social system that preceded it; and to determine what was lost and what was gained by that vast upheaval. Finally, I will venture on some speculation as to what the future holds in store for us.

Part of this second work has been roughed out, but much still has to be done before it is ready for publication. Whether I shall be able to bring it to a successful conclusion remains to be seen since the destinies of individuals are often as uncertain as those of nations.

I hope and believe that I have written the present book without any *parti pris*, though it would be futile to deny that my own feelings were engaged. What Frenchman can write about his country and think about the age in which he lives in a spirit of complete detachment? Thus I confess that when studying our old social system under its infinitely various aspects I have never quite lost sight of present-day France. Moreover, I have tried not merely to diagnose the malady of which the sick man died but also to discover how he might have been saved. In fact, my method has been that of the anatomist who dissects each defunct organ with a view to eliciting the laws of life, and my aim has been to supply a picture that while scientifically accurate, may also be instructive. Whenever I found in our forefathers any of those virtues so vital to a nation but now well-nigh extinct—a spirit of healthy independence, high ambitions, faith in oneself and in a cause—I have thrown them into relief. Similarly, wherever I found traces of any of those vices which after destroying the old order still affect the body politic, I have emphasised them; for it is in the light of the evils to which they formerly gave rise that we can gauge the harm they yet may do.

With this in mind I have not shrunk from wounding the feelings of individuals and classes in present-day France, or of affronting certain opinions and ancient loyalties, laudable though these may be. In so doing I have often felt regret but never any qualms of conscience, and I can only hope that those who may be inclined to take offence at anything in this book will realize that its author has aimed at complete honesty and impartiality.

There may be some to accuse me of making overmuch of

liberty—that watchword of the past. Nowadays, so I am told, no one in France sets any store on it. All I would say (for what it is worth) in my defence is that my devotion to freedom is of very long standing. Over twenty years have passed since, apropos of another social group, I made the observations which are reproduced below almost verbatim.

Though there can be no certainty about the future, three facts are plain to see in the light of past experience. First, that all our contemporaries are driven on by a force that we may hope to regulate or curb, but cannot overcome, and it is a force impelling them, sometimes gently, sometimes at headlong speed, to the destruction of aristocracy. Secondly, that those peoples who are so constituted as to have the utmost difficulty in getting rid of despotic government for any considerable period are the ones in which aristocracy has ceased to exist and can no longer exist. Thirdly, that nowhere is despotism calculated to produce such evil effects as in social groups of this order; since, more than any other kind of régime, it fosters the growth of all the vices to which they are congenitally prone and, indeed, incites them to go still farther on the way to which their natural bent inclines them.

For in a community in which the ties of family, of caste, of class, and craft fraternities no longer exist people are far too much disposed to think exclusively of their own interests, to become self-seekers practising a narrow individualism and caring nothing for the public good. Far from trying to counteract such tendencies despotism encourages them, depriving the governed of any sense of solidarity and interdependence; of good-neighbourly feelings and a desire to further the welfare of the community at large. It immures them, so to speak, each in his private life and, taking advantage of the tendency they already have to keep apart, it estranges them still more. Their feelings toward each other were already growing cold; despotism freezes them.

Since in such communities nothing is stable, each man is haunted by a fear of sinking to a lower social level and by a restless urge to better his condition. And since money has not only become the sole criterion of a man's social status but has also acquired an extreme mobility—that is to say it changes hands incessantly, raising or lowering the prestige of individuals and families—everybody is feverishly intent on making money or, if already rich, on keeping his wealth intact. Love of gain, a fondness for business careers, the desire to get rich at all costs, a craving for material comfort and easy living quickly become ruling passions under a despotic government. They affect all classes, even those to whom they have previously been most foreign, and tend to lower the moral standards of the nation as a whole if no effort be made to check their growth. It is in the nature of despotism that it should foster such desires and propagate their havoc. Lowering as they do the national morale, they are despotism's safeguard, since they divert men's attention from public affairs and make them shudder at the mere thought of a revolution. Despotism alone can provide that atmosphere of secrecy which favours crooked dealings and enables the freebooters of finance to make illicit fortunes. Under other forms of government such propensities exist, undoubtedly; under a despotism they are given free rein.

Freedom and freedom alone can extirpate these vices, which, indeed, are innate in communities of this order; it alone can call a halt to their pernicious influence. For only freedom can deliver the members of a community from that isolation which is the lot of the individual left to his own devices and, compelling them to get in touch with each other, promote an active sense of fellowship. In a community of free citizens every man is daily reminded of the need of meeting his fellow men, of hearing what they have to say, or exchanging ideas, and coming to an agreement as to the conduct of their common interests. Freedom alone is capable of lifting men's minds above mere mammon worship and the petty personal worries which crop up in the course of everyday life, and of making them aware at every moment that they belong each and all to a vaster entity, above and around them—their native land. It alone replaces at certain critical moments their natural love of material welfare by a loftier, more virile ideal; offers other objectives than that of getting rich; and sheds a light enabling all to see and appraise men's vices and their virtues as they truly are.

True, democratic societies which are not free may well be

prosperous, cultured, pleasing to the eye, and even magnificent, such is the sense of power implicit in their massive uniformity; in them may flourish many private virtues, good fathers, honest merchants, exemplary landowners, and good Christians, too—since the patrimony of the Christian is not of this world and one of the glories of the Christian faith is that it has produced such men under the worst governments and in eras of the utmost depravity. There were many such in the Roman Empire in its decline. But, I make bold to say, never shall we find under such conditions a great citizen, still less a great nation; indeed, I would go so far as to maintain that where equality and tyranny coexist, a steady deterioration of the mental and moral standards of a nation is inevitable.

Such were my views and thus I wrote twenty years ago, and nothing that has taken place in the world since then has led me to change my mind. And, having proclaimed my love of freedom at a time when it was made much of, I can hardly be blamed for championing it today, when it is out of fashion.

Moreover, as regards my love of freedom, I differ less from those who disagree with me than they may imagine. Can there exist a man so mean-spirited that he would rather be at the mercy of a tyrant's whim than obedient to laws which he himself has helped to enact—provided of course that he believes his nation to have the qualities enabling it to make a proper use of freedom? Even despots do not deny the merits of freedom; only they wish to keep it for themselves, claiming that no one else is worthy of it. Thus our quarrel is not about the value of freedom *per se*, but stems from our opinion of our fellow men, high or low as the case may be; indeed, it is no exaggeration to say that a man's admiration of absolute government is proportionate to the contempt he feels for those around him. I trust I may be allowed to wait a little longer before being converted to such a view of my fellow countrymen.

Much labour has gone to the making of this book—sometimes over a year's research work lies behind the writing of a quite short chapter—but I venture to hope, and to believe, it was not labour lost. I might have cluttered up my pages with footnotes, but it seemed better to insert only a few and to relegate the rest to an appendix, with the page references indicated.

These notes comprise illustrations and documentary evidence of the points I make. Should any of my readers feel that further evidence is needed and express a wish for this, I could supply many more.

# PART ONE

### CHAPTER ONE

## Conflicting opinions of the Revolution at its outbreak

No great historical event is better calculated than the French
Revolution to teach political writers and statesmen to be
cautious in their speculations; for never was any such event,
stemming from factors so far back in the past, so inevitable
yet so completely unforeseen.

Despite all his political acumen even Frederick the Great
had no inkling of what was in the air. He was very near to the
Revolution yet he failed to see what was happening under his
eyes. More remarkable still, his management of public affairs
fell in line with the new ideas; he was a precursor, one might
almost say a promoter, of the Revolution. Nevertheless, even he
failed to perceive the signs of the long-impending storm, and
similarly, when at last it broke, the features distinguishing it
from a  host of previous revolutions passed unnoticed—anyhow, to begin with.

It was watched with extreme interest by foreigners all the
world over; everywhere it gave rise to a vague awareness that
a new order was in the making and to equally vague hopes of
changes and reforms. But nobody as yet had any idea what
form these were to take. The European Kings and their
Ministers, unlike their subjects, completely failed to realise the
way events were shaping and regarded the French Revolution
as one of those passing maladies to which all nations are subject from time to time and whose only practical effect is to open
up new political possibilities to enterprising neighbours. On the
rare occasions when they spoke the truth about it they did so
unwittingly. True, at the conference of Pillnitz in 1791 the
leading German potentates declared that the peril of the French
monarchy was shared by all other European sovereigns, but at
heart they believed nothing of the sort. Confidential records of
the time prove that such declarations were disingenuous pre-

texts intended to mask the speakers' true designs or to present them to the masses in a false light.

At bottom they were convinced that the French Revolution was no more than a local, transient phenomenon which they could probably exploit to their advantage. With this in mind they hatched up schemes for their own aggrandisement, made proposals, contracted secret treaties of alliance. They even haggled amongst themselves about the division of the spoils that were soon (as they supposed) to fall into their hands; they split up into opposing camps or else joined forces and were, in fact, prepared for almost every eventuality—except what actually took place.

Even the English, who had the lessons of their own past to guide them and, thanks to their long experience of political freedom, could take a more realistic view, watched the gradual advance of this epoch-making revolution as if through a thick veil. They, too, failed to perceive its true aspect and the effects it was to have on the future of continental Europe and theirs as well. Even Arthur Young, who was travelling in France on the eve of the Revolution and foresaw its outbreak, so completely misunderstood its character as to suspect that its effect might well be to increase the power of the privileged classes. "As for the nobility and clergy, if this revolution were to give them still more preponderance, I think it would do more harm than good."

Burke, though his loathing of the Revolution from the very start seems to have stimulated his powers of observation, even Burke was in two minds about its probable effects. His first impression was that France would be weakened almost to the point of extinction. "We may assume," he said, "that for a long time to come France need no longer be reckoned with as a military power. Indeed, she may be destroyed, as such, forever and men of the next generation may repeat those ancient words: *Gallos quoque in bellis floruisse audivimus* [We have heard say that the Gauls, too, once excelled in warfare]."

The opinions of the eyewitnesses of the Revolution were no better founded than those of its foreign observers, and in France there was no real understanding of its aims even when it was on the point of breaking out. Amongst the mass of *cahiers* (statements drawn up by the Three Estates, nobility, clergy and commons, at the beginning of the Revolution) I can find only two expressing any real fear of the insurgent masses. What was apprehended was that the monarchy, "the Court" as it still was called, would now feel called on to tighten up its control over the nation. The weakness of the Estates-General and the shortness of their sessions were viewed with alarm, and there was a fear that their rights and powers would be overruled. The nobility were particularly uneasy on this score. In one of the *cahiers* we find a recommendation that the Swiss mercenaries should be required to take an oath that, even in cases of riot and revolt, they would never fire on a French citizen. Only let the Estates-General function in freedom and all abuses would be easily remedied; true, sweeping reforms were needed, but there should be no difficulty in putting them through.

Meanwhile the Revolution followed its destined course. And the attitude of the outside world towards it gradually changed, the more it revealed its monster's head and bared its bizarre and terrible countenance; when, after destroying political institutions, it abolished civil institutions; when, after changing laws, it tampered with age-old customs and even the French language; when, not content with wrecking the whole structure of the government of France, it proceeded to undermine the social order and seemed even to aim at dethroning God himself; when worse still, it began to operate beyond the frontiers of its place of origin, employing method's hitherto unknown, new tactics, murderous slogans—"opinions in arms", as Pitt described them. Not only were the barriers of kingdoms swept away and thrones laid low, but the masses were trampled underfoot—and yet, amazingly enough these very masses rallied to the cause of the new order. Thus the change of attitude mentioned above is easily accounted for. What, to start with, had seemed to European monarchs and statesmen a mere passing phase, a not unusual symptom of a nation's growing pains, was now discovered to be something absolutely new, quite unlike any previous movement, and so widespread, extraordinary, and incalculable as to baffle human understanding. Some were convinced that this unknown force, which nothing could control and which seemingly would carry on indefinitely by its own acquired momentum, could but lead to a complete and final disintegration of the social fabric throughout the civilised world. Many, indeed, regarded it as the work of the devil himself. "There is a satanic element in the French Revolution," M. de Maistre declared as early as 1797. But on the other hand, there were some who saw in it a benevolent intervention of Divine Providence, with a view to the rejuvenation not of France alone but of the whole world, and the creation of nothing short of a new human race. In the works of many writers of the period we sense something of that numinous awe which the sight of the barbarians inspired in Salvianus. Burke made no secret of his horror at the way events were shaping in France. "Deprived of her old government, or rather without any government, France seemed an object of pity or contempt rather than fated to become the scourge and terror of the human race. But out of the tomb of this murdered monarchy has arisen a formless spectre in a far more terrible guise than any of those which in former times have overpowered and subdued the imagination of mankind. Going straight forward to its end, undeterred by peril, unchecked by remorse, this strange and hideous phantom is crushing out men who cannot even understand how such a creature can exist."

Was the phenomenon in fact so extraordinary as contemporaries supposed? Was it as unprecedented, as profoundly subversive and world-changing as they thought? What was its true significance, its real nature, and what were the permanent effects of this strange and terrifying revolution? What exactly did it destroy, and what did it create?

I believe that the time has come when these questions can be answered; that today we are in a position to see this memorable event in its true perspective and pass judgment on it. For we now are far enough from the Revolution to be relatively unaffected by the frenzied enthusiasm of those who saw it through; yet near enough to be able to enter into the feelings of its promoters and to see what they were aiming at. Soon it will be difficult to do this; since when great revolutions are successful their causes cease to exist, and the very fact of their success has made them incomprehensible.

CHAPTER TWO

*How the chief and ultimate aim of the Revolution
was not, as used to be thought, to overthrow religious
and to weaken political authority in France*

One of the earliest enterprises of the revolutionary movement
was a concerted attack on the Church, and among the many
passions inflamed by it the first to be kindled and the last to be
extinguished was of an anti-religious nature. Even after the urge
to a new freedom had spent its force and Frenchmen asked for
nothing better than to be left in peace, even at the cost of servitude, the revolt against Church authority lost nothing of its
virulence. Napoleon succeeded in quelling the libertarian spirit
of the early revolutionaries, but he was quite unable to remove
their anti-Christian bias. Even in our own time we find men
who seek to compensate for their grovelling servility to the
meanest jack-in-office by declaiming against God and who,
while going back on all that was freest, noblest, most inspiring
in the revolutionary ideal, pride themselves on keeping faith
with its true spirit by remaining hostile to religion.

Nevertheless, it is easy enough to see today that the campaign
against all forms of religion was merely incidental to the
French Revolution, a spectacular but transient phenomenon, a
brief reaction to the ideologies, emotions, and events which led
up to it—but in no sense basic to its programme.

The philosophical conceptions of the eighteenth century have
rightly been regarded as one of the chief causes of the Revolution and it is undeniable that our eighteenth-century philosophers were fundamentally anti-religious. But it should be noted
that in this philosophy there were two quite distinct and
separable trends of thought.

One of them embodied all the new (or resuscitated) opinions
regarding the nature of human society and the underlying
principles of civil and political jurisprudence; the belief, for
example, that all men are born equal and its corollary, the abolition of all privileges of class, caste, and profession. To the same

category belonged the theories of the sovereignty of the people, of equal laws for all, of the vesting of the supreme power in the nation as a whole. Such ideas were not merely antecedent to the French Revolution; they formed part and parcel of it and, in the light of subsequent events, can be seen to be its most fundamental, durable, and authentic characteristics.

But—and this was a quite different aspect of their doctrines— our eighteenth-century philosophers attacked the Church with a sort of studious ferocity; they declaimed against its clergy, its hierarchy, institutions, and dogmas, and, driving their attack home, sought to demolish the very foundations of Christian belief. This part of eighteenth-century philosophy, stemming as it did from special conditions that the Revolution did away with, inevitably tended to lose its appeal once those conditions had been removed and it was, so to speak, submerged by its own triumph. I will add but a word to make my meaning clear at this point, for I shall revert elsewhere to this important topic. It was far less as a religious faith than as a political institution that Christianity provoked these violent attacks. The Church was hated not because its priests claimed to regulate the affairs of the other world but because they were landed proprietors, lords of manors, tithe owners, and played a leading part in secular affairs; not because there was no room for the Church in the new world that was in the making, but because it occupied the most powerful, most privileged position in the old order that was now to be swept away.

We need only point out how the march of time has brought this fact into prominence and is indeed confirming it more and more as the years go by. The more the political achievement of the Revolution is consolidated, the more its anti-religious elements are being discredited. The more thoroughly the ancient political institutions it assailed have been demolished, while the prerogatives and class distinctions which were anathema to it have been suppressed for good and all, with the result that even the rancours they arouse have lost their sting and the clergy have cut themselves adrift from all that fell with them—the more the Church has tended to recover its hold upon men's minds.

It must not be thought that this phenomenon is peculiar to France; there is hardly any Christian church in Europe that has not acquired a new lease of life in the period following the French Revolution. For the notion that democratic régimes are necessarily hostile to religion is based on a total misconception of the facts; nothing in the Christian faith or even in Roman Catholicism is incompatible with democracy and, on the contrary, it would seem that a democratic climate is highly favourable to Christianity. The facts of history go to show that in all periods the religious instinct has had its most abiding home in the hearts of the common people and it was there that all the religions which have passed away found their last refuge. It would indeed be surprising if institutions which reflect the aspirations and feelings of the masses should inevitably and persistently foster the growth of an anti-religious spirit among them.

What I have said about Church authority applies even more strongly to the authority of the central power. Those who saw the Revolution overthrowing all the institutions and customs which had hitherto shored up the social hierarchy and prevented men from running wild were naturally inclined to think that the Revolution spelled the end of all things; not merely of the old order, but of any order in the State, not merely that of any given form of government, but of any government at all—that in fact the nation was heading towards sheer anarchy. Yet, in my opinion, those who held this view were misled by appearances. Less than a year after the outbreak of the Revolution Mirabeau wrote thus (in a confidential letter to the King): "Only compare the present state of affairs with the old order and you will find that it has reassuring features and gives grounds for hope. The majority of the edicts issued by the National Assembly are obviously favourable to monarchical government. Is it not something to be done with parlements, with *pays d'états,* with an all-powerful priesthood, with privilege and the nobility? The modern idea of a single class of citizens on an equal footing would certainly have pleased Richelieu, since surface equality of this kind facilitates the exercise of power. Absolute government during several successive reigns could not have done as much as this one year of revolution to make good the King's authority." Capable as he was of shaping the course of the Revolution singlehanded, Mirabeau knew what he was talking about.

Since the object of the Revolution was not merely to change an old form of government but to abolish the entire social structure of pre-revolutionary France, it was obliged to declare war simultaneously on all established powers, to destroy all recognised prerogatives, to make short work of all traditions, and to institute new ways of living, new conventions. Thus one of its first acts was to rid men's minds of all those notions which had ensured their obedience to authority under the old régime. Hence its so markedly anarchic tendencies.

But beneath the seemingly chaotic surface there was developing a vast, highly centralised power which attracted to itself and wielded into an organic whole all the elements of authority and influence that hitherto had been dispersed among a crowd of lesser, unco-ordinated powers: the three Orders of the State, professional bodies, families, and individuals. Never since the fall of the Roman Empire had the world seen a government so highly centralised. This new power was created by the Revolution or, rather, grew up almost automatically out of the havoc wrought by it. True, the governments it set up were less stable than any of those it overthrew; yet, paradoxically, they were infinitely more powerful. Indeed, their power and their fragility alike were due to the same causes, as will be explained in a later chapter of this work.

It was this simple yet grandiose form of government that Mirabeau glimpsed from the very start; a massive, four-square structure rising from the wreckage of the half-demolished institutions of the past. Despite its magnitude it was as yet invisible to the eyes of the multitude, but gradually time has made amends and contemporary monarchs, in particular, are fully alive to its significance. They contemplate it with envy and admiration; not only those who owe their present eminence to the Revolution but also those who are least in sympathy with, or frankly hostile to, its achievement. Thus we see all these rulers doing what they can to abolish privileges and remove immunities within their territories. Everywhere they are breaking down class distinctions, levelling out inequalities, replacing members of the aristocracy with trained civil servants, local charters with uniform regulations, and a diversity of powers with a strong, centralised government. They are putting through these revolutionary measures with unflagging energy and sometimes even have recourse to the methods and maxims of the Great Revolution when obstacles arise. Thus we often find them championing the poor man's cause against the rich man's, the commoner's against the nobleman's, the peasant's against his lord's. In short, the lesson of the Revolution has not been lost even on those who have most reason to detest it.

CHAPTER THREE

*How, though its objectives were political, the French Revolution followed the lines of a religious revolution and why this was so*

Whereas all social and political revolutions had so far been confined to the countries in which they took their rise, the French Revolution aspired to be world-wide and its effect was to erase all the old national frontiers from the map. We find it uniting or dividing men throughout the world, without regard to national traditions, temperaments, laws, and mother tongues, sometimes leading them to regard compatriots as foes and foreigners as their kinsmen. Or, perhaps, it would be truer to say that it created a common intellectual fatherland whose citizenship was open to men of every nationality and in which racial distinctions were obliterated.

In all the annals of recorded history we find no mention of any *political* revolution that took this form; its only parallel is to be found in certain *religious* revolutions. Thus when we seek to study the French Revolution in the light of similar movements in other countries and at other periods, it is to the great religious revolutions we should turn.

Schiller rightly points out in his *History of the Thirty Years' War* that one of the most striking effects of the reformation that took place in the sixteenth century was the bringing together of races which knew next to nothing of each other and the creation of a novel sense of fellow feeling between them. So it was that when Frenchmen were fighting against Frenchmen, the English intervened, while men hailing from remote Baltic hinterlands advanced into the heart of Germany to defend the cause of Germans of whose very existence they had until then been almost unaware. Foreign wars tended to assume the nature of civil wars, while in civil wars foreigners came to take a hand. Former interests were superseded by new interests, territorial disputes by conflicts over moral issues, and all the old notions of diplomacy were thrown into the melting pot—much to the horror and dismay of the professional politicians of the age. Precisely the same thing happened in Europe after 1789.

Thus the French Revolution, though ostensibly political in origin, functioned on the lines, and assumed many of the aspects, of a religious revolution. Not only did it have repercussions far beyond French territory, but like all great religious movements it resorted to propaganda and broadcast a gospel. This was something quite unprecedented: a political revolution that sought proselytes all the world over and applied itself as ardently to converting foreigners as compatriots. Of all the surprises that the French Revolution launched on a startled world, this surely was the most astounding. But there was more to it than that; let us try to carry our analysis a stage further and to discover if this similarity of effects may not have stemmed, in fact, from an underlying similarity of causes.

Common to all religions is an interest in the human personality, the man-in-himself irrespective of the trappings foisted on him by local traditions, laws, and customs. The chief aim of a religion is to regulate both the relations of the individual man with his Maker and his rights and duties towards his fellow men on a universal plane, independently, that is to say, of the views and habits of the social group of which he is a member. The rules of conduct thus enjoined apply less to the man of any given nation or period than to man in his capacity of son, father, master, servant, neighbour. Since these rules are based on human nature, pure and simple, they hold good for men in general all the world over. To this is due the fact that religious revolutions have often ranged so far afield and seldom been con-

fined, like political revolutions, to their country of origin or
even to a single race. Moreover, when we look more deeply
into the matter, we find that the more a religion has the universal, abstract qualities described above, the vaster is its sphere of
influence and the less account it takes of differences of laws,
local conditions, and temperaments.

The pagan religions of antiquity were always more or less
linked up with the political institutions and the social order
of their environment, and their dogmas were conditioned to
some extent by the interests of the nations, or even the cities,
where they flourished. A pagan religion functioned within the
limits of a given country and rarely spread beyond its frontiers.
It sometimes sponsored intolerance and persecutions, but very
seldom embarked on missionary enterprises. This is why there
were no great religious revolutions in the Western World before
the Christian era. Christianity, however, made light of all the
barriers which had prevented the pagan religions from
spreading, and very soon won to itself a large part of the human
race. I trust I shall not be regarded as lacking in respect for this
inspired religion if I say it partly owed its triumph to the fact
that, far more than any other religion, it was catholic in the
exact sense, having no links with any specific form of government, social order, period, or nation.

The French Revolution's approach to the problems of man's
existence here on earth was exactly similar to that of the religious
revolutions as regards his afterlife. It viewed the "citizen" from
an abstract angle, that is to say as an entity independent of
any particular social order, just as religions view the individual,
without regard to nationality or the age he lives in. It did not
aim merely at defining the rights of the French citizen, but
sought also to determine the rights and duties of men in general
towards each other and as members of a body politic.

It was because the Revolution always harked back to universal, not particular, values and to what was the most "natural"
form of government and the most "natural" social system that
it had so wide an appeal and could be imitated in so many
places simultaneously.

No previous political upheaval, however violent, had aroused
such passionate enthusiasm, for the ideal the French Revolution

set before it was not merely a change in the French social system but nothing short of a regeneration of the whole human race. It created an atmosphere of missionary fervour and, indeed, assumed all the aspects of a religious revival—much to the consternation of contemporary observers. It would perhaps be truer to say that it developed into a species of religion, if a singularly imperfect one, since it was without a God, without a ritual or promise of a future life. Nevertheless, this strange religion has, like Islam, overrun the whole world with its apostles, militants, and martyrs.

It must not be thought, however, that the methods employed by the Revolution had no precedents or that the ideas it propagated were wholly new. In all periods, even in the Middle Ages, there had been leaders of revolt who, with a view to effecting certain changes in the established order, appealed to the universal laws governing all communities, and championed the natural rights of man against the State. But none of these ventures was successful; the firebrand which set all Europe ablaze in the eighteenth century had been easily extinguished in the fifteenth. For doctrines of this kind to lead to revolutions, certain changes must already have taken place in the living conditions, customs, and manners of a nation and prepared men's minds for the reception of new ideas.

There are periods in a nation's life when men differ from each other so profoundly that any notion of "the same law for all" seems to them preposterous. But there are other periods when it is enough to dangle before their eyes a picture, however indistinct and remote, of such a law and they promptly grasp its meaning and hasten to acclaim it. In fact, the most extraordinary thing about the Revolution is not that it employed the methods which led to its success or that certain men should have conceived the ideas which supplied its driving force. What was wholly novel was that so many nations should have simultaneously reached a stage in their development which enabled those methods to be successfully employed and that ideology to be so readily accepted.

CHAPTER FOUR

*How almost all European nations had had the same institutions and how these were breaking down everywhere*

The various races which, after overthrowing the Roman Empire, ended up by forming the nations of modern Europe had different ethnic origins, came from different regions, and spoke different languages—indeed, the only thing they had in common was their barbarism. Once these races were firmly entrenched within the boundaries of the Empire, there followed a long period of inter-tribal warfare, and when at last this period ended and their respective territorial limits had been stabilised, they found themselves isolated from each other by the ruins they themselves had caused. Civilisation was practically extinct, public order nonexistent; communications had become difficult and precarious, and the great European family was split up into a number of hostile communities, each an independent unit. Yet within this incoherent mass there developed with remarkable suddenness a uniform system of law.

These institutions were not an imitation of Roman law; indeed, they were so unlike it that those who at a later date set out to transform them lock, stock, and barrel took Roman law as the starting-off point for their reforms.[1*] The system we are now discussing was an original creation, vastly different from any other code of laws devised for the maintenance of the social structure. Its various elements dovetail neatly into each other, forming a symmetrical whole quite as coherent as our modern legal and constitutional codes, and were skilfully adapted to the needs of semi-barbarian peoples.

An inquiry into the circumstances under which this system of law took form, developed, and spread throughout Europe would take me too far afield, and I merely draw attention to the undoubted fact that it prevailed to a greater or lesser extent

*Notes elaborating on the text are to be found at the end of the volume, beginning on page 240.

in every part of Europe during the Middle Ages and to the exclusion of all other forms of law in many countries.

I have had occasion to study the political institutions of medieval France, England, and Germany, and the more deeply I went into the subject, the more I was struck by the remarkable similarity between the laws and institutions in all three countries; indeed, it seemed extraordinary that nations so unlike and having so little intercourse with each other should have built up systems of law so close akin. True, they vary greatly, almost infinitely on points of detail (as was only to be expected), but their basis is everywhere the same. Whenever in my study of the constitution of ancient Germany I came on a political institution, a law, a local authority, I felt sure that if I searched long enough I would find its exact parallel, or something substantially the same, in France and England—and thus it always was. With the result that each of the three nations helped me to a better understanding of the other two.

The administration of all three countries derived from the same general principles; the political assemblies were composed of the same elements and invested with the same powers. The community was divided up on the same lines and there was the same hierarchy of classes. The nobles held identical positions, had the same privileges, the same appearance; there was, in fact, a family likeness between them, and one might almost say they were not different men but essentially the same men everywhere.

Urban administrations were alike and the rural districts governed in the same manner. The condition of the peasant varied little from one country to another; the soil was owned, occupied, and cultivated in the same way and the cultivator subject to the same taxes. From the Polish frontier to the Irish Sea we find the same institutions: the manor (*seigneurie*), the seigneurial court presided over by the lord; the fief, the quitrent, feudal services, trade and craft guilds. Sometimes the names were identical in all countries and, more surprising still, behind all these institutions, and sponsoring them, was the same ideology. It is not, I think, going too far to say that in the fourteenth century the political, social, administrative, judicial, and financial institutions—and even the literary productions—of the various European countries had more resemblance to each other than they have even in our time, when the march of progress seems to have broken down all barriers and communications between nations have so vastly improved.

It is no part of my present plan to trace the gradual decline of this ancient constitution of Europe, and I confine myself to pointing out that by the eighteenth century its disintegration had progressed so far that it was half in ruins.[2] Generally speaking, this disintegration was less pronounced in the east of the continent than in the west, but its effects were visible in every part of Europe.

This progressive decay of the institutions stemming from the Middle Ages can be followed in records of the period. It is well known that each *seigneurie* maintained the registers of landed property known as *terriers*, in which were recorded the boundaries of the various fiefs and *censives* (dependent holdings paying rent), the dues payable, the services to be rendered, the local customs. In the thirteenth- and fourteenth-century registers I examined I was much impressed by the skill with which they were drafted, their clarity, and the intelligence of the men compiling them. In later periods, however, there is a very definite falling off; the *terriers* become more and more obscure, ill ordered, incomplete, and slovenly despite a rise in the general level of intelligence in France. In fact, it would seem that while the French people were advancing towards a high standard of civilisation, their political structure was relapsing into barbarism.

Even in Germany, where the old European constitution had retained its primitive features to a greater extent than in France, many of its institutions had already passed out of existence. But it is not so much by noting what had disappeared as by studying the condition of such institutions as survived that we best can measure the ravages of time. True, the forms of municipal government, thanks to which the chief German towns had developed during the fourteenth and fifteenth centuries into small, enlightened republics, thriving and self-sufficient, still existed; but they were now a mere empty show.[3] To all appearances their mandates were still in force, the officers appointed to see to their observance bore the same titles and seemed to carry on as in the past. But the spirit of local patriotism and

strenuous endeavour, and the virile, pioneering virtues it promoted, had passed away. In short, these ancient institutions,
while keeping their original forms, had been drained of their
substance.

All such public powers, creations of the Middle Ages, as
still survived were affected by the same disease; it sapped their
vitality and they fell into a decline. What was still worse, a
number of institutions which, though not actually deriving
from that period, linked up with it and bore traces of this association to any marked extent followed suit. Even that political
freedom which had given rise to so many fine achievements
in the Middle Ages now seemed doomed to sterility whenever it still bore the slightest imprint of its medieval origin;
even the aristocracy seemed to be falling into a senile decay.
Wherever the provincial assemblies had kept unchanged their
ancient structure they hindered rather than helped the march
of progress; indeed, they seemed impervious to the spirit of the
age. Moreover, they were ceasing to hold the allegiance of the
populace at large, who were growing more and more inclined
to put their faith in the royal house. The antiquity of these
institutions did not ensure respect for them. On the contrary,
the older they grew, the more they were discredited and,
paradoxically enough, the weaker they became and the more
they seemed to have lost their power to harm, the more they
were disliked. "The present state of affairs," wrote a contemporary German whose sympathies were with the old régime,
"seems to be in bad odour with nearly everybody and heartily
despised. This sudden aversion for everything that is old is
indeed a strange phenomenon. The 'new ideas' are bandied
about within the family circle, creating an atmosphere of
restlessness, and we find our modern German housewives
clamouring to get rid of furniture that has been in the family
for generations." Nevertheless, it was a period of steadily increasing prosperity in Germany no less than in France. But—
and this is a point on which I would lay stress—all that was
vital, most active in the life of the day, was of a new order;
indeed, not merely new but frankly hostile to the past.

It must be remembered that the royalty of this time had no
longer anything in common with the royalty of the Middle

Ages. It had different prerogatives, was animated by a different spirit, played a different part, and inspired sentiments of quite another order. It must be remembered, too, that local governments had broken down and made way for a central administration staffed by a bureaucracy that was steadily undermining the power of the nobility. These new authorities employed methods and were guided by ideas which the men of the Middle Ages had never dreamed of and would certainly have discountenanced, since the social system to which they applied was, to the medieval mind, inconceivable.

The same thing was happening in England, though at first sight one might think that the ancient European constitution still functioned there. True, the old names and the old offices were retained; but in the seventeenth century feudalism was to all intents and purposes a dead letter, classes intermingled, the nobility no longer had the upper hand, the aristocracy had ceased to be exclusive, wealth was a stepping-stone to power, all men were equal before the law and public offices open to all, freedom of speech and of the press was the order of the day. All this lay quite outside the purview of the medieval mind, and it was precisely these innovations, gradually and adroitly introduced into the old order, that, without impairing its stability or demolishing ancient forms, gave it a new lease of life and a new energy. Seventeenth-century England was already a quite modern nation, which, however, venerated and enshrined within its heart some relics of the Middle Ages.

To facilitate my readers' understanding of what follows, it seemed best to cast a rapid glance beyond the frontiers of France; for, in my opinion, some knowledge of the course of events abroad is essential to a proper understanding of the French Revolution.

CHAPTER FIVE

*What did the French Revolution accomplish?*

The object of the foregoing pages was solely to throw light on the subject in a general way and make it easier to understand my answers to the questions raised in a previous chapter. What was the true aim of the Revolution? What was its specific character? Why did it take place and what exactly did it achieve?

The aim of the Revolution was not, as once was thought, to destroy the authority of the Church and religious faith in general. Appearances notwithstanding, it was essentially a movement for political and social reform and, as such, did not aim at creating a state of permanent disorder in the conduct of public affairs or (as one of its opponents bitterly remarked) at "methodising anarchy". On the contrary, it sought to increase the power and jurisdiction of the central authority. Nor was it intended, as some have thought, to change the whole nature of our traditional civilisation, to arrest its progress, or even to make any vital changes in the principles basic to the structure of society in the Western World. If we disregard various incidental developments which briefly modified its aspect at different periods and in different lands, and study it as it was essentially, we find that the chief permanent achievement of the French Revolution was the suppression of those political institutions, commonly described as feudal, which for many centuries had held unquestioned sway in most European countries. The Revolution set out to replace them with a new social and political order, at once simple and more uniform, based on the concept of the equality of all men.

This in itself was enough to constitute a thorough-paced revolution since, apart from the fact that the old feudal institutions still entered into the very texture of the religious and political institutions of almost the whole of Europe, they had also given rise to a host of ideas, sentiments, manners, and customs which, so to speak, adhered to them. Thus nothing short of a major operation was needed to excise from the body politic these accretions and to destroy them utterly. The effect was to make the Revolution appear even more drastic than it actually was; since what it was destroying affected the entire social system.

Radical though it may have been, the Revolution made far fewer changes than is generally supposed, as I shall point out later. What in point of fact it destroyed, or is in process of destroying—for the Revolution is still operative—may be summed up as everything in the old order that stemmed from aristocratic and feudal institutions, was in any way connected with them, or even bore, however faintly, their imprint. The only elements of the old order that it retained were those which had always been foreign to its institutions and could exist independently of them. Chance played no part whatever in the outbreak of the Revolution; though it took the world by surprise, it was the inevitable outcome of a long period of gestation, the abrupt and violent conclusion of a process in which six generations had played an intermittent part. Even if it had not taken place, the old social structure would nonetheless have been shattered everywhere sooner or later. The only difference would have been that instead of collapsing with such brutal suddenness it would have crumbled bit by bit. At one fell swoop, without warning, without transition, and without compunction, the Revolution effected what in any case was bound to happen, if by slow degrees.

Such then was the achievement of the Revolution, and it may appear surprising that even the most clear-sighted contemporaries should have missed the point of an event whose purport seems so clear to us today. Even Burke failed to understand it. "You wish to correct the abuses of your government," he said to the French, "but why invent novelties? Why not return to your old traditions? Why not confine yourselves to a resumption of your ancient liberties? Or, if it was not possible to recover the obliterated features of your original constitution, why not look towards England? There you would have found the ancient common law of Europe." Burke did not see that what was taking place before his eyes was a revolution whose aim was precisely to abolish that "ancient common law of Europe", and that there could be no question of putting the clock back.

But why did the storm that was gathering over the whole of Europe break in France and not elsewhere, and why did it acquire certain characteristics in France which were either absent in similar movements in other countries, or if present, assumed quite different forms? Obviously this question raises points of much importance; these will be dealt with at some length in the second part of this work.

# PART TWO

### Why feudalism had come to be more detested in France than in any other country

At first sight it may appear surprising that the Revolution, whose primary aim, as we have seen, was to destroy every vestige of the institutions of the Middle Ages, should not have broken out in countries where those institutions had the greatest hold and bore most heavily on the people instead of those in which their yoke was relatively light.

At the close of the eighteenth century serfdòm had not yet been completely abolished anywhere in Germany; indeed, in most parts of that country the peasants were still literally bound to the land, as they had been in the Middle Ages.[4,5] The armies of Frederick II and Maria Theresa were composed almost entirely of men who were serfs on the medieval pattern.

In most German states in 1788 the peasant was not allowed to quit his lord's estate; if he did so, he was liable to be tracked down wherever he was and brought back in custody. He was subject to the jurisdiction of his lord, who kept a close eye on his private life and could punish him for intemperance or idleness. He could neither better his social position, change his occupation, nor even marry without his master's consent, and a great number of his working hours had to be spent in his master's service. The system of compulsory labour, known in France as the *corvée*, was in full force in Germany, and in some districts entailed no less than three days' work a week. The peasant was expected to keep the buildings on his lord's estate in good repair and to carry the produce of the estate to market; he drove his lord's carriage and carried his messages. Also he had to spend some years of his youth in his lord's household as a member of the domestic staff. However, it was possible for the serf to become a landowner, though his tenure was always hedged round with restrictions. He had to cultivate his land in a prescribed manner, under his lord's supervision, and could neither alienate nor mortgage it without permission. In some cases he was compelled to sell its produce, in others forbidden to sell it; in any case he was bound to keep the land under cultivation. Moreover, his children did not inherit his entire estate, some part of it being usually withheld by his lord.

It must not be thought that I am describing ancient or obsolete laws; these provisions can be found even in the code drawn up by Frederick the Great and put in force by his successor at the very time when the French Revolution was getting under way.[6]

In France such conditions had long since passed away; the peasants could move about, buy and sell, work, and enter into contracts as they liked. Only in one or two eastern provinces, recent annexations, some last vestiges of serfdom lingered on; everywhere else it had wholly disappeared. Indeed, the abolition of serfdom had taken place in times so remote that its very date had been forgotten. However, as a result of recent research work it is now known that as early as the thirteenth century serfdom had ceased to exist in Normandy.

Meanwhile another revolution, of a different order, had done much to improve the status of the French peasant; he had not merely ceased to be a serf, he had also become a landowner. Though this change had far-reaching consequences, it is apt to be overlooked, and I propose to devote some pages to this all-important subject.

Until quite recently it was taken for granted that the splitting up of the landed estates in France was the work of the Revolution, and the Revolution alone; actually there is much evidence in support of the contrary view. Twenty years or more before the Revolution we find complaints being made that land was being subdivided to an unconscionable extent. "The practice of partitioning inheritances," said Turgot, writing at about this time, "has gone so far that a piece of land which just sufficed for a single family is now parcelled out between five or six sons. The result is that the heirs and their families soon find that they cannot depend on the land for their livelihood and have to look elsewhere." And some years later Necker declared that there was "an inordinate number" of small country estates in France.

In a confidential report made to an Intendant shortly before the Revolution I find the following observations: "Inheritances are being subdivided nowadays to an alarming extent. Everybody insists on having his share of the land, with the result that estates are broken up into innumerable fragments, and this process of fragmentation is going on all the time." One might well imagine these words to have been written by one of our contemporaries.

I have been at great pains to make, as it were, a cadastral survey (i.e., of the distribution of land) of the old order and have to some extent, I think, succeeded. Under the provisions of the law of 1790, which imposed a tax on land, each parish was required to draw up a return of all the privately owned land within its boundaries. Most of these documents are lost, but I have discovered some in certain villages and on comparing them with their modern equivalents have found that in these villages the number of landowners was as high as half, often two thirds, of the present number. These figures are impressive, and all the more so when we remember that the population of France has risen by over twenty-five per cent since that time.

Then, as in our own day, the peasant's desire for owning land was nothing short of an obsession and already all the passions to which possession of the soil gives rise in present-day France were active. "Land is always sold above its true value," a shrewd contemporary observer remarked, "and this is due to the Frenchman's inveterate craving to become a land-owner. All the savings of the poorer classes, which in other countries are invested in private companies or the public funds, are used for buying land."

When Arthur Young visited France for the first time, among a multitude of new experiences, none impressed him more than the extent to which ownership of the soil was vested in innumerable peasant proprietors; half the cultivable land was owned by them. "I had no idea," he often says, "that such a state of affairs existed anywhere"—and in fact none such existed outside France.

There had once been many peasant proprietors in England, but by now their number had greatly dwindled. Everywhere in Germany and in all periods a limited number of free peasants had enjoyed full ownership of the land they worked.[7] The special, often highly peculiar laws regulating the cultivator's ownership of land are set forth in the oldest German *Books of Customs*, but this type of ownership was always exceptional, there never were many of these small landed proprietors.

It was chiefly along the Rhine that at the close of the eighteenth century German farmers owned the land they worked and enjoyed almost as much freedom as the French small proprietor; and it was there, too, that the revolutionary zeal of the French found its earliest adepts and took most permanent effect.[8] On the other hand, the parts of Germany which held out longest against the current of new ideas were those where the peasants did not as yet enjoy such privileges—and this is, to my mind, a highly suggestive fact.

Thus the prevalent idea that the breakup of the big estates in France began with the Revolution is erroneous; it had started long before. True, the revolutionary governments sold the estates owned by the clergy and many of those owned by the nobility; however, if we study the records of these sales (a rather tedious task, but one which I have on occasion found rewarding) we discover that most of the parcels of land were bought by people who already had land of their own. Thus, though estates changed hands, the number of landowners was increased much less than might have been expected. For, to employ the seemingly extravagant, but in this case correct, expression used by Necker, there were already "myriads" of such persons.[9]

What the Revolution did was not to parcel out the soil of France, but to "liberate" it—for a while. Actually these small proprietors had much difficulty in making a living out of the land since it was subject to many imposts from which there was no escaping.

That these charges were heavy is undeniable, but, oddly enough, what made them seem so unbearable was something that, on the face of it, should have had the opposite effect: the fact that, as in no other part of Europe, our agriculturists had been emancipated from the control of their lords—a revolution no less momentous than that which had made them peasant proprietors.

Although the old order is still so near to us in time—every day we meet persons born under its laws—it already seems buried in the night of ages. So vast was the revolution that has intervened that its shadow falls on all that it did not destroy, and it is as if centuries lay between the times we live in and the revolutionary epoch. This explains why so few people know the answer to the quite simple question: How was rural France administered previous to 1789? And indeed it is impossible to give a full and accurate answer without having studied not the literature but the administrative records of the period.

I have often heard it said that though they had long ceased to play a part in the government of the country as a whole, the nobility kept in their hands, right up to the end, the administration of the rural districts; that, in fact, the landed proprietor "ruled" his peasants. This idea, too, seems based on a misconception of the true state of affairs.

In the eighteenth century all that touched the parish, the rural equivalent of the township, was under the control of a board of officials who were no longer agents of the seigneur or chosen by him. Some were nominated by the Intendant of the province, others elected by the local peasantry. Amongst the many functions of these officials were those of assessing the tax to be paid by each member of the community, of keeping churches in repair, of building schools, of summoning and presiding over the parish assemblies. They supervised the municipal funds, decided how these were to be expended, and in litigation to which the parish was a party acted as its representatives. Far from controlling the administration of parish affairs the lord had no say at all in it. All members of the parish councils were ex officio public servants or under the control of the central power (as will be explained in the following chapter). As for the lord, he rarely figured as the King's representative in the parish or as an intermediary between him and its inhabitants. He was no longer expected to see to the maintenance of law and order, to call out the militia, to levy

taxes, to publish royal edicts, or to distribute the King's bounty
in times of shortage. All these rights and duties had passed
into the hands of others and the lord was in reality merely one
of the inhabitants of the parish, differentiated from the others
by certain exemptions and privileges. His social rank was higher,
but he had no more power than they. In letters to their sub-
delegates the Intendants were careful to point out that the lord
was only "the first resident".

When we turn from the parish to the larger territorial unit,
the canton, we find the same arrangement; the nobles play no
part, collectively or individually, in the administration of public
affairs. This was peculiar to France; in all other countries what
was the chief characteristic of ancient feudalism persisted to
some extent and possession of the land carried with it the right
to govern the people living on it.

England was administered as well as governed by the great
landed proprietors. Even in those parts of Germany, for example
Prussia and Austria, where the ruling Princes had been most
successful in shaking off the control of the nobility in the conduct of affairs of State, they had allowed the nobles to retain to
some extent the administration of the rural areas. Though in
some places they kept a firm hand on the local lord, they had
not, as yet, supplanted him.

The French nobility, however, had long ceased to play any
part in public administration, with one exception: the administration of justice. The leading nobles retained the right of
delegating to judges appointed by them the trial of certain kinds
of suits and still issued police regulations, from time to time,
that held good within the limits of their domains. But the central
authority had gradually curtailed and subordinated to itself the
judicial powers of the landed proprietor; to such an extent that
the lords who still exercised them regarded them as little more
than a source of revenue.

The same thing had happened to all the special powers of
the nobility; on the political side these powers were now defunct
and only the pecuniary advantages attaching to them remained
(and in some cases had been much increased). At this point
something must be said about those lucrative privileges which
our forefathers usually had in mind when they spoke of "feudal

rights", since it was these that most affected the life of the general public.

It is hard to say to-day which of these rights were still in force in 1789 and in what they consisted. There had been a vast number of them and by then many had died out or been modified almost out of recognition; indeed, the exact meaning of the terms in which they are described (about which even contemporaries were not very clear) is extremely hard to ascertain to-day. Nevertheless, my study of works by eighteenth-century experts on feudal law and my researches into local usages have made it clear to me that the rights still functioning in 1789 fell into a relatively small number of categories; others survived, no doubt, but they were operative only in exceptional cases.

Of the old seigneurial *corvée,* or statutory labour obligation, traces remained everywhere, but half obliterated. Most of the toll charges on the roads had been reduced or done away with, though there were few provinces in which some had not survived. Everywhere the resident seigneur levied dues on fairs and markets, and everywhere enjoyed exclusive rights of hunting. Usually he alone possessed dovecotes and pigeons, and it was the general rule that farmers must bring their wheat to their lord's mill and their grapes to his wine press. A universal and very onerous right was that named *lods et ventes*; that is to say an impost levied by the lord on transfers of land within his domain. And throughout the whole of France the land was subject to quitrents, ground rents, dues in money or in kind payable by the peasant proprietor to his lord and irredeemable by the former. Varied as they were, all these obligations had one common feature: they were associated with the soil or its produce, and all alike bore heavily on the cultivator.

The lord spiritual enjoyed similar privileges. For though the Church derived its authority from a different source and had aims and functions quite different from those of the temporal power, it had gradually become tied up with the feudal system and, though never fully integrated into it, was so deeply involved as to seem part and parcel of it.[10][11]

Bishops, canons, and abbots owned fiefs or quitrents in virtue of their ecclesiastical status, and usually a monastery had seigneurial rights over the villages on whose land they stood.[12] It had serfs in the only part of France where serfdom had survived, employed forced labour, levied dues on fairs and markets, had the monopoly of the communal wine press, bakehouse, mill, and the stud bull. Moreover, the clergy enjoyed in France—as indeed in all Christian Europe—the right of levying tithes.

The point, however, on which I would lay stress is that exactly the same feudal rights were in force in every European land and that in most other countries of the continent they pressed far more heavily on the population than in France. Take, for example, the lord's right to forced labour, the *corvée*. It was rarely exercised and little oppressive in France, whereas in Germany it was stringent and everywhere enforced.

Moreover, when we turn to the feudal rights which so much outraged our fathers and which they regarded as opposed not merely to all ideas of justice but to the spirit of civilisation itself (I am thinking of the tithe, irredeemable ground rents, perpetual charges, *lods et ventes,* and so forth, all that in the somewhat grandiloquent language of the eighteenth century was styled "the servitude of the land"), we find that all these practices obtained to some extent in England and, indeed, are still found there to-day. Yet they do not prevent English husbandry from being the best organised and most productive in the modern world; and, what is perhaps still more remarkable, the English nation seems hardly aware of their existence.

Why then did these selfsame feudal rights arouse such bitter hatred in the heart of the French people that it has persisted even after its object has long since ceased to exist? One of the reasons is that the French peasant had become a landowner, and another that he had been completely emancipated from the control of his lord. No doubt there were other reasons, but these, I think, were the chief ones.

If the peasant had not owned his land he would hardly have noticed many of the charges which the feudal system imposed on all real estate. What could the tithe matter to a man who had no land of his own? He could simply deduct it from the rent. And even restrictions hampering agriculture mean nothing to an agriculturist who is simply cultivating land for the benefit of someone else.

Moreover, if the French peasant had still been under his lord's control, the feudal rights would have seemed much less obnoxious, because he would have regarded them as basic to the constitution of his country.

When the nobles had real power as well as privileges, when they governed and administered, their rights could be at once greater and less open to attack. In fact, the nobility was regarded in the age of feudalism much as the government is regarded by everyone today; its exactions were tolerated in view of the protection and security it provided. True, the nobles enjoyed invidious privileges and rights that weighed heavily on the commoner, but in return for this they kept order, administered justice, saw to the execution of the laws, came to the rescue of the oppressed, and watched over the interests of all. The more these functions passed out of the hands of the nobility, the more uncalled-for did their privileges appear—until at last their mere existence seemed a meaningless anachronism.

I would ask you to picture to yourself the French peasant as he was in the eighteenth century—or, rather, the peasant you know to-day, for he has not changed at all. His status is different, but not his personality. See how he appears in the records from which I have been quoting: a man so passionately devoted to the soil that he spends all his earnings on buying land, no matter what it costs. To acquire it he must begin by paying certain dues, not to the government but to other land-owners of the neighbourhood, who are as far removed as he from the central administration and almost as powerless as he. When at long last he has gained possession of this land which means so much to him, it is hardly an exaggeration to say that he sinks his heart in it along with the grain he sows. The possession of this little plot of earth, a tiny part, his very own, of the wide world, fills him with pride and a sense of independence. But now the neighbours aforesaid put in an appearance, drag him away from his cherished fields, and bid him work elsewhere without payment. When he tries to protect his seedlings from the animals they hunt, they tell him to take down his fences, and they lie in wait for him at river crossings to exact a toll. At the market there they are again, to make him pay for the right of selling the produce of his land, and when on his return home he wants to use the wheat he has put aside for his daily needs, he has to take it to their mill to have it ground, and then to have his bread baked in the lord's oven. Thus part of the income from his small domain goes to supporting these men in the form of charges which are imprescriptible and ir-redeemable. Whatever he sets out to do, he finds these tiresome neighbours barring his path, interfering in his simple pleasures and his work, and consuming the produce of his toil. And when he has done with them, other fine gentlemen dressed in black step in and take the greater part of his harvest. When we remember the special temperament of the French peasant proprietor in the eighteenth century, his ruling interests and passions, and the treatment accorded him, we can well under-stand the rankling grievances that burst into a flame in the French Revolution.[13]

For even after it had ceased to be a political institution, the feudal system remained basic to the economic organisation of France.[14] In this restricted form it was far more hated than in the heyday of feudalism, and we are fully justified in saying that the very destruction of some of the institutions of the Middle Ages made those which survived seem all the more detestable.

CHAPTER TWO

*How administrative centralisation was an institution of the old order and not, as is often thought, a creation of the Revolution or the Napoleonic period*

In the bygone years when we still had political assemblies in France I remember hearing one of the speakers referring to the centralisation of our country's government as "a glorious achievement of the Revolution, the envy of all Europe". Far be it from me to deny that this centralisation was a glorious achievement and that other nations envy us in this respect, but I do deny that it was an achievement of the Revolution. On the contrary, it was a legacy from the old order and, I may add, the only part of the political constitution of that régime which survived the Revolution—for the good reason that it alone could be adapted to the new social system sponsored by the Revolution. I venture to think that readers who have the patience to read with care the present chapter will be satisfied that this assertion is fully justified by the facts.

Let us for the moment disregard the so-called *pays d'états,* that is to say the provinces which managed their own affairs or, rather, had the appearance of enjoying relative autonomy. Situated on the outskirts of the kingdom, the *pays d'états* contained barely a quarter of the population and only two of them were free in any real sense, that is to say self-governing. I shall revert later to this subject and show how far the central power had forced even the *pays d'états* into line with the over-all administrative pattern.

Here, however, I am chiefly concerned with what in the official terminology of the period were described as *pays d'élection*—though in actual fact there were fewer elections in them than anywhere else. They formed a compact bloc, surrounding Paris on all sides, the nucleus of the kingdom and its vital core.

A first glance at the administration of France under the old order gives the impression of a vast diversity of laws and authorities, a bewildering confusion of powers. In all parts of the kingdom we find administrative bodies and officials vested with rights acquired by purchase, which could not be withdrawn from them. There was no co-operation between them and often their functions overlapped to such an extent that they hampered each other or came into conflict when their activities covered the same ground.

The courts of justice indirectly took a hand in legislation; they had the right to frame administrative rules which had the force of law within their jurisdictions. Sometimes they made a stand against the central administration, vigorously censured its procedures and even issued writs against its representatives. Local magistrates drew up police regulations for the town and boroughs where they resided.

In the towns systems of administration were very varied; the chief officials had different titles and derived their powers from different sources. In some towns there were "Consuls", in others "Syndics", in others Mayors. Some were appointed by the King, others by the seigneur or a princely holder of the appanage. Some were elected annually by their fellow townsmen, others bought the right of governing the latter in perpetuity.

Obviously we here have vestiges of the old system of a multiplicity of powers, but meanwhile there had gradually arisen new or greatly modified methods of local government, which I shall now describe.

At the heart of the realm, very near the throne, an administrative body, vested with high authority and combining in a new manner all the pre-existing powers, had little by little taken form; this was the *conseil du roi* or Royal Council. Though it was of ancient origin, most of its functions were of recent date. It was at once the supreme court of appeal (for it could set aside the judgments of all ordinary courts) and the highest administrative authority, for on it depended in the last resort all the "special jurisdictions". Moreover, as a governing council it also possessed, subject to the King's approval, the power of legislation. Most of the new laws were proposed and debated by the Council, which also fixed the sums to be levied by taxation and their distribution. As the highest administrative body in the land it was called on to enact the regulations determining the duties of government officials in their various spheres. It made decisions on all important matters and supervised the work of the subordinate civil authorities. In fact, all the affairs of the realm came before it in the last instance and it gave directives in every field of the administration. All the same, it had no inherent right of jurisdiction; this remained vested in the King even when, ostensibly, decisions emanated from the Council. Indeed, even in the administration of justice the powers of the Council were merely those of an advisory board— as was pointed out by the parlement* in one of its *remonstrances* addressed to the King.

The Royal Council was composed not of great lords but of persons of middle-class or even low extraction: former Intendants and others who had practical experience in the handling

---

*The parlements, located in Paris and provincial cities, were the chief judiciary bodies of the old order. The Parlement of Paris was important politically because royal edicts had to be registered with it before they became law, and at that time it could "remonstrate" against them.

of public business, and any of its members could be dismissed at the King's will. As a rule the Council acted with discretion, never flaunting the power which, in fact, it wielded. It discountenanced publicity regarding its activities or, rather, always functioned in the shadow of the throne, with which it was so closely associated. The Council was so powerful that it took a hand in everything; yet so inconspicuous that most historians hardly mention it.

In the same way as the general administration of the country was in the hands of a single group of men, almost the entire management of internal affairs was in the hands of a single official, the Controller-General. When we examine any of the yearbooks issued under the old order we find that nearly every province had its own Minister of State; but when we turn to public records of the administration, it soon becomes apparent that the provincial Minister was given few opportunities of acting independently. It was the Controller-General who had the whip hand in the conduct of public business and he had gradually brought under his control everything that had to do with money, in other words almost the entire administration of the country, and we find him acting as Finance Minister, Minister of the Interior, of Public Works, of Commerce.

Just as the central administration had to all intents and purposes only one executive officer in Paris, so it had only one such representative in each province. True, in the eighteenth century we still find great lords bearing the title of Governors of Provinces, these men being traditional, often hereditary representatives of the feudal monarchy of the past. But though they still were treated with deference, they had ceased to have any power now that all real authority was vested in the Intendants.

The Intendant was a young man of humble extraction, who had still his way to make and was never a native of the province to which he was posted. He did not obtain his office by purchase, by right of birth, or by election, but was chosen by the government from amongst the junior members of the Council and he was always liable to dismissal. In the official jargon of the time he was described as a *commissaire départi*, because he had been "detached" from the Council to act as its provincial agent. Most of the powers possessed by the Council itself were vested in him and he was entitled to use them as he thought fit. Like those of the Council these were both administrative and judicial; he corresponded directly with Ministers and was sole executant of all the measures enacted by the government in the province to which he had been posted.

Under him and appointed by him were the officials known as "sub-delegates", one for each canton, and he could dismiss them at will. The Intendant was usually a man who had recently been raised to noble rank, the sub-delegate always a commoner. Nevertheless, within his smaller sphere of influence the latter —like the Intendant as regards the *généralité* (administrative district) as a whole—was a plenary representative of the government. He was subordinate to the Intendant in the same way as the latter was subordinate to the Minister of State. In his *Memoirs* the Marquis d'Argenson cites a remark made to him by the famous Scots financier John Law. "Until I held the post of Controller-General I could hardly believe that such a state of affairs existed. Believe it or not, the French kingdom is ruled by thirty Intendants. Your parlements, Estates, and Governors simply do not enter into the picture. The Intendants play the part of 'Masters of Requests' assigned to the provinces, whose fortunes, for better or for worse, rest entirely in the hands of these thirty men."

All-powerful though he was, the Intendant cut a relatively humble figure beside the last representatives of the feudal aristocracy, which had lost nothing of its ancient glamour, and this explains why, though he made his authority felt at every turn, he attracted so little notice. Socially the nobles had the advantage of the Intendants, being not only wealthier but bene-fitting by the prestige that always attaches to ancient institu-tions. Moreover, as members of the Court, the nobles were in touch with the King and they commanded the French fleet and armies; in a word, their activities were of the showy kind that most impresses contemporaries and all too often focuses the attention of posterity. A great lord would have felt insulted by the proposal that he should be given the post of Intendant, and a gentleman by birth, however impoverished, would normally have disdained any such offer. To his thinking these Intendants were the creations of a usurped authority, upstarts whose task it was to superintend the middle class and the peasants—and, anyhow, not the kind of people a gentleman would wish to associate with. Yet, as Law noticed, these were the men who governed France.

Let us begin by considering the right of levying imposts, which in a way contains within itself all other powers. It is common knowledge that some taxes were farmed out; as regards these, it was the Royal Council that negotiated with companies of tax farmers, drew up the contracts, and regulated the methods of collection. All other imposts, such as the *taille*, capitation tax, and the *vingtièmes*, were assessed and levied directly by agents of the central government or under their absolute control.

It was the Council that each year voted, in secret session, the amount of the *taille* and the subsidiary imposts annexed to it, also its apportionment between the various provinces. It had been increased from year to year, without notice to the taxpayer or any sort of warning. Originally the assessment and collection of the *taille*, a very ancient form of taxation, had been entrusted to local officials who were more or less independent of the central government since they held their posts by the right of birth or election, or in some cases by purchase. These were the seigneur, the parish tax collector, the Treasurers of France and the *élus*, authorities which still existed in the eighteenth century. By then, however, some of them had altogether ceased to have anything to do with the *taille*, while the powers of the others had been gradually whittled down till they were mere subordinates. For in this field, too, all real power had passed into the hands of the Intendant and his underlings; it was he alone who, appearances notwithstanding, apportioned the incidence of the *taille* between the various parishes within his jurisdiction, supervised the tax collectors, granted remissions or extensions of time for payment.

As for the other imposts such as capitation tax, which were new creations, the government had a still freer hand since it was not hampered by precedents and could act alone, without regard to local authorities. The Controller-General, Intendants, and Council fixed the amount to be levied by each tax.

So much for the fiscal system. Let us now consider the position of the individual Frenchman as regards his civic duties.

Surprise is sometimes expressed at the fact that the French should have so meekly accepted the rigours of conscription at the time of the Revolution, and that they still put up with it today. But we must not forget that they had long been inured to obligations of this order and before conscription there had been service in the militia, which, though fewer men were called up, involved many hardships. Periodically all the young men in a rural area were compelled to draw lots for military service, this being the method of recruiting for the militia regiments, in which they had to serve six years. Since the militia was a relatively modern institution, none of the old feudal authorities had anything to do with it; recruiting was solely in the hands of representatives of the central government. The Council fixed the total number of men to be called up and the share to be borne by each province. Next, the Intendant decided on the number of men to be enrolled in each parish and his sub-delegate presided over the drawing of lots, settled applications for exemption, announced which men could stay at home and which must enrol in the militia; then made the latter over to the military authorities. There was no appeal except to the Intendant and the Council.

Moreover, outside the *pays d'états* all public works, even those of purely local interest, were decided on and carried out by agents of the central power alone.

True, there still existed independent local authorities such as the seigneur, the finance committee, and the district surveyors, who were entitled to take an active part in this branch of the administration.

In practice, however, they exercised their ancient powers very little and had, in many cases, relinquished them altogether; even the most cursory perusal of the administrative records makes this clear. All the great highways and even the local roads from one township to another were maintained by the public funds and it was the Council that drew up plans for them and made the contracts. The Intendant supervised the work of the engineers, while the sub-delegate recruited the forced labour it involved. The activities of the local authorities were confined to the upkeep of parish roads, which gradually fell into a shocking state of disrepair.

As far as public works were concerned the chief executive of the central government was then as now the Highways Department (*Ponts et Chaussées*). Despite the lapse of time this department has undergone remarkably little change. The *Ponts et Chaussées* included a governing board and a school; had travelling road surveyors who sent in annual reports on the condition of all the roads in France, and civil engineers with fixed headquarters who supervised, under the control of the Intendant, the making or repairing of the roads. Though far more institutions of the old order were carried over into the new social order than is generally supposed, they usually changed their names in the process, even when their general structure remained the same. Exceptionally, the *Ponts et Chaussées* retained both its name and its original composition.

Seconded by its subordinates, the central government alone saw to the maintenance of public order in the provinces. Small brigades of mounted police under the direct control of the Intendants were posted to every part of France. The Intendants used them for coping with all sudden emergencies (calling in the army if these were serious), for arresting vagabonds, preventing begging, and quelling the riots which frequently broke out owing to the price of grain. The ordinary citizen was never called on, as in the past, to aid the government in the task of keeping order—except in towns where there was a civic guard, whose members were enrolled, and its officers appointed, by the Intendant.

The judiciary had retained, and often exercised, the right of making police regulations, but these applied only to local areas, usually to a single town. The Council could always annul these regulations and often did so when they emanated from judicial bodies of an inferior status. Meanwhile the Council constantly issued regulations of its own, which were binding on the whole kingdom. These either dealt with matters other than those on which the courts of law passed orders, or with the same matters in cases where the Council thought fit to overrule the orders issued by the courts. These *arrêts du conseil*, as they were called, were promulgated in ever increasing numbers as the Revolution drew near. Indeed, there was hardly any detail of the internal economy and political organization of the nations that was not modified by *arrêts du conseil* during the forty years preceding the Revolution.

Under the feudal system the lord, while possessing extensive powers, had no less imperative duties, one of these being to succour the needy within his domain. A last vestige of this ancient obligation, which once obtained throughout Europe, can be found in the Prussian Code of 1795, where we read that "the lord must see to it that poor peasants are given education. As far as possible he should provide means of livelihood for such of his vassals as have no land, and if any are reduced to poverty he must come to their aid."

In France, however, no such law had existed for a long while; having been divested of his power, the lord no longer felt bound by his traditional obligations. And no local authority, no poor relief committee or parish council had taken them over. Now that nobody was bound by law to see to the welfare of the poor in rural areas, the central government had, somewhat venturesomely, accepted sole responsibility for this duty. Every year the Council allotted to each province a sum of money taken from the public funds for poor relief. This was divided up by the Intendant between the parishes under his control and it was to him that the cultivator had to apply in time of need. It was he, too, who made distributions of wheat or rice when the crops had failed. Each year the Council issued orders for the setting up in various places (specified by itself) of poor-houses, in which impoverished peasants were given work at a low wage.[15] For obvious reasons a system of relief operating from such a distance was bound to be capricious, sometimes misdirected, and always quite inadequate.[16]

However, the central government did not limit itself to coming to the rescue of the peasantry when times were hard; it aspired to teach them how to become rich and to help them to make their land pay, even if this meant using what was little short of compulsion. Pamphlets on agricultural science were issued periodically by the Intendants and their sub-delegates, farmers' associations were founded and prizes awarded; moreover, nurseries, whose seed grains were available to all, were maintained at considerable expense. Still one cannot help feeling that it would have been more to the point to have lightened some of the fiscal burdens under which the agriculturist was labouring and equalised their incidence. But as far as one can see, no such idea ever crossed the minds of the authorities.

Sometimes the Council tried to force workers to make more money, willy-nilly. Dozens of laws were passed ordering artisans to use "improved" methods and to manufacture certain specified kinds of goods. Since the Intendants were unable to cope with the work involved in the enforcement of all these regulations, "Inspectors-General of Industry" were appointed who toured the provinces to make sure they were complied with.[17]

We find decrees prohibiting the growing of certain crops on land which the Council declared unsuitable for them; thus vinegrowers were ordered to uproot their vines when these were planted—according to the omniscient Council—on a bad soil. In short, the central power had taken to playing the part of an indefatigable mentor and keeping the nation in quasi-paternal tutelage.

CHAPTER THREE

*How paternal government, as it is called today, was practised under the old order*

Municipal autonomy survived the feudal system, and long after the lords had ceased to administer the country districts French towns retained the right of governing themselves. Indeed, until almost the end of the seventeenth century some towns were still to all intents and purposes small democratic republics, their officials being elected by the townsfolk and answerable to them alone. In short, there was an active municipal life in which all took part, and the communities of French towns still prided themselves on their ancient rights and set much store in their independence.

It was not until 1692 that free municipal elections were everywhere abolished. In that year appointments to municipal posts were, to use the official jargon of the day, "put in offices," which meant that the King now sold to certain members of the community the right of governing in perpetuity their fellow citizens.

This dealt a serious blow not only to the independence but also to the prosperity of the towns. True, the system of making public offices purchasable may often work well enough where judicial posts are concerned, since the criterion of a good judge is his incorruptibility and the purchaser of such a post may be presumed to be a man of substance. But the system of selling offices has always had disastrous effects when applied to administrative and executive posts, the chief qualifications for which are a sense of responsibility combined with zeal and a habit of obedience. The monarchical government had no illusions on the subject and took good care not to apply to its own personnel the system foisted on the towns. Thus, for example, it never put up to sale the post of Intendant or sub-delegate.

A circumstance on which historians may justly pour scorn is that this vast, not to say revolutionary, innovation had no political aim in view. True, Louis XI had curtailed the towns-folk's liberties because he was afraid of their democratic character;[18] Louis XIV destroyed them without fearing them. This is proved by the fact that he was quite willing to sell back their rights to such towns as could raise the sums required. In fact, he was less concerned with destroying local autonomy than with making money out of it. If the result in many cases was the ex-tinction of the municipal freedom of the past, this was merely incidental to his financial policy and, one almost might say, un-intended. Strangest of all, this curious process went on for eighty years, during which period towns were invited on no less than seven occasions to buy the right of electing their executive officials; then, after they had tasted for a while the pleasure of self-government, the right was withdrawn and sold back to them once more. This was always done for the same reason, and often the central government made no secret of it. Thus in the preamble of the Edict of 1722 we read: "Given the present financial stringency, we must needs employ the most effective methods of reducing it." The methods in question were certainly effective, but ruinous for those on whom the burden fell. "I am appalled," wrote an Intendant to the Controller-

General in 1764, "by the huge sums that this town has disbursed from time to time to repurchase the right of choosing its
own officials. Had the money been employed on works of public
utility, all the townsfolk would have greatly benefitted; as it
is, they have had to bear the brunt of the expenditure entailed
by these offices and the privileges they carry with them." To my
thinking, this was the most shameful feature of the old order.

It is by no means easy to find out how French towns were
administered in the eighteenth century for, apart from the fact
that the source from which municipal authority derived was
constantly changing (as explained above), each town still kept
some vestiges of its ancient constitution and customs peculiar to
itself.[19] Yet, though perhaps no two French towns were administered in exactly the same way, there was an underlying similarity. In 1764 the government proposed to draw up
a charter for the administration of the towns throughout the
country, and to this end instructed the Intendants to submit
reports on the system currently prevailing in each town. I have
unearthed some of the records of this inquiry and, after studying
them, have come to the conclusion that municipal business
was conducted in much the same way everywhere. There are
superficial differences but the basic structure is always the same.

Usually urban administration was in the hands of two assemblies; this holds good for all large towns and most small ones.
The first of these assemblies was composed of the municipal
officials, whose numbers varied according to the size of the
town in question. This, the executive of the community, was
known as the *corps de ville*, i.e. town corporation. In towns
where the King had revived the right of election or the offices
had been repurchased, the members of this body held their posts
for a limited period and were elective. Elsewhere they held their
posts in perpetuity, in consideration of a cash payment—in
towns, that is to say, where the King had resumed his right to
dispose of offices. However, he did not always succeed in
finding purchasers, since for obvious reasons the value of this
peculiar kind of merchandise depreciated the more the municipal authorities came under the domination of the central
power. Though these town officials were unpaid, they enjoyed
certain privileges, such as exemption from taxation. They were

all on an equal footing and their administration was collective, there being no one official with special powers and personal responsibility. The Mayor was merely president of the corporation, not its chief executive authority.

A second body known as the "General Assembly" elected the corporation—in towns where the system of election still prevailed—and in all cases continued to take part in the conduct of municipal affairs. During the fifteenth century the General Assembly was often composed of all the townsfolk; this, as was pointed out in one of the Intendants' reports, was "in accordance with the popular spirit of our forefathers." Thus in those early times the entire population of the town elected its municipal officials; moreover, it was sometimes convened to decide on matters of importance and the corporation had to justify its acts to the Assembly. This state of affairs continued in some districts as late as the close of the seventeenth century.

In the eighteenth century, however, it was no longer the entire population that sat in the General Assembly; this was almost always a committee of representatives. But—and this is an important point—these representatives were not elected by the community as a whole or even, one might say, in sympathy with it. Everywhere it was composed of notables, some of whom sat in it in virtue of some special right, while others were nominees of guilds or trade corporations, each being in duty bound to carry out the mandate given him by the group he represented.

As the century went on, the number of notables figuring as of right in the Assembly tended to increase, while the deputies of trade and craft guilds became fewer and fewer or even ceased to sit in it. The result was that the Assembly now consisted of members of the middle class, representatives of the business corporations, and contained very few artisans. Not so easily hoodwinked as many have imagined, the "common people" ceased to take any active part in local government and lost all interest in it. Time and again the authorities tried to reawaken that fine spirit of local patriotism which had worked such wonders in the Middle Ages—but without success. The ordinary citizen seemed wholly indifferent to the interests of the town he lived in. In towns where a semblance of free-elections had been retained he was pressed to go to the voting urns, but he usually preferred to stay at home. Every student of history knows that this phenomenon is a common one; rulers who destroy men's freedom commonly begin by trying to retain its forms— and so it has been from the reign of Augustus to the present day. They cherish the illusion that they can combine the prerogatives of absolute power with the moral authority that comes from popular assent. Almost all have failed in this endeavour and learned to their cost that it is impossible to keep up such appearances for long when there is no reality behind them.

Municipal government in the eighteenth century had everywhere degenerated into a petty oligarchy. A few families kept a watchful eye on their own interests, out of sight of the public and feeling no responsibilities toward less privileged citizens. Everywhere in France the local governments were stricken with this disease, and all Intendants drew attention to it. But the only remedy they could think of was to tighten the central government's control over the local authorities. Actually, however, it was difficult to go farther in this direction. Aside from the modifications decreed from time to time in the general structure of rural administration, local laws were often thrown into confusion by hastily framed regulations issued at the instance of the Intendants without preliminary investigation and sometimes without the citizens being given any notice of them.[20]

The protest of a town thus treated figures in the records. "This measure has taken all of us, from the highest to the lowest, by surprise; we had absolutely no warning it was coming."

Towns were not allowed to institute a toll or to levy a rate, to mortgage, lease or sell, or litigate about their property, or to make use of any surplus revenue without first obtaining an authorisation from the Council, sponsored by the Intendant. All public works had to conform to plans and estimates expressly sanctioned by an Order in Council, and it was under the auspices of the Intendant or his sub-delegates that contracts were allotted; moreover, their execution was usually supervised by a government survey or architect. This, I venture to think, will come as a surprise to those who believe that what is happening in France today is new.

But the interference of the central government in municipal affairs went much farther; indeed, it often flagrantly overstepped its statutory powers. Thus in a circular addressed (towards the middle of the century) by the Controller-General to all Intendants I find the following passage: "You are enjoined to pay particular attention to all that takes place in municipal assemblies. Exact records must be kept of all the resolutions voted, and these must be dispatched to me forthwith, together with your comments."

From letters that passed between Intendants and sub-delegates we learn that the government took a hand in all local affairs, even the most trivial. Nothing could be done without consulting the central authority, which had decided views on everything. Even village fêtes were regulated by it; in some cases it was the government that gave orders for public rejoicings, ordered bonfires to be lit, and houses to be illuminated. One Intendant actually imposed a fine of twenty *livres* on members of a civic guard who missed attending a *Te Deum* !

Town councillors were nothing short of abject in their deference to the representatives of government. "We humbly crave your good will and protection, and we shall prove ourselves not unworthy of them by our strict obedience to all the orders Your Excellency may deign to issue." And another group of municipal officials, magnificently styling themselves the "Town Peers", tried to ingratiate themselves with the Intendant by reminding him that "never once had they failed to comply with His Excellency's wishes." Thus it was that the middle class prepared itself for governing, and the French people for liberty !

If their subservience to authority had at least benefitted the finances of the French townships, something might have been said for it. But it did nothing of the sort. True, it was argued at the time that but for governmental control the towns would have rapidly become insolvent. Perhaps—but one thing is certain, this eighteenth-century centralisation did not prevent their ruining themselves. All administrative records of the day testify to the chaotic state of their finances.[21]

When we turn from towns to villages we find other powers, other methods; but the same subordination.[22] I have found much evidence in support of the view that during the Middle Ages the inhabitants of each French village formed a commonalty independent in many ways of the seigneur. No doubt he requisitioned their services, watched over and governed them; but the village held property in common and had exclusive ownership of it. The villagers elected their own officials and governed themselves on democratic lines.

This early type of parochial self-government was common to all once-feudal nations and in all countries into which these nations had imported vestiges of their ancient laws. Traces of it can be found everywhere in England and it was still in full force in Germany as recently as sixty years ago—as is proved by the legislative code of Frederick the Great. In France, too, some vestiges of it could still be seen in the eighteenth century.

I well remember my surprise when I was for the first time examining the records of an intendancy with a view to finding out how a parish was administered under the old order. For in the organisation of this small community, despite its poverty and servile state, I discovered some of the features which had struck me so much in the rural townships of North America: features which I then had—wrongly—thought peculiar to the New World. Neither had permanent representatives, that is to say a town council in the strict sense of the term, and both were administered by officials acting separately, under instructions from the whole community. General assemblies were convened from time to time in both and at these the townsfolk, acting in concert, elected their own officials and passed orders on matters affecting the interests of the community. In short, the French and the American systems resembled each other— in so far as a dead creature can be said to resemble one that is very much alive.

For these two systems of local government, though their ways soon parted, had in fact a common origin. Transported overseas from feudal Europe and free to develop in total independence, the rural parish of the Middle Ages became the township of New England. Emancipated from the seigneur, but controlled at every turn by an all-powerful government, it took in France the form which we shall now describe.

During the eighteenth century the number and the titles of parish officials varied from province to province. Old records show that they once had been most numerous where there was a vigorous communal life and fewest where it had decayed. By the eighteenth century their number had been reduced to two in most parishes; one being styled the Collector and the other, usually, the Syndic. Theoretically these officials were still elected by the community, but in practice they had everywhere become agents of the central power rather than representatives of the community. The Collector saw to the levying of the impost known as the *taille,* under the personal supervision of the Intendant. The Syndic, briefed daily for this purpose by the sub-delegate, represented him in all matters concerning public order and the central administration, and was his chief executive as regards the militia, public works, and the enforcement of the laws.

The lord, as we have seen, played no part in any of these activities; he stood aloof, neither co-operating with nor hindering the agents of the central authority. Indeed, he now regarded such activities, hitherto the token and the mainstay of his power, as unworthy of notice, and the more his power declined, the less they interested him. He would have felt offended had he been asked to busy himself with such petty details of the daily life of the community. Yet, though he no longer governed, his very presence in the parish and his privileges put difficulties in the way of establishing a good parochial government in replacement of his own. For the mere fact that there existed within the community an individual so highly privileged, so independent and different in kind from all its other members, told against the due enforcement of laws, which, in theory, applied to all alike.

What was still worse, his social pre-eminence had (as I shall show later) caused most of the wealthier or more cultivated residents to migrate, one by one, to the more congenial atmosphere of the towns. Thus, apart from him, the population was little more than a horde of ignorant, uneducated peasants, quite incapable of administering local affairs. "A French parish,"

Turgot rightly said, "is a congeries of huts and countryfolk as inert as their huts."

Eighteenth-century records are full of complaints regarding the incompetence, stupidity, or slackness of the Collectors and Syndics in the country districts. Ministers of State, Intendants, and even private individuals, of the better classes constantly lament this state of affairs; yet none of them traces it to its true cause.

Right up to the Revolution local government in France retained some of the democratic qualities it had possessed in the Middle Ages. For the election of municipal officials, or when some matter concerning the populace at large was to be discussed, the church bell summoned everyone to the porch of the parish church, and poor and rich alike were entitled to attend the meeting. True, there was no organised debate, no voting; yet everyone was allowed to air his views and a notary was always in attendance to take down what was said and draw up minutes of the proceedings.

Yet it was but an empty show of freedom; these assemblies had no real power. Indeed, we have here a small-scale illustration of the way in which governments of a wholly despotic order can assimilate some of the features of the most thorough-paced democracy, and, as if oppression were not enough, it can be combined with the ostrich-like absurdity of feigning not to see it. For though these democratic assemblies in the parishes could give voice to their wishes they—like the town councils— had ceased to have the right of putting them into effect. They could not even open their mouths until permission to speak had been requested from and granted by the Intendant; in fact, it was only "under his good pleasure", as the saying went, that these meetings could take place at all. Even when they came to a unanimous decision, they were unable to enforce it; they could neither buy nor sell, lease property nor go to law without permission from the Royal Council. Even the rural parishes farthest from Paris were as strictly controlled as those nearest the capital. I have found cases where parishes had to ask permission from the Council to disburse sums as small as twenty-five *livres*.

No doubt in most localities the countryfolk had retained

the right of electing their officials by an open vote, but as a rule, when such posts had to be filled, the Intendant sponsored a candidate chosen by him, and this candidate rarely failed to secure unanimous election. Sometimes too, when a man had been elected by the members of the community on their own initiative, the Intendant quashed the election, himself appointed the Collector or the Syndic, and postponed all future elections *sine die*. I have come across thousands of instances of these highhanded methods.

Once elected, these parochial officials were treated without the least consideration and were forced to truckle to the whims, however absurd, of the lowest representative of the central government, the sub-delegate. Often he imposed fines on them and sometimes even had them sentenced to imprisonment; for the laws ordinarily protecting individuals from highhanded treatment of this order did not here apply. In a report dated 1750 made by an Intendant we find him saying: "I have had sentences of imprisonment passed on some of the principal persons in villages that have been prating about their 'grievances', and made these villages defray the expenses of the visit of the mounted constabulary. So I have had no trouble in bringing them to heel." Indeed, appointment to any of these local official posts was regarded less as an honour than as a calamity to be avoided at all costs.

Nonetheless, the peasants clung to these last vestiges of the old system and local self-government; indeed, even today it is the only form of freedom which, by and large, means much to them. A French peasant may be willing enough to leave the government of the nation as a whole in the hands of an autocratic central power, but he bitterly resents the idea of not having a say in the local administration of his village: so much does even the hollowest of forms retain its glamour!

What has been said about the towns and parishes applies to all corporate bodies which were self-contained and owned property collectively. Under the old order, as nowadays, there was in France no township, borough, village, or hamlet, however small, no hospital, factory, convent,[23] or college which had a right to manage its own affairs as it thought fit or to administer its possessions without interference. Then, as today, the central power held all Frenchmen in tutelage. The term "paternal government" had not yet been invented, but the reality already existed.

CHAPTER FOUR

*How administrative justice and the immunity of public servants were institutions of the old order*

In no other European country were the ordinary courts so independent of the government as in France, but in no other country was so much use made of "exceptional" courts of justice. There was a closer connexion between these two aspects of the French judicial system than one might at first suppose. Since the King had little or no hold on the judges, being unable to dismiss them, transfer them to new posts, or even (as a general rule) promote them—since, in short, he could neither play on their ambition nor inspire them with fear—he very soon came to find their independence irksome. Hence arose the custom, more prevalent in France than elsewhere, of withdrawing from the ordinary courts the right of trying cases in which the King's authority or interest was in any way involved. Such cases were heard by special courts presided over by judges more dependent on the King, which, while offering his subjects a semblance of justice, could be trusted to carry out his wishes.

In countries, Germany for instance (or, more exactly, certain parts of it), where the ordinary courts had never been as independent as they then were in France, precautions of this kind were unnecessary and administrative justice—that is to say courts dealing specially with cases in which the administration was involved—never existed. For in the countries I have in mind their rulers felt sure enough of the subservience of the judges to be able to dispense with special tribunals.

When we read the royal decrees and edicts issued in the last century of the monarchy, and the orders enacted by the Council during the same period, we find few in which the government, when publishing a regulation, fails to add that any controversies or legal proceedings arising out of it will be decided exclusively by the Intendants and the Council. ''Furthermore, His Majesty orders that all disputes arising from the execution of this decree and its appurtenances shall be heard by the Intendant, who will pass final judgment on them, subject to a right of appeal to the Council." This is the usual formula.

In matters covered by laws and customs of the past, where this precaution had not been taken, the Council frequently exercised the right of "evocation", as it was called; that is to say it withdrew from the jurisdiction of the ordinary judges any suit in which the administration was implicated, and itself decided it. The records of the Council are full of orders of this sort. Little by little what was theoretically an exception became the general rule, indeed, a fixed principle. Though there was no provision for this in the common law, those who administered it came to take it for granted that all suits in which matters of public interest were at issue or which concerned the interpretation of an official regulation did not fall within the purview of the ordinary courts, whose sole function was to try suits between private parties. Thus the practice obtaining today is no innovation; it existed under the old order, and the only change has been to codify it.

From now on most legal proceedings relating to the assessment and collection of taxes were subject to the exclusive jurisdiction of the Intendant and the Council. The same applied to everything connected with traffic regulations, public conveyances, the upkeep of the highways, inland navigation, and the like. In a word, all suits in which the public authority was in any way concerned were heard by administrative tribunals.

The Intendants saw to it that the scope of this "exceptional" jurisdiction was continually enlarged; their reports to the Controller-General and the Council were full of recommendations in this sense. The arguments put forward by one such official with a view of procuring an "evocation" are revealing. "The ordinary judge is bound by rules which compel him to penalise certain offences against the law, but the Council can always override the provisions of the law when this seems advisable."

With this in mind the Intendant and the Council often with-

drew from the ordinary courts and themselves decided cases
which had only the vaguest connexion, or even none at all
with public administration. Thus when a certain gentleman,
being involved in a court case with a neighbour, was dissatisfied with the procedure of the trying judge, he applied to
the Council to "evoke" the case. The petition was referred to
the Intendant, who expressed the following opinion in the course
of his report. "Though only private rights are in issue and the
cognisance of this suit pertains to the ordinary court, His
Majesty is always entitled, if such be his good pleasure, to take
cognisance of suits of any and every nature, without assigning
reasons for so doing."

As a rule all members of the lower classes who were accused
of breaches of the public peace accompanied by violence were
tried by the Intendant or the Provost of the Mounted Constabulary, in pursuance of an "evocation". Most of the riots due
to the high price of flour were dealt with in this manner.
In association with a certain number of persons of high standing
—a kind of vigilance committee selected by himself *ad hoc*—the
Intendant sat as a criminal judge. I have come on records of
judgments passed by the courts of this order in which the accused persons were given sentences of penal servitude, even of
death. The trial of criminal cases by Intendants was still frequent at the close of the seventeenth century.

Our modern jurists assure us that much progress has been
made since the Revolution as regards the relations between the
administrative and judicial powers. Formerly, they tell us, they
tended to overlap, whereas nowadays they are kept distinct,
neither being allowed to encroach on the other. But when we
seek to evaluate the "progress" made in this respect, we do well
to bear in mind the fact that while under the old régime the
judicial power was constantly tending to range beyond its
proper field of action, by the same token it never wholly filled
that field. If we limit our attention to one or other of
these two facts we have but a partial, indeed misleading, idea
of the true state of affairs. Sometimes, no doubt, courts of law
were allowed to make decisions on matters of public administration which were obviously outside their competence; but sometimes, on the other hand, they were debarred from hearing

cases between private parties and thus excluded from their proper sphere. True, we have ousted the judiciary from the administrative field, on which, under the old order, it had been improperly encroaching; but we have permitted the government to continue intermeddling, as in the past, in matters which, by common consent, should be left to the decision of our ordinary courts of law. And this confusion of powers which exists today may well be deemed no less pernicious, if not more so, than its predecessor. For when the judiciary intervenes in administrative matters, only material interests suffer; but when the State tampers with the course of justice, the effect is to unsettle men's minds and to make them at once servile and revolutionary.

Among the nine or ten "definitive" constitutions which have been drawn up in France during the last sixty years, one contains a provision that no government servant shall be prosecuted in an ordinary court of law unless and until his prosecution has been sanctioned by higher authority. The advisability of this provision seemed so obvious to all concerned that when the form of constitution in which it was included went the way of previous constitutions, care was taken to salvage it from the wreckage, and ever since then, revolutions notwithstanding, it had been preserved intact. Government servants have a habit of describing the immunity from prosecution they enjoy as one of the benefactions of 1789. But this, too, is a misconception; under the old monarchy the government was mindful, as are our modern governments, of protecting its servants from the annoyance of being haled before the courts like common malefactors. The only real difference is this: before the Revolution the government had to use methods that were arbitrary, not to say illegal, for this purpose; whereas nowadays it is legally entitled to allow its employees to violate the law with impunity.

Under the old order when proceedings against a government servant of whatever rank were pending in an ordinary court, the Council usually stepped in with a notice withdrawing the case from it and directing the defendant to appear before a board nominated by the Council. For otherwise, as a Councillor of State, speaking of a contemporary case, observed, "a government official brought before an ordinary court would certainly find the judges prejudiced against him, and the effect would be to undermine the King's authority." "Evocations" of this sort were not exceptions but the general rule and concerned not only high officials but the humblest government employees. Indeed, if a man had even the slightest connexion with any branch of the administration he had nothing to fear from any other authority. Thus when a foreman employed by the *Ponts et Chaussées* to supervise the forced-labour gangs working on a road was prosecuted by one of his men for alleged ill-treatment, the Intendant reported on the case as follows. "Undeniably the foreman behaved improperly, but this is not a reason for letting the law take its course. It is of vital importance to the *Ponts et Chaussées* that the ordinary courts should not be allowed to deal with complaints against their foremen laid by conscripted labourers. Were this case allowed to proceed, a precedent would be created and the execution of public works impeded by the constant litigation which, given the unpopularity of these foremen, would certainly ensue."

On another occasion an Intendant wrote as follows to the Controller-General. (The offender in this case was a contractor employed by the government who had taken building materials from privately owned land near the place where he was working.) "I cannot impress on you too strongly how prejudicial it would be to the interests of the administration were its contractors exposed to prosecution in the ordinary courts, whose conceptions of the law are bound to conflict with those of the government."

That was written just a hundred years ago, in 1756—but the words might well be those of one of our present-day officials.


CHAPTER FIVE

*How the idea of centralised administration was established among the ancient authorities, which it supplanted, without, however, destroying them*

At this stage it may be well to sum up briefly the state of affairs set forth in the three preceding chapters. We find a single central power located at the heart of the kingdom and controlling public administration throughout the country; a single Minister of State in charge of almost all the internal affairs of the country; in each province a single representative of government supervising every detail of the administration; no secondary administrative bodies authorised to take action on their own initiative; and, finally, "exceptional" courts for the trial of cases involving the administration or any of its officers. Is not this exactly the highly centralised administration with which we are familiar in present-day France? True, its forms were less clearly defined, its procedures less co-ordinated, and the government machinery ran less smoothly than it does today; nonetheless, it was the same in all essentials. Nothing vital has been added to or taken from it. The only change is that the centralisation of power in France has become far more conspicuous now that all the relics of the past have been pruned away.[24]

Most of the institutions described above were subsequently adopted by other countries—indeed, replicas of them can now be seen in many parts of the world—but at the time of which I am writing they were peculiar to France and they had, as I shall now set forth, a very great influence not only on the Revolution itself but on its aftermath.

That it was possible to build up modern institutions of this kind in France within the shattered framework of feudal society may seem surprising at first sight. It was a task calling for much patience and adroitness rather than for the exercise of force and authoritarian methods. When the Revolution broke out, very little of the old administrative structure had actually been destroyed; but a new substructure, so to speak, had gradually been pieced together.

There is nothing to show that in carrying out this difficult task the government of the old order was following any premeditated scheme. It merely yielded to the instinctive desire of every government to gather all the reins of power into its own hands and, despite the multiplication of secondary powers, this instinct never failed to take effect. Representatives of the former ruling class retained their rank and titles, but all effective authority was gradually withdrawn from them. They were not so much expelled from their former spheres of influence as edged out of them. Taking advantage of the apathy of some and the unenlightened egotism of others, the central administration stepped into their place; far from seeking to amend their short-comings it made these serve its turn, and ended up, almost everywhere, by replacing them with a single representative of government named the Intendant, whose very title was a new creation.

The only obstacle the central power encountered in carrying out its vast programme was the judiciary; but even in this domain it succeeded in grasping the substance of power, leaving only the shadow of it to its rivals. It did not exclude the parlements from the administration but little by little extended its authority so as to usurp practically the whole field assigned to them. In certain states of emergency, during periods of famine for example, when feelings ran high amongst the people and the local authorities saw a chance of asserting themselves, the central government allowed the parlements to take charge for the duration of the crisis and to make a great show of bene-ficent activity (historians have tended to give prominence to these episodes). But once the crisis was over, the government stepped in again, and discreetly but firmly resumed its control of everything and everyone within the affected areas.[25]

When we closely study the conflicts between the parlements and the royal power we find that it was almost always in the field of politics, not in that of administration, that these clashes took place. Usually the bone of contention was a new tax; that is to say the matter at issue was not of an administrative order but concerned exclusively the power of legislation—a power which, constitutionally, neither of the parties involved had any better right than the other to arrogate to itself.

These disputes are found to intensify in violence the nearer we come to the revolutionary period. And with the rising tide of popular feeling, the parlements tended more and more to take a hand in politics while, as a result of the increasing efficiency (due to long, cumulative experience) of the central power and its officers, the parlements concerned themselves less and less with matters of an administrative order in the strict sense. Thus the French parlement became less and less an administrative and more and more a demagogic body.

Moreover, with the passing years the central power constantly opened up new fields of action into which the courts of law, owing to their inadaptability and conservatism, were incapable of following it. For they had no precedents to go on and were inhibited by routine. The social order was in the throes of a rapid evolution, giving rise to new needs, and each of these was an added source of power to the central government, since it alone was in a position to satisfy them. Whereas the activities of the courts were limited to a well-defined field, those of the central government were being steadily extended, along with civilisation itself.

With the approach of the Revolution the minds of all the French were in a ferment; a host of new ideas were in the air, projects which the central government alone could implement. Thus, before overthrowing it, the Revolution increased its powers. That, like so much else, the State machine had been brought to a high state of perfection is evidenced by all the records of the period. The Controller-General and the Intendants of 1790 were quite other than the Controller-General and the Intendants of 1740. The administration had been thoroughly overhauled, and though it employed the same officials, they were actuated by a very different spirit. In proportion as the central power at once widened its sphere of action and paid more heed to details, it had become more systematic in its methods and more efficient. Moreover, now that it had the entire nation under its control, it could afford to be more lenient, to give more suggestions, fewer peremptory orders.

That ancient institution, the French monarchy, after being swept away by the tidal wave of the Revolution, was restored in 1800. It was not, as is often supposed, the principles of 1789 that triumphed at that time (and are still incorporated in the French administrative system); on the contrary, it was the principles of the old order that were revived and have been endorsed by all successive governments.

If I am asked how it was possible for this part of the old order to be taken over *en bloc* and integrated into the constitution of modern France, my answer is that the reason why the principle of the centralisation of power did not perish in the Revolution is that this very centralisation was at once the

Revolution's starting-off point and one of its guiding principles.
Indeed, I would go so far as to say that whenever a nation
destroys its aristocracy, it almost automatically tends towards a
centralisation of power; a greater effort is then needed to hold
it back than to encourage it to move in this direction. All the
authorities existing within it are affected by this instinctive urge
to coalesce, and much skill is needed to keep them separate.
Thus the democratic revolution, though it did away with so
many institutions of the past, was led inevitably to consolidate
this one; centralisation fitted in so well with the programme of
the new social order that the common error of believing it to
have been a creation of the Revolution is easily accounted for.

### CHAPTER SIX

*Of the methods of administration under the old
order*

Anyone who reads letters that passed between the Intendants
and their superiors or subordinates cannot fail to be struck by
the family likeness between the government officials of the past
and those of modern France. They seem to join hands across the
abyss made by the Revolution and, indeed, the same may be said
of the people they administered. Never, perhaps, has the extent
to which systems of government shape the mentality of the
governed been so clearly demonstrated.

Long before the Revolution, Ministers of State had made a
point of keeping a watchful eye on everything that was happening in the country and of issuing orders from Paris on every
conceivable subject. As time went on and with the increasing
efficiency of administrative technique, this habit of surveillance
became almost an obsession with the central government. Towards the close of the eighteenth century it was impossible
to arrange for poor-relief work in the humblest village of a
province hundreds of miles from the capital without the
Controller-General's insisting on having his say about the exact
sum to be expended, the site of the workhouse, and the way it
was to be managed. When an almshouse was established, he

insisted on being supplied with the names of the paupers using it, the dates of their arrival and departure. In 1733 M. d'Argenson observed that "the amount of office work imposed on our heads of departments is quite appalling. Everything passes through their hands, they alone decide what is to be done, and when their knowledge is not as wide as their authority, they have to leave things to subordinate members of their staffs, with the result that the latter have become the true rulers of the country."

The Controller-General did not merely call for reports on matters of public interest; he insisted also on being given detailed information, often of a trivial kind, about private persons. In such cases the Intendant directed his sub-delegates to make inquiries and in his report to the Controller-General he repeated verbatim what they had told him, without mentioning that he knew the facts only at second hand.

Owing to this system of centralising information and controlling everything from Paris, a most elaborate machinery had to be set up for coping with the flood of documents that poured in from all sides, and even so the delays of the administration were notorious. On studying the records I found that it took a year at least for a parish to get permission to repair a church steeple or the priest's house. Oftener than not the time required was much longer: two or three years.

The Council itself took notice of this regrettable state of affairs in one of its minutes (29 March, 1773). "The transaction of public business is delayed to an almost incredible extent by administrative formalities and the public has all too often just cause for complaint. Nevertheless," the writer makes haste to add, "all these formalities are indispensable."

I used to think that our present rulers' obsession with statistics was a new development; but I was mistaken. Towards the end of the old order small printed forms with blanks to be filled in were frequently circulated among the Intendants, who had the necessary entries made by their sub-delegates and the Syndics of parishes. The Controller-General called for reports from each district on the nature of the soil, on the way it was cultivated, on the kind and quantity of crops, on the number of livestock in each rural district, on the activities and habits of the local population. The information thus supplied was hardly less detailed, and no more reliable, than that provided nowadays by our sub-prefects and Mayors. As a rule, the opinions expressed by sub-delegates on the manners of those they governed were far from favourable; we often find them complaining that the peasants were congenitally lazy and would never do a stroke of work if their livelihood did not depend on it. This was an economic doctrine much in vogue, it would seem, with the local representatives of the central power.

Even the official terminology of the two periods is remarkably similar. In both we find the same flat style, the same vagueness and insipidity; it is as though the writers made a point of effacing their personalities in the manner of the modern bureaucrat. Indeed, the reports of any present-day Prefect might well be the work of an old order Intendant.

Not until the century's end, when the literary methods we associate with Rousseau and Diderot had had time to diffuse themselves and to affect the spoken language, did the rather maudlin sensibility affected by these authors creep into the style of our administrators, and even of our businessmen. Formerly so stiff and dessicated, our official style now frequently became unctuous, almost lush. Thus we find a sub-delegate lamenting in a letter to the Intendant in Paris that he often experiences "a grief most harrowing to a sensitive soul" in the execution of his duties.

As in our own time, the government provided poor relief in country parishes on condition that the well-to-do inhabitants should help with voluntary contributions. When the sum contributed was adequate, the Controller-General noted in the margin of the list of subscribers: "Good. Express satisfaction." When it was more than adequate, he wrote: "Good. Express satisfaction and our heartfelt gratitude."

Most official posts were staffed by men belonging to the middle class, which had its own traditions, its code of honour, and its proper pride. This was, in fact, the aristocracy of the new and thriving social order which had already taken form and was only waiting for the Revolution to come into its own.

Already characteristic of the French civil service was its intense dislike for all outsiders, whether of noble or of middle-class extraction, who showed a wish to take a hand, on their own initiative, in public affairs. Any independent group, however small, which seemed desirous of taking action otherwise than under the aegis of the administration filled it with alarm, and the tiniest free association of citizens, however harmless its aims, was regarded as a nuisance. The only corporate bodies tolerated were those whose members had been hand-picked by the administration and which were under its control. Even big industrial concerns were frowned upon. In a word, our administration resented the idea of private citizens having any say in the control of their own enterprises, and preferred sterility to competition. But since, given our national temperament, the French must always be allowed a little rope, so as to console them for their servile state, the government permitted them to air their views freely on general or abstract subjects: on religion, philosophy, ethics, and even politics. Thus it raised no objection to attacks on the basic principles of the existing social order and even to discussions on the nature and existence of God, provided no adverse criticisms were levelled at any of its representatives, however insignificant. To its thinking, none of these matters were of any practical importance.

Though our eighteenth-century newspapers (or "gazettes" as they then were called) contained more light verse than polemics, the government took umbrage at their influence, slight as it was. While tolerant in its attitude to books, it already exercised a strict control over the newspapers and, being unable to suppress them altogether, tried to enlist them in its service. In 1761 a circular was sent out to all Intendants in the kingdom announcing that the King (Louis XV) had decided that henceforth the *Gazette de France* was to be edited under the direct supervision of government. "His Majesty wishes this Gazette to be as interesting as possible and universally recognised as superior to all other newspapers. To this end," the Minister continues, "I request you to send me a description of anything that takes place within your *généralité* which is likely to interest the reading public. Articles that have anything to do with physical science and natural history will be particularly acceptable, as well as accounts of unusual and interesting events." Accompanying the circular was a leaflet announcing that the new gazette, though appearing oftener and containing more news than the journal it replaced, would cost much less to subscribers.

When in compliance with the circular an Intendant wrote to his sub-delegates asking them to furnish "copy" of this kind, they began by reporting there was no such news available. Whereupon another letter came from the Minister of State to the Intendant, complaining angrily of the "barrenness" of the province in question. "His Majesty instructs me to say that he wishes you to take this matter seriously and to issue peremptory orders to your subordinates." The sub-delegates did what they could. One reported that a man caught smuggling salt had been hanged and had displayed much courage at his execution; another that a woman in his district had given birth to triplets, all girls; another that there had been a terrific storm which (he had to admit regretfully) had done no damage. And yet another, when reporting that though he had done his best he had failed to get any news of the kind required, tried to make amends by adding that not only had he personally taken out a subscription to the gazette but he had invited "all right-minded people" to do likewise. Yet it would seem that all this display of energy was unavailing, for in a later circular we read that "the King, who has so graciously deigned to study in detail the best ways and means of making the Gazette a success and ensuring for it the first place among all French newspapers and the popularity it should enjoy, has expressed profound dissatisfaction with the poor results so far obtained." History, indeed, is like a picture gallery in which there are few originals and many copies.

One fact, however, should be noted in this context: that in France the central government never followed the example of those governments in Southern Europe which seem to have laid hands on everything and sterilized all they touched. The French Government always displayed much intelligence and quite amazing energy in handling the tasks it set itself. But, unfortunately, its activities were often sterile, and even harmful, since some of the things it tried to do were beyond its powers and in much of what it did it acted irresponsibly.

It rarely undertook (or very soon abandoned) reforms which were a vital necessity but, if they were to succeed, called for a long-term effort; while, on the other hand, it was continually making changes in relatively trivial laws and regulations. Indeed, our eighteenth-century government seems to have made a fetish of tinkering with the laws of the land; new regulations followed on each other's heels so rapidly that executive officers could not keep track of them and were often at a loss how to act. We even find town officials protesting to the Controller-General himself against the incessant changes in the field of municipal legislation. "In the sphere of finance alone there are now such frequent changes that a municipal officer who wished to keep abreast of them would have to devote his whole time to this task, and neglect his other duties."

Even where the actual wording of a law was not altered, the manner of putting it into execution varied from day to day. A study of confidential records of this period throws a singularly revealing light on the methods of the administration under the old order at the time when there no longer existed any political assemblies or newspapers to act as a check on the caprices and the erratic, often misdirected activities of high officials and their staffs. Reading these documents, we are not surprised at the contempt which then was felt for the laws of the land, even by those whose duty it was to put them into effect.

We find new Orders in Council in which reference is not made to existing laws, often of very recent origin, which had been promulgated but never put into practice. In point of fact, there were no royal edicts or decrees, no letters patent duly embodied in the code book that did not lend themselves to a host of different interpretations when it was a matter of applying them to particular cases. Letters from the Controller-General and the Intendants show that government was always ready to countenance deviations from the orders issued by it. It rarely did violence to a law, but from time to time, in special cases, it allowed a law to be discreetly turned if this made for the smooth running of public affairs.

Thus when a public works contractor was seeking exemption from certain toll dues, an Intendant wrote as follows to his superior: "It is obvious that on a strict interpretation of the edicts and decrees cited above, no man in the kingdom can claim exemption from these dues. All the same, it is well known to all experienced government officials that these sweeping provisions are like the penalties imposed: although one finds them in almost all edicts, declarations, and decrees establishing taxes, that does not mean there may not be exceptions." There we have the old order in a nutshell: rigid rules, but flexibility, not to say laxity, in their application.

Were we in fact to try to form an opinion of the way France was governed at this time in the light of the laws that then existed, we should be led to the most preposterous conclusions. Thus in 1757 the King issued an edict to the effect that any author publishing tracts or books "contrary to religion" was to be sentenced to death, and this fate would befall not only the printers of such works but also the booksellers and itinerant peddlers vending them to the public. One might well fancy one was back in the age of St. Dominic. Actually this was the very period when Voltaire was being hailed on all sides as a leading light of French literature!

One often hears people lamenting the modern Frenchman's outspoken contempt for the laws of his country; but when could the French have learned to respect them? It might almost be said that under the old order everything was calculated to discourage the law-abiding instinct. It was the normal thing for a man filing a petition to ask that in his case a departure should be made from the strict letter of the law, and petitioners showed as much boldness and insistence in such requests as if they were claiming their legal rights. Indeed, whenever the authorities fell back on the letter of the law, this was only a polite expedient for rejecting a petition. The population was still submissive to authority, but this was more a matter of habit than of a law-abiding disposition. When their passions were roused (as sometimes happened), the least incident became the signal for an outbreak of mob violence, and usually such movements were followed by summary and brutal reprisals, not by trials of the offenders.

During the eighteenth century the central power had not as yet developed the healthy, robust constitution which it has today. All the same, since by then it had succeeded in eliminating all intermediate authorities and since there was a vast gulf between the government and the private citizen, it was accepted as being the only source of energy for the maintenance of the social system, and as such, indispensable to the life of the nation.

This is borne out even in the writings of its bitterest adversaries. In the long period of rankling unrest and rising discontent preceding the Revolution all sorts of schemes were worked up for the establishment of a new social order and a new method of government. The ends proposed by the reformers varied greatly, but the means were always the same. They wished to make use of the central power, as it stood, for shattering the whole social structure and rebuilding it on lines that seemed to them desirable. For, to their thinking, only the central authority could bring this "ideal State" into being, and there should be no limit to its might, as there was none to its right. The one thing needed was to persuade it to exercise its power in the right direction. Even Mirabeau *père*, a man of high birth so firmly convinced of the prerogatives of the nobility that he dubbed the Intendants "intruders", and so hostile to the idea that appointments to the magistracy should be made solely by the government as to declare that if this were done, the courts of justice would soon become no more than "gangs of commissaries"—even Mirabeau was convinced that only the central power was capable of implementing his dream of an ideal State.

Such notions were not confined to books; they had taken root in people's minds and were implicit in their ways of living; in fact, they entered into the very texture of everyday life throughout the country.

It never occurred to anyone that any large-scale enterprise could be put through successfully without the intervention of the State. Even the cultivators—and the French cultivator has always had a shrewd mistrust of his would-be mentors—came to believe that the government was largely to blame for the backwardness of agriculture in France because it did not give the peasants adequate assistance and advice. In the recriminatory tone of a letter written by a farmer to an Intendant we sense something of the spirit of the impending revolution. "Why does government not appoint inspectors to tour the provinces once a year and examine the condition of the crops and explain to the cultivators how to improve them, how to rear their cattle, fatten them and sell them, and at what places they can count on the best markets? These inspectors should draw good salaries and the farmer producing the best crops in each district should be given a badge of merit." (This idea of touring inspectors and badges of merit would certainly have tickled an English farmer of the day!)

To the mind of the great majority of people only the government was capable of maintaining order in the land. The populace had a salutary dread of the mounted police, and of them alone, while the landed proprietors regarded them as the only force in which they could feel some confidence. The mounted policeman was, in fact, the embodiment of law and order, not merely its chief defender. "No one," we read in the minutes of the Provincial Assembly of Guienne, "can have failed to notice how the mere sight of a mounted policeman is enough to bring to heel even the most truculent disturbers of the peace."[26] For this reason every man of property wanted to have a detachment of mounted police posted at his door, and the records of the intendancies are full of such requests. No one seemed to have had the faintest inkling that the protector might one day become the master.

One of the features of English life which most impressed our *émigrés* was the absence of any military police of this kind. All were surprised, and some saw in it a piece of typically English obtuseness. The comments of a Frenchman, no fool but a man whose upbringing had not prepared him for what he was to see in England, are enlightening. "It is the literal truth that the average Englishman consoles himself for having been robbed with the reflection that at any rate his country has no mounted police! However great his indignation at a breach of the public peace, the Englishman can console himself for the fact that the offenders are enabled to return to the bosom of society, scoundrels though they are, by the thought that anyhow the letter of the law has been respected. However, these mistaken notions are not shared by all; an enlightened few refuse to entertain them—and counsels of wisdom will certainly prevail in the long run."

Obviously it never occurred to him that these "eccentricities" were bound up with the whole British concept of freedom; so he fell back on a would-be scientific explanation of the peculiarities of the English. "In a country where the climate is so damp and the air so turgid, people naturally tend to fix their minds on serious topics. Thus the Englishman takes a great interest in constitutional and administrative problems, whereas the Frenchman is indifferent to such matters."

The government having stepped into the place of Divine Providence in France, it was but natural that everyone, when in difficulties, invoked its aid. We find a vast number of petitions which, though the writers professed to be speaking on behalf of the public, were in reality intended to further their small private interests.[37] The files in which they figure are perhaps the only places in which all the various classes of pre-revolutionary France rub shoulders, so to speak. They make depressing reading. We find peasants applying for compensation for the loss of their cattle or their homes; wealthy landowners asking for financial aid for the improvement of their estates; manufacturers petitioning the Intendant for monopolies protecting them from competition. Often, too, businessmen report to the Intendant confidentially that their affairs are in a bad way and request him to approach the Controller-General for a loan to tide them over this emergency. (It would seem, in fact, that special funds were earmarked for such eventualities.)

Sometimes even the gentry did not disdain to play the part of suppliants: their class scarcely appearing save in the loftiness with which they begged. What they most resented was having to pay the *vingtième*. Since their quota of the total sum to be levied under this head was fixed by the Council on the basis of reports submitted to it by the Intendants, it was to the latter that they usually applied for exemption or an extension of the time of payment. I have read a number of such petitions from members of the upper classes, mostly titled and sometimes of the highest rank, in which poverty or temporary financial straits were pleaded. In the ordinary way persons of this social rank always addressed the Intendant as "Monsieur", but I have noticed that in these petitions they follow the example of the middle class and address him as "Monseigneur".

Sometimes we find a quaint mixture of obsequiousness and

pride in these letters. In one the petitioner appeals to the Intendant in the following terms: "Surely your natural good feeling will prevent you from taxing for the full *vingtième* a man of my position with a family to support, as you would tax a member of the lower class in such a case."

In times of dearth—and these were frequent in the eighteenth century—everyone expected the Intendant to come to the rescue as a matter of course. For the government was held responsible for all the misfortunes befalling the community; even when these were "acts of God", such as floods or droughts, the powers-that-be were blamed for them.[28]

For all these reasons we need not be surprised at the remarkable ease with which centralisation was re-established in France at the beginning of the nineteenth century. Though the men of '89 had overthrown the ancient edifice, its foundations had been laid immutably in the minds of all Frenchmen, even its destroyers; thus there was little trouble in re-establishing it not only rapidly but in a more stable, shockproof form.

CHAPTER SEVEN

*How in France, more than in any other European country, the provinces had come under the thrall of the metropolis, which attracted to itself all that was most vital in the nation*

It is not the geographical position of a capital, nor its size or wealth, that gives it political supremacy over the rest of the country; that depends, rather, on the nature of the country's government.

London, for example, though its population is as great as that of some entire kingdoms, has not so far had any determinant influence on the political destinies of Great Britain. Nor does any citizen of the United States imagine that the populace of New York can shape the course of the American Union—not even the residents in New York State would advance any such claim. Nevertheless, present-day New York can boast of

a population as large as that of Paris at the outset of the
Revolution.

During the Wars of Religion the population of Paris stood
in the same proportion to that of the rest of France as it stood
in 1789; yet its voice was not decisive in national affairs. And
at the time of the Fronde insurrection Paris was still no more
than the largest town in France. But by 1789 things were very
different; it is no exaggeration to say that Paris *was* France.

In 1740 Montesquieu wrote in a letter to a friend: "In France
there is only Paris—and a few outlying provinces Paris hasn't
yet found time to gobble up." And in 1750 the Marquis de
Mirabeau, who, if fanciful in his ideas, could be a shrewd
observer, wrote, with Paris in mind (though without naming
it specifically): "Capitals are indispensable, but when the head
becomes too swollen, the body develops apoplexy, with fatal
results. What, then must we expect if the provinces are reduced
to a state of dependence on the capital, their inhabitants treated
as a sort of inferior species and given no outlet for their ambitions, with the result that everyone with any ability migrates
to the metropolis?" He goes on to describe this gradual draining
of the provinces of their natural leaders, their best businessmen
and intellectuals as "a sort of bloodless revolution".

Those of my readers who have read the foregoing chapters
with some care already know the reasons for this momentous
change, and I need not revert to them.

The government saw only the most obvious aspect of what
was taking place in France, that aspect being the steady growth
of the metropolis. From day to day Paris was extending her
boundaries and the authorities feared that the proper administration of so big a city might soon become impracticable. Thus
many royal edicts issued in the seventeenth and eighteenth
centuries were intended to put a stop to this expansion, and the
paradoxical situation arose that at the very time when our Kings
were concentrating more and more the public life of France in
the capital, or its near vicinity, they were also trying to keep
Paris a small town. People were either forbidden altogether to
build new houses, or else forced to build on the costliest scale
and on specified—often definitely unattractive—sites. Each edict

takes regretful notice of the fact that, despite previous ordinances, Paris is continuing to expand. Six times during his reign
Louis XIV tried to check the growth of Paris, yet all-powerful
as he proved himself in many other fields, he failed in this.
Meanwhile the capital's authority over the rest of France was
being enlarged even more rapidly than the city's area, this being
due less to what was being done within its walls than to what
was taking place outside them. For throughout this period local
autonomy was everywhere becoming a dead letter; the
characteristic traits of the ancient provinces were steadily being
ironed out and the last traces of an independent public life
obliterated. Not that the nation was sinking into lethargy; far
from it, there was increased activity throughout the land, but
the driving force behind it came exclusively from Paris. I shall
cite only one instance out of many. Reports made to the Minister
concerned with the state of the book trade show that whereas
in the sixteenth century and at the beginning of the seventeenth
there had been printing presses in many provincial towns, these
had closed down at the time when the report was made, as no
work was forthcoming. Yet it is common knowledge that at
the end of the eighteenth century vastly more printed matter
of all sorts was being turned out than in the sixteenth. What
had happened was that by then Paris had absorbed the intellectual life of the whole country at the expense of the provinces.

When shortly after the meeting of the Estates-General and a
few days before the taking of the Bastille that famous English
traveller Arthur Young set out from Paris to the country, he was
greatly struck by the different atmosphere he found once he had
left the capital. Paris had been all agog with excitement, a steady
stream of propaganda was flowing from the presses—it was
reckoned that no less than ninety-two political pamphlets were
issued in a single week. "Never," Young says, "had I seen
such a craze for pamphleteering, even in London." Outside
Paris, however, he got an impression of inertia and apathy; no
newspapers and few brochures were being printed. Yet appearances were deceptive and the provinces were only biding their
time, waiting for a signal to embark on violent action. On
the rare occasions when the citizens got together it was to listen

to the latest news from Paris. In every country town he visited
Young asked the people he met what they proposed to do.
Everywhere he got the same answer. "We are only a provincial
town; we must wait till Paris gives us a lead." These people,
he ironically observes, seemed not to dare even to form an
opinion until they knew what was being thought in Paris!

Some have been surprised at the extraordinary ease with
which the Constituent Assembly annihilated at one fell swoop
all the historic divisions of France—the provinces—and split
up the kingdom into eighty-three well-defined units—the
departments—almost as if they were partitioning not an ancient
kingdom but the virgin soil of the New World. Nothing surprised and, indeed, shocked the rest of Europe more than this.
"It is the first time," Burke said, "that we have seen men hack
their native land to pieces in so barbarous a manner." But
though it might seem that living bodies were being mutilated,
actually the "victims" were already corpses.

During the same period as that in which Paris was coming
to dominate the entire country another change was taking place
within the city itself, a change which all historians do well to
take into account. Besides being at once a business and commercial centre, a city of pleasure seekers and consumers, Paris
had now developed into a manufacturing city—a change which,
in conjunction with the political ascendancy of Paris described
above, was destined to have great and dangerous consequences.

As a matter of fact, this was not a new development and
its origins can be traced back to the remote past; already in the
Middle Ages, Paris was by all accounts the most hard-working
as well as the largest town in the kingdom. This becomes still
more apparent as we approach modern times. Along with the
centralisation of administrative power, industrial activities tended to converge on the capital. And now that Paris was becoming
more and more the national arbiter of taste, sole centre of
authority and of the arts, the focal point of all that was most
vital in France, it was natural enough that big industrial
concerns throughout the country should be attracted to the capital
and make it their headquarters.

Though the statistical records of the old order are far from trustworthy, we are justified, I think, in saying that during the sixty years preceding the Revolution the number of workers employed in Paris more than doubled, while in the same period the general population of the city rose by hardly a third.

Aside from these considerations of a general order there were specific reasons for the influx of workers into Paris from all parts of France and the development of districts of the city inhabited almost exclusively by the working class. The handicaps imposed on industry by the fiscal authorities were less onerous in the capital than in other parts of France, and the control exercised by the trade and craft guilds was easier to evade. Some city districts, such as the Faubourg St.-Antoine and the Faubourg du Temple, enjoyed great privileges in this respect. Those of the Faubourg St.-Antoine were much extended by Louis XVI, who did his best to convert this part of Paris into a vast workers' centre. "It is our desire," this ill-starred monarch announced in one of his decrees, "to confer on the workers of the Faubourg St.-Antoine a further token of our concern for their welfare and to free them from restrictions prejudicial both to their interests and to the freedom of trade."

The number of factories, mills, and blast furnaces increased to such an extent in the period just before the Revolution that the government took alarm, though the grounds for this alarm were in most cases purely imaginary. Several decrees were issued on the subject, one of which (an Order in Council dated 1782) ran as follows: "Fearing that the rapid increase in the number of factories may lead to a consumption of wood so great as to cause a shortage of fuel within the City of Paris, the King forbids the erection of any new factories within a radius of fifteen leagues around the capital." Meanwhile the very real dangers inherent in this concentration of labour at one spot passed quite unnoticed.

Thus Paris had mastered France, and the army that was soon to master Paris was mustering its forces.

Most qualified observers, so far as I can judge, concur in the opinion that chief among the reasons for the collapse of all the various governments that have arisen in France during the past forty years are administrative centralisation and the absolute predominance of Paris. And I shall have no difficulty in proving that the catastrophic downfall of the monarchy was largely due to the same causes. They should, indeed, rank among the chief factors of this first revolution, progenitor of all the others.

### CHAPTER EIGHT

*How France had become the country in which men were most like each other*

One of the things which cannot fail to strike an attentive student of the social system under the old order is that it had two quite contradictory aspects. On the one hand, we get an impression that the people composing it, at least those belonging to the upper and the middle classes—the only ones that is to say who catch the eye—were all exactly like each other. Nevertheless, we also find that this seemingly homogeneous mass was still divided within itself into a great number of watertight compartments, small, self-contained units, each of which watched vigilantly over its own interests and took no part in the life of the community at large.

If we bear in mind the number of these minute gradings and the fact that nowhere else in the world were citizens less inclined to join forces and stand by each other in emergencies, we can see how it was that a successful revolution could tear down the whole social structure almost in the twinkling of an eye. All the flimsy barriers between the various compartments were instantaneously laid low, and out of the ruins there arose a social order closer knit and less differentiated, perhaps, than any that the Western World had ever known.

I had pointed out how local differences between the various provinces had long since been obliterated throughout practically the entire kingdom; this had greatly contributed to making Frenchmen everywhere so much like each other. Behind such diversities as still existed the unity of the nation was making itself felt, sponsored by that new conception: "the same laws for all." For as the eighteenth century advances, we find an ever increasing number of edicts, Orders in Council, and royal man-

dates imposing the same regulations and the same procedures on
all parts of the kingdom. Not only the governing class but also
the governed endorsed this concept of a standardised legislative
system valid everywhere. Indeed, it underlies all the successive
projects of reform put forward during the three decades preceding the Revolution. Two centuries earlier any such projects
would have been quite literally unthinkable.

Not only did the provinces come to resemble each other more
and more, but within each province members of the various
classes (anyhow those above the lowest social stratum) became
ever more alike, differences of rank notwithstanding. This is
borne out conspicuously by the *cahiers* (written instructions
given to the deputies) presented by the different Orders at the
meeting of the Estates-General in 1789. Allowing for the fact
that the parties who drew up these memoranda had strongly
conflicting interests, they seem remarkably alike in tenor.

When we turn to the proceedings of the earliest Estates-
General we find a very different picture: the middle class and
the nobility then had more common interests, more points of
contact, and displayed much less antipathy towards each other
—but they still gave the impression of belonging to different
races. Though with the passing years the privileges which made
a cleavage between these two important sections of the community had not merely been maintained but in some respects
intensified, the lapse of time had worked towards a certain
levelling out of their differences in all else.

For during several centuries the French nobility had been
getting steadily poorer. "Despite its privileges," a man of gentle
birth, writing in 1755, laments, "the nobility is being starved
out, and all its wealth passing into the hands of the Third
Estate." Yet the laws protecting property owned by the nobility
had not been modified and to all appearances its economic position was unchanged. Nonetheless, the more its power declined,
the poorer it became.

It would seem that in all human institutions, as in the human
body, there is a hidden source of energy, the life principle itself,
independent of the organs which perform the various functions
needed for survival; once this vital flame burns low, the whole

organism languishes and wastes away, and though the organs seem to function as before, they serve no useful purpose. The French nobility still had entails (Burke, indeed, observed that in his day entails were commoner and more binding in France than in England), the law of primogeniture, the right to perpetual dues on the land; in fact, all their vested interests had been left intact. They had been released from the costly obligation of defraying their own expenses on active service in the army and, nevertheless, had retained their immunity from taxation; that is to say they still profited by the exemption after being relieved of the obligation. Moreover, they now enjoyed several financial advantages unknown to their ancestors. And yet, in proportion as both the instinct and the practice of leadership declined among them, their wealth passed out of their hands. This gradual impoverishment of the French nobility was largely due to the breaking up of the great landed estates, to which we have already drawn attention. The nobleman had sold his land, plot by plot, to the peasants, keeping only the seigneurial dues which safeguarded the semblance, but not the reality, of his overlordship.[29] In several French provinces—for example the Limousin, of which Turgot gives us so good a description—the erstwhile seigneurs eked out a hand-to-mouth existence; they had hardly any land of their own, and dues and quitrents were almost their only source of income.

"In this *généralité*," wrote an Intendant at the beginning of the century, "there are still several thousand noble families, but not fifteen of them have an income of twenty thousand *livres* a year." The position is lucidly summed up in a note handed by the Intendant of Franche-Conté to his successor (in 1750). "The nobles in these parts are worthy folk but very poor, and as proud as they are poor. Their prestige has sadly declined. It is not bad policy to keep them in this state, for thus they are obliged to have recourse to us and to carry out our wishes. They have formed a club, to belong to which a man must prove his right to four quarterings on his escutcheon. It meets only once a year, and it is not officially recognised; merely tolerated. The Intendant is always present at its meetings. On such occasions, after dining and attending Mass in a body, these worthy gentlemen go home, some on foot, and some on old, worn-out hacks. It's quite a comical sight—as you will see for yourself.''

This gradual impoverishment of the nobility was not peculiar to France. It was taking place in all parts of the continent where the feudal system was in process of dying out without being replaced by a new form of aristocracy. In German territory, along the Rhine, the decadence of the indigenous nobility was particularly marked and attracted much attention. England was the one exception. There the old nobility had not only retained but greatly increased its wealth; its members were still the richest and most influential of the King's subjects. True, new families were coming to the fore, but their wealth was no greater than that of the ancient houses.

In France the commoners alone seemed to be taking over the wealth that was being lost by the nobility, to be growing fat at their expense. Yet there was no law preventing the middle-class man from ruining himself or helping him to amass a fortune. All the same he steadily grew wealthier and frequently became as rich as, sometimes richer than, the nobleman. Moreover, his wealth often took the same form; though usually residing in a town, he owned land in the country and sometimes even bought up entire seigneurial estates.

Education and a similar style of living had already obliterated many of the distinctions between the two classes. The bourgeois was as cultivated as the nobleman and his enlightenment came from the same source. Both had been educated on literary and philosophic lines, for Paris, now almost the sole fountainhead of knowledge for the whole of France, had cast the minds of all in the same mould and given them the same equipment. No doubt it was still possible at the close of the eighteenth century to detect shades of difference in the behaviour of the aristocracy and that of the bourgeoisie; for nothing takes longer to acquire than the surface polish which is called good manners. But basically all who ranked above the common herd were of a muchness; they had the same ideas, the same habits, the same tastes, the same kinds of amusements; read the same books and spoke in the same way. They differed only in their rights.

I doubt if this levelling-up process was carried so far in any other country, even in England, where the different classes, though solidly allied by common interests, still differed in mentality and manners. For political freedom, though it has the admirable effect of creating reciprocal ties and a feeling of solidarity between all the members of a nation, does not necessarily make them resemble each other. It is only government by a single man that in the long run irons out diversities and makes each member of a nation indifferent to his neighbour's lot.

### CHAPTER NINE

*How, though in many respects so similar, the French were split up more than ever before into small, isolated, self-regarding groups*

Let us now turn to the other side of the picture and observe how these same Frenchmen who had so much in common were kept apart from each other to an extent hitherto unknown in France; perhaps unparalleled in any other country.

When the feudal system first struck root in Europe, the nobility (to use the term that subsequently came into currency) did not immediately, so far as we can judge, assume the form of a caste. Composed of all the leading men in the nation, it was no more than an aristocracy (in the exact sense of the term) during its early phase. There is no occasion here to go deeply into the question and I confine myself to pointing out that by the Middle Ages it had developed into a caste, by which I mean that membership of it was essentially a matter of birth and had become hereditary.

True, it retained one of the chief functions of an aristocracy, that of being a governing body; but birth alone decided who should be the leaders of the nation. Those who were not of noble blood were automatically excluded from the magic circle, and though they might hold posts of some importance in the administration, these were always of a subordinate nature.

Wherever feudalism established itself on the continent it led to the formation of a caste of this description; in England, exceptionally, it gave rise to an aristocracy. I have always been surprised that a circumstance that renders England so different from all other modern nations and which alone explains the peculiarities of her laws, history, and traditions has not received more attention from historians and statesmen—and that long familiarity has made Englishmen themselves so unaware of it. Some have had glimpses of this fact and alluded to it briefly; but never, to my knowledge, has it been adequately dealt with by observers of the English scene. Thus when Montesquieu visited England in 1739, he wrote to a friend, "Here am I in a land that is quite unlike any other European country"—but he let it go at that.

It was not merely parliamentary government, freedom of speech, and the jury system that made England so different from the rest of contemporary Europe. There was something still more distinctive and more far-reaching in its effects. England was the only country in which the caste system had been totally abolished, not merely modified. Nobility and commoners joined forces in business enterprises, entered the same professions, and—what is still more significant—intermarried. The daughter of the greatest lord in the land could marry a "new" man without the least compunction.

For when we seek to discover whether the caste system, with its age-old conventions and social barriers, has been definitely eradicated in any country, the acid test is that country's marriage customs. Even in modern France, after sixty years of democracy, we often find the old prejudices surviving. Though persons of high rank and parvenus may seem to fraternize in other respects, intermarriage between the classes is still discountenanced.

One often hears it said that the English nobility has proved itself more adroit, more worldly wise, more accessible to new ideas than any other. It would be truer to say that for a long time past there has been no nobility in England, if we use the term "nobility" in the sense it has elsewhere.

Though this curious revolution (for such in fact it was) is hidden in the mists of time, we can detect traces of it in the English language. For several centuries the word "gentleman" has had in England a quite different application from what it had when it originated, and, similarly, there is no equivalent for its French antithesis, the word *roturier*. It would have been impossible to translate into English, even in 1664 when Molière wrote it, the line:

"*Et tel que l'on le voit, il est bon gentilhomme.*"

A study of the connexion between the history of language and history proper would certainly be revealing. Thus if we follow the mutations in time and place of the English word "gentleman" (a derivative of our *gentilhomme*), we find its connotation being steadily widened in England as the classes draw nearer to each other and intermingle. In each successive century we find it being applied to men a little lower in the social scale. Next, with the English, it crosses to America. And now in America it is applicable to all male citizens, indiscriminately. Thus its history is the history of democracy itself.

In France, however, there has been no question of enlarging the application of the word *gentilhomme*, which as a matter of fact has, since the Revolution, dropped out of common use. This is because it has always been employed to designate the members of a caste—a caste that has never ceased to exist in France and is still as exclusive as it was when the term was coined many centuries ago.

I will, indeed, go further and say that this caste has become more and more exclusive and that a tendency diametrically opposed to what we have observed in England has been operative in France. For while the bourgeois and the nobleman were becoming more and more alike in many ways, the gap between them was steadily widening, and these two tendencies, far from counteracting each other, often had the opposite effect.

In the Middle Ages, and so long as the feudal system was in full force, all who held their land from a seigneur (those who in feudal terminology were properly described as vassals), many of whom were not of noble birth, were expected to co-operate with their lord in the administration of the *seigneurie*; this was in fact one of the chief duties attaching to their tenure. Not only had they to follow their lord in war, but they were bound by the terms of their vassalage to spend a stated period of each year at his court, during which time they aided him in administering justice and maintaining law and order among the dwellers on his estate. These courts were a vital element of the feudal system. In all ancient European legislative codes we find specific mention of the seigneurial courts, and vestiges of them can still be found in parts of modern Germany. Thirty years before the Revolution an expert in this field, Edme de Fréminville, published an exhaustive study of feudal rights and land tenure as revealed in the records of seigneurial estates. He tells us that the title deeds of many *seigneuries* prove that all vassals were required to make fortnightly attendances at the lord's court, where, sitting with the lord himself or his judge in ordinary, they held assizes and settled controversies between persons residing within his jurisdiction. These records show, he tells us, that in some *seigneuries* there were as many as two hundred vassals of this kind, many of them *roturiers* (men of non-noble birth). This is but one of many instances that might be cited of the close, day-to-day contacts between the country-folk and the nobility, and their joint management of local affairs. What the lords' courts did for the small landed proprietors was done by the provincial Estates and, later, the Estates-General for the town-dwelling middle class.

Indeed, when we study such records of the proceedings of the Estates-General in the fourteenth century as have survived, we cannot fail to be struck by the place assigned to the Third Estate in these assemblies and the power it exercised. Doubtless, from the point of view of his mental and moral equipment the fourteenth-century bourgeois was much inferior to his eighteenth-century counterpart; nevertheless, the middle class as a body were accorded a higher, more responsible position in those early days. Their right to participate in the government of the country was taken for granted, their opinions always carried weight in political assemblies and often were preponderant, and the other classes never forgot that theirs was a force to be reckoned with.

But most striking of all is the fact that the nobility and the Third Estate found it so much easier in those days than at any later time to co-operate in the management of public affairs. We find ample evidence of this not only in records of the proceedings of the fourteenth-century Estates-General (several of which indulged in turbulent, not to say revolutionary, manifestations owing to the troubled conditions of the age), but

also in those of the provincial Estates whose sessions, so far
as we can judge, were conducted in an orderly, traditional
manner.[30] Thus in Auvergne we find the three Orders passing
important measures in joint session, and delegates from each
Order superintending their execution. The same thing happened
in the province of Champagne. A famous example of this co-
operation between the classes is the association jointly formed
by the nobles and the citizens of many French towns at the
beginning of the fourteenth century with a view to defending
the liberty of the nation and the ancient rights of the provinces
against encroachments of the royal power.[31] Many such incidents
took place in this period, incidents which one would expect to
figure in a history of England rather than in ours. But nothing
of this sort happened in the following centuries.

For as the lords' administration of their *seigneuries* gradually broke down; as convocations of the Estates-General became
fewer or altogether ceased; and as our nation-wide freedoms
succumbed, dragging down with them all local liberties, there
was a tendency for the upper and the middle classes to co-
operate less and less in public affairs and thus to draw apart.
Every day the rift between them widened until, by the eighteenth
century, nobleman and bourgeois never met except by chance
in private life. And by then the two classes were not merely
rivals, they were foes.

What seems peculiar to France is that at the very time when
the nobility, *qua* Order, was losing its political power, the
nobleman as an individual was granted privileges he had never
hitherto enjoyed and was even extending those he had already.
It seemed as if individuals were enriching themselves at the
expense of the Order as a corporate body. More and more the
nobility was being divested of its right to rule, but by the
same token the nobles enjoyed more and more the exclusive
prerogative of being the chief servitors of their supreme overlord, the King. It was easier for a man of humble extraction to
become a high official under Louis XIV than it was under
Louis XVI. (The same thing had been often happening in
Prussia at a time when in France it was as yet unheard of.)
Each privilege, once granted, became hereditary and inalienable.

Thus in the course of ceasing to be an aristocracy, the nobility tended more and more to become a caste, thriving on vested rights.

The privilege most resented by the general public, that of exemption from taxation, became progressively more valuable from the fifteenth century up to the Revolution. For its value obviously kept pace with the steady increase in the financial burdens imposed on the mass of the people. When (under Charles VII) a mere 1,200,000 *livres* were brought in by the tax known as the *taille*, the advantages of exemption were relatively slight. But when, under Louis XVI, the sum raised by taxation was eighty millions the value of the privilege was enormous. So long as the *taille* was the only impost to which the rest of the population was subject, the nobleman's immunity attracted little attention. But when taxes of this order were multiplied under a host of names and in various forms; when four other imposts were assimilated to the *taille*; and when obligations unknown in the Middle Ages—notably forced labour requisitioned by the Crown for public works and compulsory service in the militia—were superadded, with a complete disregard for equality, keen resentment was felt for the privileged position of the nobility.[32] True, the inequality, though great, was not so bad as it seemed, since the nobleman was often affected indirectly, through his tenants, by taxes from which ostensibly he was exempted. But in such cases injustice that is glaring causes more irritation than actual injury.

Harassed by the perpetual financial crises of the last years of his reign, Louis XIV had recourse to two new taxes which took no account of class distinction: a poll tax (capitation) and the *vingtième*. But so strong was the feeling that exemption from taxation was too venerable, not to say too sacrosanct, to be roughly handled that though the new taxes were borne by all alike, care was taken that the manner of their collection was very different: [33, 34, 35] harsh to the point of brutality for one section of the population and, for the other, courteous, indulgent.[36]

Although inequality of taxation prevailed all over Europe, there were few countries in which it had become so flagrant and so much detested as in France. In a great part of Germany taxation was mostly indirect, and even as regards direct taxation the nobles did not escape altogether, their privilege often consisting merely in being assessed at a somewhat lower rate than other taxpayers. Moreover, there were some taxes falling on the nobility alone; these took the place of the unpaid military service which otherwise would have been exacted from them.

Of all the various ways of making men conscious of their differences and of stressing class distinctions unequal taxation is the most pernicious, since it creates a permanent estrangement between those who benefit and those who suffer by it. Once the principle is established that noblemen and commoners are not to be taxed at the same rates, the public is reminded of the distinction drawn between them year by year when the imposts are assessed and levied. Thus on these occasions each member of the privileged class takes notice of the practical interest he has in differentiating himself from the masses and in stiffening the barriers between himself and them.

Since so many debates on public affairs concern an existing tax or the imposition of a new one, it is obvious that when one section of the community is exempt and another subject to it, they will rarely see eye to eye or wish to meet together and exchange ideas. Thus little or no effort is required to keep them apart, there being no incentives or any inclination to act in concert.

In his flattering picture of the old French constitution Burke mentioned as a point in favour of the French nobility the ease with which a commoner could obtain a title by securing one of the official posts that automatically ennobled their holders. Here, to his thinking, was something analogous to the "open" aristocracy of England. No doubt Louis XI had distributed titles lavishly, but his aim was to lower the prestige of the nobility. If his successors were equally lavish of titles, this was for a different motive: that of raising money. Necker tells us that in his day no less than four thousand official posts carried titles with them. Nothing of this sort was to be seen in any other country on the continent; yet the parallel drawn by Burke between France and England was due to a misconception of the facts.

The reason why the English middle class, far from being actively hostile to the aristocracy, inclined to fraternise with it was not so much that the aristocracy kept open house as that its barriers were ill defined; not so much that entrance into it was easy as that you never knew when you had got there. The result was that everyone who hovered on its outskirts nursed the agreeable illusion that he belonged to it and joined forces with it in the hope of acquiring prestige or some practical advantage under its aegis.

But the barriers between the French nobility and the other classes, though quite easily traversed, were always fixed and plain to see; so conspicuous, indeed, as to exasperate those against whom they were erected. For once a man had crossed them he was cut off from all outside the pale by privileges injurious both to their pockets and their pride.

Far from reducing the dislike of the nobility felt by their "inferiors" the practice of ennobling commoners had the opposite effect. The envy with which the newly made nobleman inspired his former equals intensified their sense of being unfairly treated. This explains why the Third Estate in its petitions for radical changes always shows more animosity towards the recent creations than towards the old nobility, and far from asking that the ways of access to the privileged class should be more widely open to commoners, constantly demands that they be narrowed.

In no other period of French history was it so easy to acquire a title as in 1789, yet never had the gap between the middle class and the nobility been so great. Not only did the nobles refuse to tolerate in their electoral body anything that savoured in the least of the bourgeoisie, but the bourgeois showed an equal distaste for anything and anyone of high extraction. In some provinces newly ennobled men were given the cold shoulder by the former because they were not thought highborn enough, and by the latter because they were already too much so! (This happened, we are told, to that famous man Lavoisier.)

When we turn from the nobility to the middle class we find a very similar state of affairs; the bourgeois was almost as aloof from the "common people" as the noble from the bourgeois.

Under the old order nearly all the middle class preferred to live in the towns, and there were two causes for this preference: the privileges of the nobility and the *taille*. The lord who lived on his estate usually displayed a certain bonhomie towards his peasants—in fact, they got on very well together—but he made no secret of his disdain for his middle-class neighbours. This disdain had continuously increased, keeping pace with the decline of his political influence, and in fact because of it. For one thing, now that he no longer held the reins of power, there was no need to humour people who might have aided him in his public duties; and also (as has often been remarked) he tried to console himself for the loss of real power by an exaggerated insistence on such prerogatives as still were his. Even when he lived away from his estate, this did not make things any more agreeable for his neighbours; on the contrary, they felt all the more aggrieved, since privileges flaunted by a deputy seemed still more odious.

Yet I am inclined to think that the *taille* and the other imposts linked up with it were more to blame. It would be easy to explain, relatively briefly, why the incidence of the *taille* and the taxes assimilated to it made itself felt more strongly in rural districts than in towns. But for my present purpose it is enough to point out that the urban middle class, acting as a group, had many means of reducing the impact of the *taille* and sometimes of escaping it altogether; whereas an isolated member of that class, living in the country on his own land, had no such means of escape. One of the chief advantages of the town dwellers was that they were not concerned with collecting the *taille*—an obligation dreaded even more than that of having to pay it. Indeed, there was no post under the old order (or, for that matter, any other that I know of) so unenviable as that of the rural tax collector, as I shall have occasion to point out later, in another context. No one living in a French village (except members of the nobility) was exempted from this duty; many rich commoners left their lands and moved to the nearest town so as to avoid it. All the records I have studied bear out Turgot's statement that "the obligation to collect the *taille* was changing all rural landowners, noblemen excepted, into town dwellers." (This, by the way, is one of the reasons why there are so many more towns, small towns especially, in France than in most other European countries.)

Living within the four walls of a town, the rich bourgeois soon lost any taste he might have had for country life and came to regard the activities and ways of living of the men of his own class who stayed on the land as all but incomprehensible. For he had now, to all intents and purposes, only one ambition: that of securing an official post of some kind in the place where his lot was cast. For it is a great mistake to suppose that the keen desire for office displayed by the modern Frenchman, in particular the bourgeois, developed only after the Revolution. This peculiar passion took its rise several centuries before, and since then it has never ceased to grow, thanks to the encouragement given it by the powers-that-be.

The posts available under the old order were not the same in all cases as they are today, but they were, I think, even more numerous; indeed, the number of minor civil servants was legion. Within no more than sixteen years, from 1693 to 1709, it would seem that some forty thousand new official posts, for the most part open to members of the lower middle class, were created. On examining the statistics of quite a small provincial town I found that in 1750 a hundred or more of its inhabitants were engaged in the administration of justice and a hundred and twenty-six in the execution of judgments passed by the courts.

There can be few, if any, parallels for this intense desire of the middle-class Frenchman to cut an official figure; no sooner did he find himself in possession of a small capital sum than he expended it on buying an official post instead of investing it in a business. This deplorable propensity had a worse effect than the guilds or even the *taille* on the progress of trade and agriculture in France. When there was a shortage of available posts, the office seekers were quick to think up new ones. Thus we find a man named Lemberville publishing an "open letter" to the effect that it is in the public interest to appoint an inspector for the supervision of an industry which he names—and winding up by suggesting he should be given the post. A familiar type, this M. Lemberville—we have all met him! To a man of some education and with a little money of his own it seemed unbecoming to go to his grave without having held an official post sometime in his career. "Everybody according to his walk in life," wrote a contemporary, "wishes to be a 'somebody' by royal appointment."

The chief difference between the times of which I now am speaking and modern France is that the government then sold official posts, whereas now it gives them. To obtain one a man no longer pays in hard cash; he goes one better—and sells himself.

Segregated from the peasantry by his place of residence and still more by his way of living, the bourgeois was usually estranged from them no less by a conflict of interests. There were many justified complaints about the privileges enjoyed by the nobility in the matter of taxation, but there were equal grounds for complaint as regards the middle class. For thousands of official posts existed which carried with them partial or total exemption from the burdens imposed on the general public: one post exonerated its holder from service in the militia, another from forced labour, another from the *taille*. Where is there a parish, asked a writer of the day, which does not contain, apart from nobles and ecclesiastics, a number of citizens who have secured immunity from taxation in virtue of the official posts they hold or public duties they perform? One of the reasons which led now and again to the abolition of certain official posts ear-marked for the middle class was the diminution of revenue caused by so many exemptions from payment of the *taille*. I am convinced that the number of persons thus exempted was as great among the bourgeoisie as among the nobility, and indeed often greater.

While enraging all who did not share in them, these odious prerogatives inspired their possessors with a pride as inordinate as it was shortsighted. Throughout the eighteenth century the hostility of the urban middle class towards the peasantry living around the towns and the jealousy of the latter were common knowledge. "Every town," wrote Turgot, "is bent on promoting its own interests at the expense of the rural districts in its vicinity." Elsewhere he says, addressing his sub-delegates, "You have often been obliged to check the tendency of the towns to overstep their lawful rights in dealing with the rural population within their spheres of influence."

Even the common people living beside the bourgeois in the towns came to regard the peasantry almost as members of an alien race and often to dislike them. Most of the local dues levied by the townsfolk were so contrived as to bear most heavily on the humblest members of the community. I have found ample evidence in support of Turgot's opinion that the middle class had found means of arranging city tolls in such a way that they themselves were unaffected by them.

But what perhaps strikes us most in the mentality and behaviour of our eighteenth-century bourgeois is their obvious fear of being assimilated in the mass of the people, from whose control they strained every effort to escape. "Should it be His Majesty's pleasure," the burgesses of a town suggested in a memorandum to the Controller-General, "to restore the elective system for the post of Mayor, it would be well to enact that the electors must choose their candidates among the notables of the town or even limit these to members of the presidial court."

We have seen that the policy of our Kings was gradually to withdraw the exercise of their former political rights from the ordinary townsfolk; this is the keynote of all royal legislation from the reign of Louis XI to that of Louis XV. Often the middle class joined in promoting measures of this kind; sometimes, indeed, suggested them.

In 1764, when reforms were being made in urban administration, an Intendant invited the municipal officials of a small town to give their opinion as to whether or not the artisans "and other humbler classes" should retain the right of electing magistrates. The answer given was that though in practice "the people had never misused this right and it would certainly seem more gracious to let them, as in the past, choose those who were to govern them, nevertheless, in the interest of good order and the public peace it seemed advisable to vest this power in the assembly of notables." The sub-delegate, for his part, reported that he had invited "the six most worthy citizens" to his house for a secret conference and they had expressed a unanimous opinion that the wisest course was to restrict the electorate in these cases not merely to the assembly of notables (as the municipal officials had proposed) but to a small committee representing the various corporations of which the assembly was composed. In transmitting this opinion to his chief the subdelegate, whose views were more liberal than those of the six gentlemen in question, remarked that "it seemed unfair to expect the working population to pay the sums imposed by their fellow citizens without their having any say about the manner in which the money raised was to be expended; the aforesaid fellow citizens being very likely men who, thanks to their exemption from taxation, were least affected by levies of this kind."

To complete the picture, let us now examine the position of the middle class as distinct from the common people in the same way as we examined that of the nobility vis-à-vis the middle class. The first thing to catch our notice in this small section of the nation is the immense number of separate elements of which it was composed. Like those substances once thought indivisible in which modern scientists, the more closely they examine them, find more and more separate particles, the French bourgeoisie, while seemingly a uniform mass, was extremely composite. Thus I find that the notabilities of a quite small town were split up into no less than thirty-six distinct groups. Small as they were, these groups kept trying still further to narrow themselves down by expelling all such elements as seemed in any way out of sympathy with their aims. Indeed, this exclusiveness was carried to such a pitch that some of these groups comprised only three or four members. But this made them all the more vocal, the more determined to assert themselves. Each group was differentiated from the rest by its right to petty privileges of one kind or another, even the least of which was regarded as a token of its exalted status. Thus they were constantly wrangling over questions of precedence, so much so that the Intendant and the courts were often at a loss for a solution of their differences. "At last an order has been passed that the holy water is to be given to the judges of the presidial court before being given to members of the town corporation. The parlement had been unable to come to a decision, so the King took the matter up in Council and has decided it himself. It was high time, too, as the whole town was in a ferment." When a group was not given the precedence it claimed

in the general assembly of notables, it ceased to attend, preferring to withdraw from public affairs altogether rather than to
stomach such an affront to its dignity. In a small provincial
town, La Flèche, the guild of wig-makers ventilated its "just
indignation" in this manner when the bankers' union was given
precedence of it. In another town we find several of the leading
men refusing to perform their civic functions because (as the
Intendant reports) "some artisans have been admitted to the
assembly and the notables deem it beneath them to consort with
persons of this kind." "If a mere notary is appointed sheriff,"
another Intendant tells his chief, "the notables will feel affron-
ted, since all the notaries here are men of low extraction and started out as clerks." The above-mentioned "six most worthy citizens", who had so lightheartedly decided that "the common
people" should be mulcted of their political rights, found themselves in a curious quandary when it came to decide who the
notables in question were to be and what order of precedence
should obtain between them. On this delicate question they were
far less categorical and even expressed a fear of wounding the
susceptibilities of some of their fellow citizens.

These disputes about questions of prestige between small
groups of men gave many occasions for the display of that personal vanity which seems innate in Frenchmen—to the exclusion of the honest pride of the self-respecting citizen. Most
of the corporate bodies of which I have been speaking were in
existence as far back as the sixteenth century, but in those
early days their members, after having settled among themselves
such matters as concerned their group interests, made a point
of conferring with all the other inhabitants of the town or city
when matters affecting the community at large were to be discussed. By the eighteenth century, however, these groups had
withdrawn to a great extent from this wider sphere of action,
since municipal business was much reduced in volume and
transacted by specially empowered officials. Thus each of these
small groups lived only for itself and, quite literally, minded its
own business.

That word "individualism", which we have coined for our
own requirements, was unknown to our ancestors, for the good

reason that in their days every individual necessarily belonged
to a group and no one could regard himself as an isolated unit.
Nevertheless, each of the thousands of small groups of which the
French nation was then composed took thought for itself alone;
in fact, there was, so to speak, a group of individualism which
prepared men's minds for the thorough-paced individualism
with which nowadays we are familiar.

What is still more singular is that all these men, split up
into compact groups though they were, had become so similar
as to be almost interchangeable; that is to say anyone might have
moved out of his group into another without one's noticing any
difference in his practices or personality. Moreover, had anyone
with a gift for psychology delved into their inmost feelings,
he would have found that these very men regarded the flimsy
barriers dividing people so much alike as contrary both to the
public interest and to common sense and that already, theoretically anyhow, these ancestors of ours were all for unity. Each
set store on his status as member of a particular group because
he saw others asserting their personalities in this way; yet all
were quite ready to sink their differences and to be integrated
into a homogeneous whole, provided no one was given a
privileged position and rose above the common level.

CHAPTER TEN

*How the suppression of political freedom and the
barriers set up between classes brought on most of the
diseases to which the old order succumbed*

In the preceding chapters I have described the most pernicious
of the diseases from which the old order suffered and which
ultimately proved fatal to it. I will now revert to the origin of
this strange and fateful malady and show how many other ills
were likewise due to it.

If with the passing of the Middle Ages the English, like the
French, had been deprived not only of political freedom but also
of those local franchises which, once the former is extinct, can-

not survive for long, we may be fairly sure that the various classes of which their aristocracy was composed would have become estranged from each other (as was the case in France and, to a greater or lesser extent, in all parts of the continent), and that all alike would have set up barriers between themselves and their "inferiors". But, by reason of the political freedom obtaining in England, the aristocracy and the lower orders were obliged to maintain contact with each other so as to be able to join forces if and when the need arose.

Particularly noteworthy is the skill with which the English nobility, in order to safeguard their position, were quite ready, whenever it seemed advisable, to fraternise with the common people and to profess to regard them as equals. Arthur Young (whose *Travels* contain one of the most judicious accounts we have of the state of France just before the Revolution) tells us that when visiting the Duke of Liancourt he expressed a wish to meet some of the richest and most knowledgeable local farmers and the Duke told his agent to arrange for this. Young observes that had the Duke been an Englishman, he would have invited three or four farmers to his residence and they would have dined at the family table in company with ladies of the highest rank. Such a thing, he adds, would have been quite out of the question anywhere in France, from Calais to Bayonne.

True, the English aristocrats were haughtier by nature than the French and even less disposed to demean themselves by hobnobbing with persons of lower rank; nevertheless, they were compelled to do so by the force of circumstances. No sacrifice was too great if it ensured their power. For many centuries the only inequalities of taxation existing in England have been those successively introduced in favour of the poorer classes. It is curious to see how a difference in political principles led to a complete divergence in the social system of two countries separated only by a narrow arm of sea. In England during the eighteenth century it was the poor who enjoyed exemption from taxation; in France it was the rich.[37] The English aristocracy voluntarily shouldered the heaviest public burdens so as to be allowed to retain its authority; in France the nobles clung to their exemption from taxation to the very end to console themselves for having lost the right to rule.

In the fourteenth century the principle of "No taxation without the people's consent" seemed as well established in France as in England herself. It was often cited; to override it was always regarded as a tyrannical gesture, and to abide by it as the due observance of an immemorial right. Indeed, at that time the political institutions in France and England were very similar. Subsequently, however, there was a parting of the ways, and as time went on, the two nations became ever more dissimilar. Thus two lines starting out from practically the same point but given slightly different directions diverge more and more, the more they are prolonged.

It was on the day when the French people, weary of the chaos into which the kingdom had been plunged for so many years by the captivity of King John and the madness of Charles VI, permitted the King to impose a tax without their consent and the nobles showed so little public spirit as to connive at this, provided their own immunity was guaranteed—it was on that fateful day that the seeds were sown of almost all the vices and abuses which led to the violent downfall of the old order. Such, anyhow, is my opinion, and I fully endorse the view of our sagacious fifteenth-century historian Commines when he writes: "Charles VII, when he succeeded in establishing the right of levying the *taille* at his own pleasure, without the consent of the Estates, laid a heavy burden on his own soul and on those of his successors, and moreover inflicted a wound on his kingdom which will continue bleeding for many years to come." Indeed this "wound" of which he speaks, far from healing, tended to enlarge itself, as is plain to see if we follow up the consequences of this disastrous innovation.

Forbonnais is right when in his *Enquiry into the Finances of France* he points out that during the Middle Ages our Kings usually lived on the revenues of their domains, and "since non-recurring expenditure was defrayed by 'extraordinary' taxation, this was borne equally by the clergy, the nobility, and the people."

Most of the nation-wide taxation voted by the Three Estates during the fourteenth century was, in fact, of this nature. For almost all these taxes were indirect; that is to say they were borne by all consumers without distinction. Such direct taxes as existed were levied not on real but on personal estate. For example, nobles, ecclesiastics, and townsfolk were ordered to remit to the King during a specified year one tenth of their total incomes. I am speaking here of taxes voted by the Estates-General; but the same applies to those imposed during this period by the provincial Estates within their several territories.

During this period, it is true, the nobleman was immune from the direct tax known as the *taille*, the reason being that he was compelled to perform military service at his own expense. But in those days the incidence of the *taille* as a tax of a general order was restricted; it concerned the *seigneurie*, the lord's domain, rather than the kingdom as a whole.

When for the first time the King decided to levy taxes on his own account he saw it would be wiser to select a kind of tax that did not seem to hit the nobility directly. For they were in a sense his rivals and a constant danger to the monarchy, and they certainly would not have tolerated an innovation prejudicial to their interests. For these reasons his choice fell on a tax from which they were exempt, the *taille*.

Thus to the existing inequalities of various kinds he added yet another of a more general order, which intensified public feeling against the others. From now on, in proportion as the needs of the exchequer grew as a result of the extended functions of the central power, the *taille* was increased and given various forms; with the result that before long it had risen tenfold and all new taxes were assimilated to it. Thus year by year the inequality of taxation created an ever wider rift between classes, dividing up the nation more and more into watertight compartments.[38] Once taxation had been so contrived as to press most heavily on those who had least means of defending themselves against it, and not on those most capable of bearing the burden, the result was as inevitable as it was detested: the rich got off scot free and the poor suffered accordingly. When Mazarin, we are told on good authority, being in need of money, tried to put through a plan of levying a tax on all the big mansions in Paris, so violent was the opposition from interested parties that he decided to raise the five additional millions needed by an increase of the *taille*. He had proposed to tax the wealthiest citizens; he ended by taxing the poorest—and the Treasury lost nothing by the change.

Obviously there were limits to the productivity of taxes so unequally distributed; but there now were none to the financial exigencies of the French Kings. Yet they would neither convene the Estates with a view to getting subsidies voted, nor by taxing the nobles run the risk of inciting them to demand the convocation of these assemblies. Hence the prodigious, wellnigh diabolical ingenuity displayed by our Finance Ministers during the last three centuries of the monarchy. When we look into the history of the administration under the old régime and the financial expedients it resorted to, we realise to what arbitrary, indeed unscrupulous, practices the lack of money may reduce an otherwise well-intentioned government when there is no public opinion to control it, once time has consecrated its authority and freed it from the fear of revolution, that last resort of an indignant nation.

In records of the period we constantly read of royal property being sold, then declared "unsaleable" and taken back; of broken pledges; of established rights being brushed aside. In every financial crisis the creditor of the State was victimised and the government broke faith with the governed.[39]

Privileges granted in perpetuity were constantly withdrawn. Indeed, if mishaps to a foolish vanity deserved any pity we could hardly help sympathising with those unlucky people who, after having acquired a patent of nobility, were forced time and again during the seventeenth and eighteenth centuries to repurchase the unjust privileges or vain honours for which they had already paid several times over. Thus Louis XIV abolished all the titles that had been conferred during the past ninety-two years, mostly by himself, but their owners were allowed to retain them on payment of a further sum of money, "all the titles having been obtained by surprise," as the edict quaintly phrases it. And, eighty years later, Louis XV was moved to imitate this lucrative precedent.

Men called up for service in the militia were not allowed to furnish substitutes, for fear, it was declared, of raising the price paid by the government for recruits. Towns, commonalties, and hospitals were forced to repudiate their commitments so as to be able to lend money to the King. Parishes were debarred from undertaking works of public utility because it was feared that if they thus depleted their resources they might be less punctual in their payments of the *taille*.

It is on record that two high officials, M. Orry and M. de Trudaine, Controller-General and Director-General of Public Works respectively, drew up a plan for replacing obligatory labour on the highways by the payment of a fixed sum to be levied from the inhabitants of each district for the upkeep of their roads. The reason why these able administrators had to abandon the project is revealing. It was feared that once this fund had been established, there was nothing to prevent the exchequer from diverting it to its own use, with the result that very soon ratepayers would be saddled with a new impost and the duty of forced labour as well. Indeed, it might be said that had a private person managed his own affairs in the same way as our great King in all his glory managed the public finances, he would soon have found himself in the clutches of the law.

When we come across any ancient medieval custom which was maintained, with its worst elements wilfully exploited in defiance of the spirit of the age, or any new and equally pernicious measure, we always find, if we go to the root of the matter, some financial expedient that has crystallised into an institution. Thus, to meet emergencies of a temporary order, new powers were frequently created which were to last for centuries.

A special impost named the *droits de franc-fief* had been instituted at a very early period, its effect being to tax commoners who owned fiefs properly accruing to the nobility. Thus it created the same distinction between landed estates as that obtaining between individuals, and each of these distinctions tended to aggravate the other. I am indeed inclined to think that this impost was more responsible than any other for the great gulf that developed between the nobleman and the non-noble, since it prevented them from making common cause regarding that form of property which more than any other causes men to pool their interests: the ownership of real estate.

Thus the noble landed proprietor and his neighbour, the non-noble landowner, were constantly reminded of the vast difference between them. In England, on the other hand, nothing has done more to bring together these two classes than the abolition (in the seventeenth century) of all distinctions between the nobleman's fief and land held by a commoner.

In the fourteenth century the feudal due of *franc-fief* was far from onerous and only rarely levied; but in the eighteenth century, when feudalism was in its death throes, it was stringently enforced, a sum equivalent to a whole year's income being exacted every twenty years. The son had to pay it when he stepped into his father's place. In 1761 the Société d'Agriculture at Tours denounced it with considerable courage. "This tax is doing infinite harm to agriculture. Of all the imposts to which the King's subjects are liable, none is more vexatious, none presses so heavily on our farmers and agricultural workers." And another contemporary observes that "this due, formerly exacted only once in a lifetime, has gradually become an intolerable burden."[40] Even the nobles would have welcomed its abolition, since it discouraged commoners from buying their land. Unfortunately, owing to financial stringency, the fiscal authorities insisted on its retention, and even increased it.

The Middle Ages are often held responsible for all the evils caused by the trade corporations. This view is mistaken; everything goes to show that at their inception the trade and craft guilds were no more than associations enabling persons engaged in the same occupation to get together and set up small, independent governing bodies whose task it was at once to protect the interests of the workers and to control them. This, in fact, was what St. Louis aimed at, so far as can be ascertained.

It was not until the beginning of the sixteenth century, in the heyday of the Renaissance, that for the first time the right to work as an artisan came to be regarded as a "privilege" purchasable from the King. Only then did each corporation develop into a small, closed oligarchy and those monopolies arise which so greatly handicapped the crafts and professions and displeased our ancestors. From the reign of Henri III, who generalised, though he did not originate, the mischief, to that of Louis XVI, who did away with it, the evils of the guild system steadily increased at the very time when social progress was making them seem less tolerable and public opinion was growing ever more resentful of such despotic methods. Year after year new branches of industry were brought under the yoke and the monopolies of the older guilds extended. Things were at their worst during the "best years" (as they are called) of the reign of Louis XIV for the good reason that never had the government needed money so badly, nor had any monarch been so determined not to appeal to the nation in such emergencies. Letronne was right when he said (in 1775) that the State had established these corporations simply with the object of making them a source of revenue, partly from the sale of licences and partly by the creation of new "offices", which the corporations were forced to buy up. "The Edict of 1673 carried the policy of Henri III to its logical conclusion when it obliged the guilds to take out 'letters of confirmation' on payment of a certain sum. All artisans who were not as yet enrolled in a guild were forced to join one, and this odious transaction brought in 300,000 *livres*."

We have already seen how in the French towns the whole system of municipal elections was changed, not for political ends, but simply with a view to raising money for the Treasury. It was this same urgent need of money, combined with a reluctance to ask it from the Estates-General, that led to the widespread sale of offices, a phenomenon perhaps unique in history. This practice, in its origin a purely financial expedient, skilfully exploited the vanity of the Third Estate, the desire of the commoner to hold some public office. Indeed, the craving to secure a place in the bureaucracy became a second nature with the Frenchman, and had much to do with the servile state to which the people were reduced and the revolutionary movement.

For the creation of new offices kept pace with the ever growing financial difficulties of the central power, and all these posts carried with them exemption from taxation or other privileges.[41] Thus since the needs of the Treasury and not those of the administration were the decisive factor, a well-nigh unbelievable number of offices, some merely superfluous, some actively pernicious, were created.[42] In 1664, when Colbert made a survey of the finances of the realm, he found that the capital invested in this egregious form of "property" amounted to almost five hundred million *livres*. Richelieu, we are told, abolished a hundred thousand offices, but they were promptly reinstituted under other names. For the sake of raising some paltry sums of money the central power deprived itself of the right to supervise efficiently the work of its own agents and to keep them under control. In the result, the administrative machinery which was thus built up year by year became so intricate and so inefficient that it had to be left running idle, so to speak, while alongside it was set up another instrument of government, at once simpler and easier to manipulate, which in practice carried out the functions nominally performed by the horde of office-holders who had bought their way into the bureaucracy.

It is obvious that none of these pernicious institutions would have survived for long had free discussion of them been permitted. Indeed, none would have been established, still less allowed thus to proliferate, had the opinion of the Estates-General been taken or had the protests made by them on the rare occasions when they were still convened been listened to. For during the last centuries of the monarchy the evils of the system were denounced by the Estates-General at every opportunity. They made no secret of their belief that at the root of these evils was the power, usurped by the King, of arbitrarily levying taxes or, as they put it in the forthright language of the fifteenth century, "the right of battening on the people's flesh and blood without discussion by the Three Estates and without their consent." The Estates-General did not merely stand up for their own rights; they vigorously and often successfully championed those of provinces and towns. At each successive meeting voices were raised against the inequalities of the burdens imposed on taxpayers; on several occasions there were demands for the abolition of the guild system, and century by century the sale of offices was denounced with ever increasing vehemence. "Trafficking in offices is tantamount to selling justice and a highly immoral act." And long after the system had become an established custom, the Estates-General continued to protest against the creation of new offices, of a host of parasitic functionaries and invidious privileges. But their protests were unavailing; indeed, these institutions were actually intended to undermine their authority, implementing as they did the King's reluctance to convene the Estates-General and his desire to hide from the French people the nature of the taxation he dared not let them see in its true colours.

Strangely enough the best Kings had recourse to these expedients no less than the worst. It was Louis XII who first made a regular practice of the sale of offices and it was Henri IV who took to selling the reversion of them—so much stronger were the vices of the system than the virtues of the men who operated it.

The same desire of breaking free of the control of the Estates-General led to the practice of vesting the parlements with numerous political functions. The effect was an entanglement of the judicial with the administrative authority highly prejudicial to the good conduct of public affairs. But it was necessary to replace the rights which had been taken away by some new constitutional guarantees, since though the Frenchman will submit patiently enough to absolute power provided it is not oppressive, he dislikes the sight of it; thus it is well to place in front of it some sort of screen which, without obstructing, masks it to some extent.

Finally, it was the desire of preventing the nation whose money was being asked for from asking back its freedom that led the government to spare no pains in maintaining the barriers between the various classes, which were thus unable to join forces and put up an organised resistance. This ensured the safety of the central power, which had to deal only with small, isolated groups of malcontents. Though in the long history of the French kingdom so many admirable monarchs occupied the throne at various periods, many of them remarkable for their practical shrewdness, some for their high intelligence, and almost all for their courage, not one of them ever made an attempt to unite classes and obliterate their distinctions otherwise than by reducing them all to a common state of dependence on the Crown. No, I am making a mistake; one of our monarchs made it his aim and, indeed, put all his heart into it, and—how inscrutable are the ways of Divine Providence!—that was the ill-starred Louis XVI.

The segregation of classes, which was the crime of the late monarchy, became at a late stage a justification for it, since when the wealthy and enlightened elements of the population were no longer able to act in concert and to take part in the government, the country became, to all intents and purposes, incapable of administrating itself and it was needful that a master should step in.

"The nation," Turgot wrote regretfully in a confidential report to the King, "is an aggregate of different and incompatible social groups whose members have so few links between themselves that everyone thinks solely of his own interests; no trace of any feelings for the public weal is anywhere to be found. Villages and towns have no more intercourse between them than have the districts in which they are included. They cannot even come to an agreement about carrying out public works indispensable for their welfare. In view of their endless bickerings and conflicting claims, Your Majesty is obliged to decide everything by yourself or through your agents. Special orders from you are needed before anyone will contribute in any way to the public good, respect his neighbour's rights, and, sometimes, even make the best use of his own."

It was no easy task bringing together fellow citizens who had lived for many centuries aloof from, or even hostile to, each other and teaching them to co-operate in the management of their own affairs. It had been far easier to estrange them than it now was to reunite them, and in so doing France gave the world a memorable example. Yet, when sixty years ago the various classes which under the old order had been isolated units in the social system came once again in touch, it was on their sore spots that they made contact and their first gesture was to fly at each other's throats. Indeed, even today, though class distinctions are no more, the jealousies and antipathies they caused have not died out.

CHAPTER ELEVEN

*Of the nature of the freedom prevailing under the old
order and of its influence on the Revolution*

Should any of my readers decide at this point to lay aside this
book, he would have only a very incomplete picture of the government of France as it was under the old order and of the social
conditions leading to the Revolution. For the fact that the
French were so profoundly divided amongst themselves and so
limited, politically speaking, in their interests, taken with the
no less obvious fact that the royal power dominated the whole
life of the country, might lead him to suppose that the spirit of
independence had died out, along with public freedom; that
the French as a nation had been tamed to servitude. Actually
this was by no means the case; though the government had
absolute control of public affairs, it was far from having broken
the spirit of the individual Frenchman.

In the midst of institutions designed to buttress absolute
power freedom survived, but a peculiar kind of freedom, of
which it is hard for us today to form a clear conception. In fact,
it needs attentive study if we wish to understand its good and
evil effects on the French social system.

While the central government was gradually taking over all
the powers of local authorities and coming more and more to
monopolise the whole administration of the country, some institutions which it had allowed to survive and even some new
ones created by itself tended to check this centripetal movement.
And certain age-old customs, ancient usages, and even ancient
abuses, had a similar effect. Thus beneath the surface of conformity there was forever stirring in the minds of many
Frenchmen a spirit of resistance and sturdy individualism.

Under the monarchy centralisation was of the same kind,
fell into the same patterns, and had the same aims as the
centralisation we know today, though it never had the far-
reaching power of our modern governments. For in its desire
to make money out of everything the old administration put

up to sale most public offices and thereby deprived itself of the right of appointing or dismissing its officials at will. Thus one of its propensities tended to counteract the other; its greed frustrated its ambition. In the result the central power was compelled to make use of a personnel which it had not shaped to its ends and was unable to discard;[43] and its enactments, even the most imperative, were often carried out halfheartedly. Indeed, these curious flaws in the constitution of the bureaucracy often acted as a political check on the absolutism of the central power; as a sort of breakwater which, ramshackle though it was, tended to disperse its strength and weaken its impact.

The government of those days had not at its disposal the immense number of subventions, favours, and honours, or the huge sums of money which nowadays it distributes with a lavish hand. In a word, it had fewer inducements to offer as well as fewer means of coercion. Moreover, it had no very clear idea of the extent of its power. None of its rights was firmly established or unequivocally defined, and though its sphere of action was already vast, it had to grope its way, so to speak, in the dark and exercise much prudence. The fact that the limits of the authority of government and the rights of all concerned were so indefinite operated in two ways: while favouring the designs of Kings upon the liberty of their subjects, it often made it easier for the latter to defend their freedom.

Painfully conscious of being a recent creation and staffed by men of relatively low birth, the administration was always chary of taking a drastic step when it encountered opposition. Reading the correspondence between our eighteenth-century Ministers of State and the Intendants, we cannot fail to be struck by the way in which a government so authoritative and self-assured (provided no one questioned its authority) suddenly took fright at the least hint of resistance, was dismayed by the least criticism, and scared by the least rumour of discontent. On such occasions it drew back, negotiated, tried to take the pulse of public opinion—and often stopped short of the full use of its legitimate powers. The easygoing egotism of Louis XV and the natural kindliness of his successor lent themselves to such procedures. It never entered their heads that anyone would dream of dethroning them. They had none of the anxieties and nothing of the cruelty inspired by fear that we find in so many rulers of a later day, and the only people they trod underfoot were those they did not see.

Many of the prejudices, false ideas, and privileges which were the most serious obstacles to the establishment of a healthy, well-ordered freedom had the effect of maintaining in the minds of Frenchmen a spirit of independence and encouraging them to make a stand against abuses of authority. The nobility had the utmost contempt for the administration properly so called, though now and again they addressed petitions to it. Even after the surrender of their former power they kept something of their ancestral pride, their traditional antipathy to servitude and subordination to the common law. True, they gave little thought to the freedom of the populace at large and were quite ready to let the authorities rule those around them with a heavy hand. But they refused to let that hand weigh on themselves and were prepared to run the greatest risks in the defence of their liberties if and when the need arose. When the Revolution broke out, the nobility, destined as they were to be swept away with the throne, still maintained in their dealings with the King an attitude vastly more arrogant and a freedom of speech far greater than those of the Third Estate, who were soon to over-throw the monarchy. Almost all the safeguards against the abuse of power which the French nation has possessed during its thirty-seven years of representative government were vigorously demanded by the nobles. When we read the *cahiers* they pre-sented to the Estates-General, we cannot but appreciate the spirit and some of the high qualities of our aristocracy, despite its prejudices and failings.[44] It is indeed deplorable that instead of being forced to bow to the rule of law, the French nobility was uprooted and laid low, since thereby the nation was deprived of a vital part of its substance, and a wound that time will never heal was inflicted on our national freedom. When a class has taken the lead in public affairs for centuries, it develops as a result of this long, unchallenged habit of pre-eminence a certain proper pride and confidence in its strength, leading it to be the point of maximum resistance in the social organism. And it not only has itself the manly virtues; by dint of its example it quickens them in other classes. When such an element of the body politic is forcibly excised, even those most hostile to it suffer a diminution of strength. Nothing can ever replace it completely, it can never come to life again; a deposed ruling class may recover its titles and possessions but nevermore the spirit of its forbears.

The priesthood, which since then has often displayed such obsequiousness (in civil matters) towards the temporal power, whatever it may be, and, indeed—provided the government has had an air of favouring the Church—truckled to it servilely, was in earlier days one of the most independent bodies in the land and the only one to enjoy a freedom none dared call in question.

The provinces had lost their independence, and the towns had kept a mere shadow of theirs. The members of the nobility could not meet to confer on any matter whatsoever without permission from the King. The Church of France, on the other hand, held its periodical assemblies right to the end.[45] Within the Church the powers of the high ecclesiastical authority had well-recognised limits; even the lowest orders of the hierarchy had effective means of defending themselves against would be tyrannical superiors. Thus they had not been tamed by all-powerful bishops to a habit of blind obedience, which as a result they might have practised likewise towards the temporal power. It is not my purpose to pass judgment on the ancient constitution of the Church; I merely wish to show that it did not pre-condition the clergy to political servility.

In any case, many ecclesiastics were men of noble blood and they brought into the Church the spirit of pride and, indeed, unruliness which was their birthright. All these men, moreover, held high positions in the State and enjoyed privileges accruing to their rank. The exercise of these secular feudal rights, while injurious to the moral authority of the Church, gave its members a feeling of independence as regards the civil power.

But what above all tended to imbue the clergy with the ideas, the aspirations, and sometimes even the passions of the laity was the ownership of land. I have been at pains to study most of the reports and records of the debates of the ancient provincial Estates, and in particular those of Languedoc, a province in which the clergy played a more active part than elsewhere in the administration. I have also read the minutes of the provincial assemblies in 1779 and 1787. Importing into the perusal our present-day notions of the clergy's functions, I was almost startled at finding bishops and abbots—many of them renowned for their saintliness and erudition—making projects for the construction of roads or canals and showing a thorough practical knowledge of the subject. They proved themselves no less competent advisers when ways and means of increasing the productivity of the land, revising the living standard of the population, or promoting trade and industry were under discussion. They were no less knowledgeable about such matters, indeed often more so, than the laymen with whom they were conferring.[46]

Dissenting from a popular and strongly held opinion, I venture to suggest that when a nation deprives the Catholic clergy of the ownership of land and replaces the income drawn from it by fixed salaries, the nation is furthering the interests of the Holy See and the temporal power and these alone, and is also suppressing one of the chief elements of freedom within its borders.

For a man who in respect of all that counts most in his spiritual life is subject to a foreign authority and is not allowed to have a family has only one possible link with the soil of the country in which he lives, and that link is the ownership of land. Cut this link and he belongs nowhere in particular. In the place where by the accident of birth he lives, he is like a foreign body in the community; none of its interests touch him personally. As for his conscience, he is dependent solely on the Pope, for his subsistence solely on the ruling power, and the only motherland to which he owes allegiance is—the Church. Thus in every political crisis the first question he asks himself is how it will affect the Church, favourably or otherwise. Provided the Church remains free and flourishes, what else matters? Where politics are concerned the attitude that comes most naturally to him is one of indifference; though an excellent member of the Christian *civitas*, he is but an imperfect citizen in the mundane sense. Such sentiments and convictions when they obtain in a group of men called on to shape the minds and morals of a country's youth are bound to have a debilitating

effect on the mores of the nation as a whole in matters touching
on public life.

If we wish to get a clear idea of the changes that the mind
of man is apt to undergo as the result of changes in his material
environment, we cannot do better than study the *cahiers* presented by the clergy in 1789. They often strike us as intolerant
and sometimes obstinately insistent on ecclesiastical privileges;
nevertheless, they show themselves as hostile to despotism, as
favourable to civil liberty, and as eager for political freedom as
the Third Estate or the nobility.[47] They claim that individual
liberty should be safeguarded not by mere promises but by legislation on the lines of the English habeas corpus; that State
penitentiaries should be abolished and likewise "exceptional"
tribunals and "evocations" (withdrawals by a higher tribunal
of suits filed in the ordinary courts). They were also in favour
of public hearings of all court cases, of the irremovability of
judges; the admissibility of all citizens to government posts,
such appointments being made on grounds of personal merit;
a less oppressive and humiliating method of recruiting to the
army, no exemptions being allowed; the buying out of all
seigneurial rights, which, deriving as they did from the feudal
system, were inconsistent with the idea of freedom; the right
to work without restraint of any kind; the abolition of internal
customs barriers; a great increase in the number of private
schools (one for each parish) and free education for all; lay
charitable organisations such as almshouses and workhouses in
all rural districts; and finally, the promotion of agriculture by
every possible means.

In the political field they proclaimed—and none were more
outspoken—the absolute right of all the people to meet together
for the purpose of passing laws and freely voting taxes. No
Frenchman, they said, should be compelled to pay a tax for
which he had not voted in person or through a deputy. The
clergy also demanded that the Estates-General, all members of
which were to be freely elected, should meet every year and
debate in public session all matters of national importance;
that they should enact laws applicable to all, against which
none had the right of setting up any ancient usage or personal
privilege; that they should draw up the budget and control even

.the King's privy purse; that their deputies should enjoy immunity from arrest and legal proceedings, and that Ministers should always be answerable to them. In conclusion, the clergy proposed that local "assemblies" of the Estates should be instituted in all provinces and that every town should have its own municipality. Of "divine right" not a word.

By and large—and despite the all too obvious shortcomings of some of its members—there has probably never been a clergy more praiseworthy than that of Catholic France just before the Revolution; more enlightened, more patriotic, less wrapped up in merely private virtues, more concerned with the public good, and, last but not least, more loyal to the Faith—as persecution clearly proved in the event. When I began my study of the old order I was full of prejudices against our clergy; when I ended it, full of respect for them. In fact, they had only the faults normal to all corporate bodies, political and religious alike, when they are highly organised and closely integrated. Among these failings are a tendency to go beyond their legitimate sphere of action, a certain intolerance, and an instinctive, sometimes unjustified attachment to the special rights of their corporation.

Under the old order the middle class was in a far better position than it is at present to assert its independence; indeed, many of the very defects inherent in it tended to that end. The public posts available were even more numerous than they are today and members of the middle class were no less eager to obtain them. But it is noteworthy how things have changed in this respect. Before the Revolution the majority of these posts, being neither granted nor alienable by the government, raised the status of their holders without putting them at the mercy of the central power. In a word, that very situation which today keeps so many Frenchmen in a state of almost abject terror of the powers-that-be was once the surest means they had of making themselves respected by their fellow citizens.

The immunities of all sorts which so perniciously estranged the middle class from the common people tended to make of the former a pseudo-aristocracy that on occasion displayed the spirit of resistance of a true aristocracy. Though in each of the small, semiprivate associations which split it into so many factions the true interest of the community tended to be slurred over, the utmost concern was shown for those of the group.[48] For its members were acutely aware that they had to defend their group privileges and prestige; no individual could play for safety and make ignoble concessions, hoping to pass unnoticed. The stage on which each played his part was small but brightly lit and there was always the same audience to applaud or hiss him.

Methods of stifling the least whisper of resistance had not been brought to their present-day perfection. France had not yet become the land of dumb conformity it is now; though political freedom was far to seek, a man could still raise his voice and count on its echoes being widely heard.

But it was our judicial system that, above all, enabled the oppressed to make known their grievances. For though as far as administration and political institutions were concerned France had succumbed to absolutism, our judicial institutions were still those of a free people. Under the old order litigation was costly, complicated, and unconscionably protracted. True, these were grave defects, but the courts showed none of that servility towards the ruling power which is a form, indeed one of the worst forms, of venality since it not only corrupts the judge himself but in time infects the nation as a whole. Our magistrates were irremovable, nor did they aspire to promotion in the judicial hierarchy. Thus two prime conditions of their independence were assured; for even though it may be impossible to apply direct compulsion to a judiciary, a government has many other means of influencing it.

It is not to be denied that the central power succeeded in removing from the jurisdiction of the ordinary courts most kinds of proceedings in which a public authority was involved; but even so it feared them. For while it could forbid their trying certain cases, it did not dare to prevent them in a general way from entertaining complaints and expressing their opinions. And since the court still used the idiom of our old French tongue, which was nothing if not forthright, the magistrates did not mince their words or fail, on occasion, to describe the methods of the high authorities as arbitrary and despotic.[49] Thus the intervention of the courts in administrative matters, though it often told against the good conduct of public business, served sometimes as a safeguard of the freedom of the nation; it was a great mischief, but limited a still greater mischief.

Within the judicature and in its sphere of influence the robust good sense of the past was conserved despite the ferment of new ideas. As for the parlements, though they were more concerned with their own interests than with those of the country as a whole, it is certain that they always showed much courage in defending their independence and their principles, and this attitude did not fail to take effect on all who came in contact with them.

When in 1770 the parlement of Paris was dissolved and the magistrates belonging to it were deprived of their authority and status, not one of them truckled to the royal will. What is more, organisations of a different kind, such as the Board of Excise, which were untouched and in no danger, voluntarily exposed themselves to the same risks, though it was certain that they would be treated with the same severity. Yet more conspicuous was the stand made by the leading members of the Bar practising before the parlement; of their own will they shared its fate, relinquished all that had assured their prestige and prosperity, and, rather than appear before judges for whom they had no respect, condemned themselves to silence. In the history of free nations I know of no nobler gesture than this; yet it was made in the eighteenth century and in the shadow of the court of Louis XV.

The practices of the law courts had entered in many ways into the pattern of French life. Thus the courts were largely responsible for the notion that every matter of public or private interest was subject to debate and every decision could be appealed from; as also for the opinion that such affairs should be conducted in public and certain formalities observed. Obviously incompatible with the concept of a servile state, such ideas were the only part of a free people's education furnished by the old régime. Even the administration had borrowed much from the terminology and usages of the law courts. The King felt it incumbent on him always to justify his edicts and to set forth his reasons for them before making them effective; decisions of the court were preceded by lengthy preambles; the Intendant made known his orders through a court usher. In all administrative bodies of ancient origin—such as the corps of Treasurers of France and the assemblies of *Élus*—public debate was the order of the day and everyone had the right of expressing his opinion. All these customs and procedures were so many obstacles to royal despotism. However, the common people (especially in rural districts) were seldom in a position to resist oppression otherwise than by a recourse to violence. For most of the means of countering oppression described above were outside their grasp; only those whose social status enabled them to make their voices heard and attract attention could employ them. But outside the humblest classes there was not a man in France who, given the necessary courage, could not defy authority up to a certain point and, while seeming to comply, put up a resistance. In addressing the nation the King spoke as a leader rather than as a master. "We glory," Louis XVI declared in his preamble to an edict issued at the beginning of his reign, "in the fact that the nation we govern is high-spirited and free." One of his ancestors expressed the same ideas in more antiquated phraseology when, in applauding the Estates-General for the boldness of their "remonstrances," he said, "We had rather converse with freemen than with serfs."

Eighteenth-century man had little of that craving for material well-being which leads the way to servitude. A craving which, while morally debilitating, can be singularly tenacious and insidious, it often operates in close association with such private virtues as family love, a sense of decorum, respect for religion, and even a lukewarm but punctilious observance of the rites of the established Church. While promoting moral rectitude, it rules out heroism and excels in making people well behaved but mean-spirited as citizens. The eighteenth-century Frenchman was, in short, both better and worse than ourselves.

France in those days was a nation of pleasure seekers, all for the joy of life. They were perhaps more irregular in their behaviour, more extravagant in their passions and ideas than our contemporaries, but on the other hand, they had nothing of that discreet, well-regulated sensualism which prevails today. The upper classes were far more interested in living beautifully than in comfort; in making a name for themselves than in making money. Even the middle classes did not devote themselves exclusively to the pursuit of material comforts; they often aspired to loftier, more refined satisfactions and were far from regarding money as the supreme good. As a contemporary writer put it, in a style that for all its oddity had a certain dignity: "I know my nation well; versed though it is in making and squandering precious metals, it is not so constituted as to bestow perpetual adoration on them, but at any moment may return to its ancient gods: valour, glory, and, I make bold to say, magnanimity."

Moreover, we must be chary of regarding submission to authority as *per se* a sign of moral abjection—that would be using a wrong criterion. However subservient was the Frenchman of the old régime to the King's authority there was one kind of subservience to which he never demeaned himself. He did not know what it was to bend the knee to an illegitimate or dubious authority, a government little honoured and sometimes heartily despised, which it is well to truckle to because it has power to help or harm. This degrading form of servitude was something quite unknown to our forefathers. Their feeling for the King was unlike that of any other modern nation for its monarch, even the most absolute; indeed, that ancient loyalty which was so thoroughly eradicated by the Revolution has become almost incomprehensible to the modern mind. The King's subjects felt towards him both the natural love of children for their father and the awe properly due to God alone. Their compliance with his orders, even the most arbitrary, was a matter far less of compulsion than of affection, so that even when the royal yoke pressed on them most heavily, they felt they still could call their souls their own. To their thinking, constraint was the most evil factor of obedience; to ours, it is the least. Yet is not that type of obedience which comes of a servile mind the worst of all? Indeed, we should be ill advised to belittle our ancestors; and would do better to regain, even if it meant inheriting their prejudices and failings, something of their nobility of mind.[50]

Thus any notion that the old order was one of servility and subservience is very wide of the mark.[51] There was far more freedom in that period than there is today, but it was a curiously ill-adjusted, intermittent freedom, always restricted by class distinctions and tied up with immunities and privileges. Though it enabled Frenchmen on occasion to defy the law and to resist coercion, it never went so far as to ensure even the most natural and essential rights to all alike. Yet partial and perverse though it was, this freedom served France well. At the very time when the forces of centralisation were deliberately crushing out all individuality and trying to impose a drab uniformity, a sort of dingy monochrome, this spirit of independence kept alive in many individuals their sense of personality and encouraged them to retain their colour and relief. More than this, it fostered a healthy self-respect and often an overmastering desire to make a name for themselves. This is why we find in eighteenth-century France so many outstanding personalities, those men of genius, proud and greatly daring, who made the Revolution what it was: at once the admiration and the terror of succeeding generations. It would be absurd to suppose that such virile virtues could have sprung from a soil on which all liberty had been extinguished.

But though this peculiar, ill-assimilated, and, as it were, unwholesome liberty prepared the French for the great task of overthrowing despotism, it made them by the same token less qualified than perhaps any other nation to replace it by stable government and a healthy freedom under the sovereignty of law.

CHAPTER TWELVE

*How, despite the progress of civilisation, the lot of the French peasant was sometimes worse in the eighteenth century than it had been in the thirteenth*

In the eighteenth century the peasant was no longer at the mercy of petty feudal overlords, nor did he often receive harsh treatment from the government. He enjoyed civil liberty and had land of his own. Nevertheless, the other classes looked down on him and he was, in fact, more isolated from the rest of the community than the peasant of any other place or period. This was a new, peculiar form of oppression and its consequences merit close and special study.

In the early seventeeth century Henri IV (so Péréfix tells us) lamented the fact that the nobility were ceasing to live in the country. By the middle of the next century this had become the general rule; all contemporary records make mention of it and deplore it: economists in their treatises, Intendants in their letters, and agricultural societies in their minutes. If further proof of the desertion of the countryside by the nobility be wanted, it can be found in the rolls of the capitation tax, which was always levied at the taxpayer's place of residence. From these we learn it was in Paris that all the high nobility and many of the lesser nobles paid this tax.

Hardly any of the gentry—except those whom poverty compelled to remain on their estates—still lived in the country. When a member of the upper class was thus marooned on his estate, his relations with the peasantry around him were of a kind that no rich landowner, I imagine, had ever entertained in earlier days.[52,53] Now that he had ceased to hold a dominant position he no longer was at pains, as he would then have been, to help "his" peasants, to further their interests, and to give them good advice. Moreover, since he was not subject to the same taxes as they, he could not easily enter into their feelings on this score and associate himself with grievances he did not share. In short, they were no longer his subjects and protégés, but he was not as yet their fellow citizen—a state of affairs unique in history.

This led to what might be called a spiritual estrangement more prevalent and more pernicious in its way than mere physical absenteeism. For in his dealings with his tenants the landowner who lived on his estate often developed sentiments and views that would, were he an absentee, have been those of his agent. Like an agent he came to regard his tenants as mere rent-payers and exacted from them the uttermost farthing to which the law, or ancient usage, still entitled him, the result being that the collection of such feudal dues as still existed was apt to seem even more galling to the peasants than it had been in the heyday of feudalism.

Always short of money and often deep in debt, he usually lived with extreme economy in his country home, his one idea being to save up all he could for the winter season in town. The common people, with their knack of hitting on the telling word, had a good name for these squireens, that of the smallest bird of prey; they called them "the hobbyhawks". I am dealing here with classes as a whole, to my mind the historian's proper study, and am quite willing to admit there were exceptions. No one, indeed, would think of denying that during this period many rich landowners did much for the welfare of the peasants, though they were under no obligation to do so and their own interests were not in any way involved. But these were the laudable few who swam against the stream and successfully resisted the forces urging them towards indifference and their former vassals towards hatred.

It is often said that some of our Kings and Ministers of State—notably Louis XIV and Richelieu—were mainly responsible for this desertion of their country homes by the nobility. Nor can it be denied that almost all our Kings during the last three centuries of the monarchy made it their policy to detach the nobles from the people, to lure them to the Court, and to encourage them to take service under the King. This was specially the case in the seventeenth century, when the King saw in them a threat to his power.

An item in a questionnaire sent to all Intendants ran as follows: "Do the nobles in your province prefer staying on their estates, or living elsewhere?" One of the replies is extant. In it the Intendant deplores the way the nobles are behaving in his province; they actually prefer living among their peasants in the country to fulfilling their duties towards the King. This is particularly interesting because the province in question is Anjou (later named La Vendée) and these very men who, according to the Intendant, refused to do their duty to the King were the only nobles who subsequently took up arms in defence of the monarchy and died fighting for it. And what made it feasible to put up this heroic resistance was the fact that they had always been on close and friendly terms with those same peasants for living amongst whom this shortsighted Intendant reproached them!

Nevertheless, we must beware of assuming that the desertion of the countryside by those who at the time were still regarded as the leaders of the nation was due to the direct influence of certain French Kings. Its principal and permanent cause was not that it was encouraged by various monarchs, but, rather, the slow, persistent action of our institutions. This is proved by the fact that when, in the eighteenth century, the government tried to put a stop to this unhealthy tendency, it could not even prevent its gaining ground. The more the nobles lost their ancient rights without being granted any new ones and local freedoms died out, the more the upper-class migration to the cities intensified. Indeed, it was no longer necessary to offer inducements to the nobles to quit their estates; they had no wish to stay on them since they found country life profoundly boring.

What I have been saying of the nobles applies equally to all rich landowners in France. Centralisation was now the order of the day and all the well-to-do and cultured residents of the country districts were moving to the towns. In this context I would suggest that one of the consequences of extreme centralisation is that agriculture ceases to be progressive and the peasant blindly keeps to the old methods of cultivation—thus confirming a famous remark of Montesquieu's: "The soil is productive less by reason of its natural fertility than because the people tilling it are free." But to develop this idea would take me too far afield.

I have already drawn attention to the fact that everywhere the middle class was migrating from the country to the towns, whose atmosphere was more congenial. This is borne out by all the records of the period. From them we learn that only one generation of rich peasants is usually to be found in country districts, for no sooner has an industrious farmer put a little money aside than he tells his son to quit the plough and move to the nearest town, where he buys for him some petty official post. To this period we can date the origin of that peculiar aversion shown by the French farmer, even today, for the occupation which brings him in a comfortable income; the effect has outlived the cause.

To tell the truth, the only well-bred and well-educated man—

the only "gentleman", as our English friends would say—who lived permanently among the peasants and in constant touch with them was the curé, and, Voltaire notwithstanding, the priests might well have come to dominate the local peasantry had they not been so closely and patently allied with the political hierarchy. And the chief reason why they shared to some extent in the odium inspired by the ruling class was that they shared several of its privileges.[54]

Thus not only was the peasant almost entirely deprived of any contacts with the upper classes; he was also separated even from those of his own class who might have been able to befriend and to advise him. For once such persons had achieved a certain culture or prosperity they turned their backs on him. He was, in fact, cold-shouldered on all sides and treated like a being of a peculiar species. This was not (or anyhow not to the same degree) the case in any other great civilised country of Europe, and even in France it was a new development. The fourteenth-century peasants had been at once more oppressed and better cared for; the great seigneurs may have sometimes treated them harshly, but they never abandoned them to their own resources.

The eighteenth-century French village was a community of poor, benighted rustics; its local officials were as little educated and as much looked down on as the ordinary villagers; its Syndic could not read; its tax collector was incapable of compiling, unaided, the returns which so vitally affected his neighbours' incomes and his own. Not only had the seigneur lost all control over local affairs, but he had come to the point of regarding any participation in them as beneath his dignity. It was for the Syndic to assess the *taille*, to call up the militia, to recruit and direct the forced labour gangs—servile functions unworthy of the lord. The villages were left entirely to the tender mercies of the central government, and since it was at a great distance and had nothing to fear from them, its primary concern was to use them as a source of revenue.

It is instructive to see what happens when a whole class of the population is thus neglected and, though no one actually wishes to oppress it, no one tries to educate and aid it. True, the heaviest burdens imposed by the feudal system on the countryfolk had by now been removed or lightened; yet (and it is a fact too often overlooked) these had been replaced by other, perhaps more onerous forms of taxation. The peasant was in some respects more leniently handled than his forefathers, but he had to put up with many impositions unheard of in the past. We must not forget that the peasants had had almost exclusively to bear the brunt of the tenfold rise in the *taille* during the preceding centuries, and something must here be said of the way in which it now was levied. This is a matter of general interest since it goes far to show what barbarous laws can be enacted or kept in force in even "enlightened" periods when the most intelligent members of a nation have no personal interest in amending them.

In a confidential letter addressed to the Intendant by the Controller-General himself in 1779, I find a description of the *taille* which, in its way, is a model of accuracy and brevity. "Arbitrary in its incidence, universal in its application, bearing on personal, not real estate throughout the greater part of France, the *taille* is subject to constant fluctuations owing to the changes taking place year by year in the means of the tax-payers." There we have, neatly summarised, the gist of the matter; indeed, it would be hard more aptly to describe this evil, and remunerative, fiscal expedient.

The total sum due from each parish was fixed each year and, as the Minister observed, it constantly varied, with the result that a farmer never knew a year in advance what he would have to pay in the following year. Within the parish the tax was apportioned between the residents by a peasant chosen at random and entitled the Collector. I mentioned in a previous chapter that I would have something more to say about this official and I shall begin by quoting a declaration made in 1779 by the Provincial Assembly of Berry. Its opinions on the point may be presumed to be impartial since it consisted almost entirely of privileged persons, chosen by the King, who were exempt from payment of the *taille*. "Since nobody wishes to be given the post of Collector, it is right that everybody should hold it in turn. So every year a new man is appointed to collect the *taille*, without regard to his ability or standing. As might be expected, the way the tax roll is drawn up reflects something of the character of the man responsible for it: his personal foibles, his fears and failings. Yet how could he be expected to do better when he is working in the dark? How can any man know just what are his neighbour's means, or the proportion of his wealth to that of someone else? Nonetheless, the Collector has to make a decision based on his own unaided opinion and he is responsible in his person as well as in his chattels for the sum collected. Usually he has to devote every other working day over a period of two years to interviews with the taxpayers. Collectors unable to read have to hunt around in the neighbourhood for someone to help them out." Shortly before, referring to another province, Turgot had said: "This post is the despair, usually the ruin, of those who are compelled to fill it; as a result, all the well-to-do families in a village are reduced to poverty one after another."

Nevertheless, the Collector wielded a power as vast as it was arbitrary; he was almost as much an autocrat as a victim. During his term of office he might ruin himself, but could, if he so wanted, ruin everyone else as well. "Partiality towards members of his family, his friends and neighbours"—it is still the Provincial Assembly speaking—"hatred and a desire to harm his enemies, the need to curry favour with influential people, and reluctance to offend some wealthy citizen who may give him work—all these motives conspire to undermine his sense of justice." Often his personal apprehensions made the Collector ruthless; there were some villages which he never dared visit except with an escort of bailiffs and their men.[55] "Unless he brings bailiffs with him," wrote an Intendant to the Minister (in 1764) "people refuse to pay their taxes." "In the district of Villefranche alone"—thus the Provincial Assembly of Guienne—"there are as many as a hundred and six process servers and bailiff's men always on the road, day in day out."

To evade these arbitrary, not to say ferocious, methods of taxation the French peasant—in that enlightened age, the eighteenth century!— acted much as the Jews did in the Middle Ages. Even when he was a man of means he put up a show of poverty, knowing to his cost that any sign of wealth was dangerous. This is proved to the hilt in a record that, this time, does not come from Guienne but from a hundred leagues away.

In its 1761 report the Agricultural Society of Maine mentioned that it had had the idea of awarding cattle by way of prizes, as incentives to good husbandry. It goes on to say that "the idea has been dropped because of the risks to which the prize winners would be exposed owing to the jealousy of the other competitors, who might well take advantage of the arbitrary methods on which taxes are assessed to make the winners suffer financially in the following year."

Such was the system of taxation that every taxpayer had an urgent and unfailing motive for spying on his neighbours and promptly notifying the Collector of any increase in their means. So it was that envy, malice, and delation flourished to an extent that might not have caused surprise in the domain of an Indian rajah, but was certainly exceptional in Europe.

Nonetheless, taxes were still levied in an orderly and considerate manner in certain parts of France, the districts known as *pays d'états*, where taxation was in the hands of the local government.[56] In Languedoc, for instance, the incidence of the *taille* was adjusted to the amount of land held by each taxpayer and did not vary with his year's income. It was based on a carefully made cadastral survey which took place every thirty years and in which the cultivable land was divided into three classes, according to its fertility. Every taxpaper knew in advance the exact share of the total tax which would be required of him. If he failed to pay he alone or, rather, his land alone was distrained on. If he thought he had been overtaxed he had the right of demanding that his quota of the total to be raised from the community should be compared with that of another dweller in the parish, specified by himself. This was, in fact, the procedure known in France today as "an appeal to proportional equality."

Indeed, all these procedures were much the same as those obtaining in present-day France; we have improved on them but little and have merely enlarged their application. In this context it is worth noting that though we have inherited from the governmental system of the old régime the forms of our public administration, we have been careful not to imitate it in other respects. It is from the provincial assemblies, not from the central power, that we have acquired whatever is most praiseworthy in our administration. While taking over the machine we have discarded what came out of it.

The notorious poverty of the countryfolk gave rise to theories little calculated to ally it. "If people are too well off," Richelieu wrote in his *Political Testament*, "they are apt to become unmanageable." Views as extreme as this were not current in the eighteenth century but it still was thought that without the necessity of earning his daily bread, the peasant would not do a stroke of work; that pauperism was the only cure for idleness. I have heard just the same ideas put forward as regards the Negroes in our colonies; indeed, this opinion is so frequent in the minds of rulers that most economists feel called on to rebut it.

It is common knowledge that the original object of the *taille* was to enable the King to hire soldiers so as to release the nobles and their vassals from service in the army. When in the seventeenth century compulsory military service was reintroduced in the form of the militia, the burden now was borne solely by the humbler classes and almost entirely by the peasantry.

The extreme unpopularity of service in the militia is proved by the great number of police reports contained in the files of the Intendants' offices relating to searches for militiamen who failed to present themselves when called up or had deserted. Indeed, it would seem that this was the form of public duty most detested by the peasants. To evade it they often took to the woods, where they were tracked down and rounded up by bodies of armed men. A surprising state of affairs when we remember how smoothly our compulsory military service operates today.

The peasants' aversion for service in the militia at that time was due less to the nature of the recruiting laws than to the way in which they were carried out. Among the chief reasons for this aversion were the prolonged uncertainty in which the system involved those subject to military service (an unmarried man was liable to be called up at any time until he reached the age of forty); the highhanded methods of the recruiting boards, which almost nullified the effect of drawing a "lucky number"; the law against procuring substitutes; distaste for a rough and dangerous profession, in which there was no prospect of promotion; and, above all, the feeling that this hateful burden was shouldered by the poorest, most helpless section of the population—a feeling that brought home to them their plight and made it still more odious.

I have perused some of the 1789 militia rolls in a number of parishes. Amongst the exempted men I found a gentleman's manservant, the janitor of an abbey, the valet of a member of the middle class—but, be it noted, "a bourgeois who lived like a lord." The mere fact of being rich was a ground for exemption; thus the sons of a farmer who figured annually among the most heavily taxed members of the community were allowed exemption from service in the militia (ostensibly "for the encouragement of agriculture"). Strongly though they advocated equality in all the rest, our economists said nothing against this form of privilege; they merely suggested it should be extended so as to cover other cases—in other words, that the burden imposed on the poorest, most defenceless peasants should be made still heavier. "Considering the meagreness of the soldier's pay," they said, "the way in which he is housed, clothed, and fed, and the rigours of military discipline, it would be sheer cruelty to conscript men not belonging to the lowest class."

Until the close of the reign of Louis XIV the highroads were either not kept up at all or kept up at the expense of their users; in other words, the State or the people living along them. About that time, however, the system of repairing the roads wholly by forced labour, that is to say at the peasants' expense, was introduced in certain districts. This method of getting good roads without paying for them was thought to be so happily conceived that it was extended in 1737 (under instructions from Orry, the Controller-General) to the whole of France, the Intendant being empowered to send constables to arrest defaulters and to sentence them to terms of imprisonment.[57]

Thereafter, when new roads were needed, either owing to increasing traffic or a public demand for them, recourse was had to forced labour, of which, needless to say, the peasants had to bear the brunt. In a report made to the assembly of the province of Berry it was estimated that the public works for which forced labour was requisitioned in this relatively poor province could be valued at 700,000 *livres* per annum, and about the same figure was given for Lower Normandy in 1787. Nothing illustrates more clearly the unhappy lot of the French country-folk. The economic and social progress which was enriching other classes drove the peasants to despair; they were the down-trodden in the march of civilisation.[58]

From letters written by Intendants at about this time I learn that it was thought fit to refuse to allow peasants to use the *corvée* for the upkeep of roads within villages; such labour, it was urged, should be employed solely on the main roads, the King's highways as they were called. New though it was, this curious idea that the cost of the highways should be borne by the poorest members of the population, those in fact who had fewest occasions for making long journeys, became so deeply rooted in the minds of those who gained by it that soon they could not conceive of any other way of keeping up the main roads. In 1776 an attempt was made to commute this obligation into a local tax; but the inequality of burdens was carried over into, and embodied in, the new impost.[59]

Originally local and seigneurial, the system of forced labour on becoming nation-wide and royal was little by little extended to public works of all descriptions. Thus I find that in 1719 forced labour was employed for building barracks. "Parishes are to be told to send their best workmen, and this should be given priority over all other public works in progress." Forced labour was used for transporting criminals to penitentiaries, beggars to workhouses, and, when a regiment was posted to a new head-quarters, its equipment, this last *corvée* being exceptionally onerous at a time when every regiment was attended by an enormous baggage train. A huge number of carts had to be requisitioned, with oxen to draw them, from a large area.[60] Little exacting to begin with, this kind of forced labour came, with the growth of standing armies, to be extremely burden-some.[61] The records tell us of government contractors vigorously insisting on being supplied with forced labour for conveying timber from the forests to the naval arsenals.[62] True, these workers usually were paid, but at rates that were always low and arbitrarily assessed. Sometimes the requisitioning of labour on such inequitable terms led collectors of the *taille* to protest. "The demands on our peasants for repairs to the roads," wrote one

of them in 1751, "will soon make it impossible for them to
pay their taxes."

We well may question if all these new forms of oppression
would have been tolerated had the peasants been able to count
on the support of wealthy, enlightened neighbours, willing and
able, if not to protect them from extortion, at least to intercede
for them with the common overlord, the State, whose grip was
tightening on poor and rich alike. I have read a letter written
by a big landed proprietor in 1774 to the Intendant of his
province asking him to have a new road constructed. This road,
he says, would greatly contribute to the prosperity of the village
it served and he gave good reasons for this opinion. He also
suggested that a market fair should be established, which, he
felt convinced, would double the prices obtained for market
produce. And this worthy citizen added that with the help of a
small subvention a school might be founded which would provide the King with more industrious subjects. These projects,
desirable though they were, had only just occurred to him;
they were the fruit of the two years' residence in his château
imposed on him by royal command. "This exile on my country
estate," as he ingenuously puts it, "has opened my eyes to the
great desirability of these measures."

But it was especially in times of dearth that the loosening or
severance of the links between the great landowners and the
peasantry became apparent. In such emergencies the central
government woke to the fact that it now was out of touch with
the people and sought to revive the personal influences and
political contacts which it had wilfully done away with. But
when it invoked their aid, no one answered the appeal. And,
preposterously enough, it often showed surprise on discovering
that those very people whom it had, itself, deprived of life were
dead.

In the poorest provinces there were some Intendants, such
as Turgot, who came to the rescue of the starving peasantry by
issuing orders—for which there was no legal sanction—compelling
rich landowners to feed their tenants until the next harvest. Also,
I have seen letters written by parish priests (in 1770) in which
it is suggested that the Intendant should tax the rich landowners,
ecclesiastics as well as laymen, of their parishes. "These men

have huge estates on which they never live and from which they
draw fat incomes that they spend elsewhere."

Even in normal times villages were infested with beggars
since (as Letronne points out) poor folk in the towns were
looked after but in the country they had no choice but to beg.
From time to time drastic measures were taken against these
unhappy people.[63] In 1767 the Duc de Choiseul decided to
abolish begging throughout France, and the Intendants' letters
show how he went about it. The police were ordered to arrest
at sight all persons caught begging in any part of the kingdom,
and it appears that over fifty thousand were arrested. Physically
fit men were to be sent to the galleys and more than forty workhouses were opened for the others—yet surely it would have
been better to open once more the hearts of the well-to-do to
charitable sentiments!

The government of the old régime, which in its dealings with
the upper classes was so lenient and so slow to take offence, was
quick to act and often harsh to a degree where members of the
lower orders, peasants especially, were concerned. Of all the
many records I have examined, not one mentions the arrest
of bourgeois under instructions from the Intendant. Peasants,
on the other hand, were constantly arrested in connection with
the levies of forced labour or the militia; for begging, for misdemeanours, and countless other minor offences. One class of the
population could count on impartial tribunals, protracted hearings, and all the safeguards of publicity; the others were tried
summarily by the provost, and there was no appeal.

"The vast gulf between the common people and all other
classes," Necker observed in 1785, "prevents us from seeing
how the man who is but one in the crowd is treated by the
powers-that-be. Were it not for the tolerance and human feeling
inherent in the French temperament (and indeed the spirit of
the age), this would be a constant source of distress to all who
can feel pity for sufferings from which they themselves are
happily immune."

But it is less the actual hardships suffered by the poorer
classes than the way they were prevented from bettering themselves mentally and materially that strikes us today as so inhuman. Though they were free and, in a small way, landowners,

they were left in a state of ignorance and often destitution worse than that of the serfs, their forefathers. In an age of industrial progress they had no share in it; in a social order famed for its enlightenment they remained backward and uneducated. Though not deficient in the shrewd common-sense characteristic of the French peasant in all ages, they had not learned how to turn it to account and get the best out of the land, their only source of livelihood since time immemorial. "The methods of agriculture I find prevailing in France," said an English expert on the subject, "are those of the tenth century." It was in soldiering alone that the peasant excelled; and in the army, anyhow, he was perforce in close daily contact with members of the other classes.

Thus the peasant lived in a state of isolation and abjection, as inaccessible to outside influences as a prisoner in jail. I was almost startled at discovering that less than twenty years before Catholic worship was peremptorily suppressed and the churches desecrated. The method sometimes adopted by local authorities for making a census of the population of a canton was as follows. The priest was asked to report the number of persons who had attended Holy Communion on Easter Sunday; to this figure was added the presumed number of non-communicants, children under age and sick persons, and the total was reported as being the number of dwellers in the parish. Nevertheless, the ideas of the age were beginning gradually to seep into the minds of the French peasantry and in those cramped, obscure retreats they often assumed peculiar forms. For the moment, however, there was no apparent change; to a superficial observer the peasant's habits, mentality, and beliefs seemed as they always had been; he was still as meek as ever—and even merry in his fashion.

But the cheerfulness the Frenchman often displays under even the most untoward circumstances can be misleading. It merely shows that feeling there is nothing to be done about it, he tries to forget his troubles and refuses to brood over them; it does not mean that he is unconscious of them. Show him a way of escape from the afflictions which seem to worry him so little and he will rush so passionately, so blindly to it that if you happen to be in his path, he will trample you underfoot, hardly noticing your presence!

From the point in time we now have reached we can see all this quite clearly, but it was otherwise with contemporary observers. Only with the utmost difficulty did members of the upper classes succeed in glimpsing something of the feelings of the common people, and particularly those of the peasants. For the peasant's upbringing and way of living gave him an outlook on the world at large peculiar to himself, incomprehensible to others. And whenever the poor and the rich come to have hardly any common interests, common activities, and common grievances, the barriers between their respective mentalities become insuperable, they are sealed books to each other even if they spend all their lives side by side. This may help to explain the singular fact that at the very moment when the Revolution was knocking at the door so few apprehensions of any kind were felt by members of the upper and the middle classes, and why they went on blithely discoursing on the virtues of the people, their loyalty, their innocent pleasures, and so forth. Such was the blindness, at once grotesque and tragic, of these men who would not see!

Before going further let us pause for a moment to reflect on one of the laws of Divine Providence which, behind these "petty details" (as they seemed to be at the time), was shaping human destiny in that momentous phase of our history.

The French nobility had stubbornly held aloof from the other classes and had succeeded in getting themselves exempted from most of their duties to the community, fondly imagining they could keep their lofty status while evading its obligations. At first it seemed they had succeeded, but soon a curious internal malady attacked them, whose effect was, so to speak, to make them gradually crumple up, though no external pressure of any kind was brought to bear. The more their immunities increased, the poorer they became. On the other hand, the middle class (of being merged into which they were so much afraid) grew steadily richer and more enlightened without their aid and, in fact, at their expense. Thus the nobles, who had refused to regard the bourgeois as allies or even fellow citizens, were forced to envisage them as their rivals, before long as their enemies, and finally as their masters. A power external to themselves had released them from the tasks of protecting, instructing, and succouring their vassals, and at the same time had left intact their pecuniary and honorific privileges. So they imagined that all was well, and that as they still were given pride of place in the social hierarchy, they were still the nation's leaders. Moreover, they were still surrounded by men to whom legal documents referred as their "subjects", others being described as their vassals, their tenants, or their farmers. In reality, however, they led nobody; they were alone, and when an attack was launched on them, their sole recourse was flight.

Though the nobility and the middle class followed divergent paths, in one respect they were alike; for the bourgeois ended up by being as isolated from the people as any nobleman. Far from showing any concern for the peasants, he shut his eyes to their misfortunes instead of making common cause with them in an attempt to correct social disabilities in which he shared; he deliberately sponsored new forms of injustice that benefitted him personally; indeed, he was quite as eager to secure preferential treatment for himself as any noble to retain his privileges. The peasantry, from whom he stemmed, had come to seem to him an alien, incomprehensible race of men. It was only after he had put arms in their hands that he realised he had kindled passions such as he had never dreamed of, passions which he could neither restrain nor guide, and of which, after being their promoter, he was to be the victim.

No doubt there will always be some to express amazement at the catastrophic downfall of that great house of France which at one time seemed destined to bring all Europe within its orbit. Yet those who, studying its history, read between the lines will have no difficulty in understanding how this happened. Almost all the vices, miscalculations, and disastrous prejudices I have been describing owed their origin, their continuance, and their proliferation to a line of conduct practised by so many of our Kings, that of dividing men so as the better to rule them.

But once the bourgeois had been completely severed from the noble, and the peasant from both alike, and when a similar differentiation had taken place within each of these three classes, with the result that each was split up into a number of small groups almost completely shut off from each other, the inevitable consequence was that, though the nation came to seem a homogeneous whole, its parts no longer held together. Nothing had been left that could obstruct the central government, but, by the same token, nothing could shore it up. This is why the grandiose edifice built up by our Kings was doomed to collapse like a card castle once disturbances arose within the social order on which it was based.

In the event this nation, which alone seems to have learned wisdom from the errors and failings of its former rulers, has been unable, though it so effectively shook off their domination, to rid itself of the false notion, bad habits, and pernicious tendencies which they had given it or allowed it to acquire. Sometimes, indeed, we find it displaying a slave mentality in the very exercise of its freedom, and as incapable of governing itself as it was once intractable vis-à-vis its masters.

# PART THREE

## CHAPTER ONE

*How towards the middle of the eighteenth century men of letters took the lead in politics and the consequences of this new development.*

I now leave behind the circumstances remote in time and of a general order which prepared the way for the great revolution, and come to the particular, more recent events which finally determined its place of origin, its outbreak, and the form it took.

For a long while the French had been the most literary-minded of all the nations of Europe, but so far our writers had not displayed that intellectual brilliance which won them world-wide fame towards the middle of the eighteenth century. True, they did not play an active part in public affairs, as English writers did; on the contrary, never had they kept so steadily aloof from the political arena. In a nation teeming with officials none of the men of letters held posts of any kind, none was invested with authority.

Nevertheless, they did not (like most of their German contemporaries) resolutely turn their backs on politics and retire to a world apart, of *belles lettres* and pure philosophy. On the contrary, they were keenly interested in all that concerned the government of nations; this, one might almost say, was an obsession with them. Questions such as the origin of human society, its earliest forms, the original rights of citizens and of authority, the "natural" and the "artificial" relations between men, of the legitimacy of custom, and even the whole conception of law—all these bulked large in the literature of the day. As a result of this incessant probing into the bases of the society in which they lived, they were led both to examine its structure in detail and to criticise its general plan. Not all our writers, it is true, made these vast problems their exclusive study; indeed, the great majority dealt with them casually, even, one might say, toyed with them. But all took notice of them in one way or another. This kind of abstract, literary politics found its way, in varying proportions, into all the writings of the day, and there was none, from the most ponderous treatise to the lightest lyric, that had not at least a grain of it.

The political programmes advocated by our eighteenth-century writers varied so much that any attempt to synthesise them or deduce a single coherent theory of government from them would be labour lost. Nonetheless, if, disregarding details, we look to the directive ideas, we find that all these various systems stemmed from a single concept of a highly general order, their common source, and that our authors took this as their premise before venturing on their personal, often somewhat eccentric solutions of the problem of good government. Thus, though their ways diverged in the course of their researches, their starting point was the same in all cases; and this was the belief that what was wanted was to replace the complex of traditional customs governing the social order of the day by simple, elementary rules deriving from the exercise of the human reason and natural law.

When we look closely into it we find that the political philosophy of these writers consists to all intents and purposes in ringing the changes on this one idea. It was no new one; it had haunted men's imaginations off and on for three millennia, but never until now had it succeeded in making itself accepted as a basic principle. How was it that at this particular point of time it could root itself so firmly in the minds of the writers of the day? Why, instead of remaining as in the past the purely intellectual concept of a few advanced thinkers, did it find a welcome among the masses and acquire the driving force of a political passion to such effect that general and abstract theories of the nature of human society not only became daily topics of conversation among the leisure class but fired the imagination even of women and peasants? And why was it that men of letters, men without wealth, social eminence, responsibilities, or official status, became in practice the leading politicians of the age, since despite the fact that others held the reins of government, they alone spoke with accents of authority? These questions I shall now try to answer, and at the same time I shall draw attention to the remarkable, not to say formidable, influence these men's writings (which at first sight might seem to concern the history of our literature alone) had on the Revolution, and, indeed, still have today.

It was not by mere chance that our eighteenth-century thinkers as a body enounced theories so strongly opposed to those that were still regarded as basic to the social order; they could hardly be expected to do otherwise when they contemplated the world around them. The sight of so many absurd and unjust privileges, whose evil effects were increasingly felt on every hand though their true causes were less and less understood, urged or, rather, forced them towards a concept of the natural equality of all men irrespective of social rank. When they saw so many ridiculous, ramshackle institutions, survivals of an earlier age, which no one had attempted to co-ordinate or to adjust to modern conditions and which seemed destined to live on despite the fact that they had ceased to have any present value, it was natural enough that thinkers of the day should come to loathe everything that savoured of the past and should desire to remould society on entirely new lines, traced by each thinker in the sole light of reason.[64]

Their very way of living led these writers to indulge in abstract theories and generalisations regarding the nature of government, and to place a blind confidence in these. For living as they did, quite out of touch with practical politics, they lacked the experience which might have tempered their enthusiasms. Thus they completely failed to perceive the very real obstacles in the way of even the most praiseworthy reforms, and to gauge the perils involved in even the most salutary revolutions. That they should not have had the least presentiment of these dangers was only to be expected, since as a result of the total absence of any political freedom, they had little acquaintance with the realities of public life, which, indeed, was *terra incognita* to them. Taking no personal part in it and unable to see what was being done by others in that field, they lacked even the superficial acquaintance with such matters which comes to those who live under a free régime, can see what is happening, and hear the voice of public opinion even though they themselves take no part whatever in the government of the country. As a result, our literary men became much bolder in their speculations, more addicted to general ideas and systems, more contemptuous of the wisdom of the ages, and even more inclined to trust their individual reason than most of those who have written books on politics from a philosophic angle.

When it came to making themselves heard by the masses and appealing to their emotions, this very ignorance served them in good stead. If the French people had still played an active part in politics (through the Estates-General) or even if they had merely continued to concern themselves with the day-to-day administration of affairs through the provincial assemblies, we may be sure that they would not have let themselves be carried away so easily by the ideas of the writers of the day; any experience, however slight, of public affairs would have made them chary of accepting the opinion of mere theoreticians.

Similarly if, like the English, they had succeeded in gradually modifying the spirit of their ancient institutions without destroying them, perhaps they would not have been so prompt to clamour for a new order. As it was, however, every Frenchman felt he was being victimised; his personal freedom, his money, his self-respect, and the amenities of his daily life were constantly being tampered with on the strength of some ancient law, some medieval usage, or the remnants of some antiquated servitude. Nor did he see any constitutional remedy for this state of affairs; it seemed as if the choice lay between meekly accepting everything or destroying the whole system.

Nevertheless, in the nation-wide debacle of freedom we had preserved one form of it; we could indulge, almost without restriction, in learned discussions on the origins of society, the nature of government, and the essential rights of man. All who were chafing under the yoke of the administration enjoyed these literary excursions into politics; indeed, the taste for them spread even into sections of the community whose temperaments or upbringing would have normally discouraged them from abstract speculations. But there was no taxpayer aggrieved by the injustices of the *taille* who did not welcome the idea that all men should be equal; no farmer whose land was devastated by a noble neighbour's rabbits who did not rejoice at hearing it declared that privilege of any kind whatever was condemned by the voice of reason. Thus the philosopher's cloak provided safe cover for the passions of the day and the political ferment was canalised into literature, the result being that our writers now became the leaders of public opinion and played for a while the part which normally, in free countries, falls to the professional politician. And as things were, no one was in a position to dispute their right to leadership.

A powerful aristocracy does not merely shape the course of public affairs, it also guides opinion, sets the tone for writers, and lends authority to new ideas. By the eighteenth century the French nobility had wholly lost this form of ascendancy, its prestige had dwindled with its power, and since the place it had occupied in the direction of public opinion was vacant, writers could usurp it with the greatest ease and keep it without fear of being dislodged.

Still more remarkable was the fact that this very aristocracy whose place the writers had taken made much of them. So completely had our nobility forgotten that new political theories, once they are generally accepted, inevitably rouse popular passions and bear fruit in deeds, that they regarded even the doctrines most hostile to their prerogatives, and in fact to their very existence, as mere flights of fancy, entertaining *jeux d'esprit*. So they, too, took a hand in the new, delightful game and, while clinging to their immunities and privileges, talked lightheartedly of the "absurdity" of all the old French customs.

Astonishment has often been expressed at this singular blindness of the upper classes of the old régime and the way they compassed their own downfall. Yet how could they have known better? Political freedom is no less indispensable to the ruling classes to enable them to realise their perils than to the rank and file to enable them to safeguard their rights. More than a century had elapsed since the last traces of free public life had disappeared in France, and those most directly interested in the maintenance of the old constitution had not been forewarned by any sound or sign of an impending breakdown. Since outwardly nothing had changed, they had no fears for its stability. In a word, their point of view was that of their fathers, they could not move with the times. In the 1789 *cahiers* we find the nobility still harping as much on the "*encroachments*" of the royal power as if they were living in the fifteenth century.

And that ill-starred King, Louis XVI, at the very moment when he was about to be engulfed by the flood tide of democracy, continued (as Burke has aptly pointed out) to regard the aristocracy as the chief danger to the throne and mistrusted it as much as if he were back in the days of the "Fronde". On the other hand, he, like his ancestors, saw in the middle class and the people the staunchest supporters of the Crown.

But what must seem still more extraordinary to us, given our experience of the aftermath of so many revolutions, is that the possibility of a violent unheaval never crossed our parents' minds. No one breathed a word of it, no one ever dreamed of it. The small disturbances which, when there is political freedom, inevitably take place from time to time in even the most stable social systems are a constant reminder of the risk of large-scale cataclysms and keep the authorities on the *qui vive*. But in the eighteenth century, on the very eve of the Revolution, there had been as yet no warning that the ancient edifice was tottering.

I have closely studied the *cahiers* drawn up by the three Orders before the meeting of the Estates-General—by all three Orders, be it noted—nobility and clergy as well as the Third Estate. In the course of ploughing my way through these voluminous documents I made many notes: here was a request for the amendment of a law, here for the suppression of a custom, and so forth. When I had reached the end of my labours and made a list of these various proposals I realised with something like consternation that what was being asked for was nothing short of the systematic, simultaneous abolition of *all* existing French laws and customs. There was no blinking the fact that what the authors of these *cahiers* jointly sponsored was one of the vastest, most catastrophic revolutions the world had ever known. Yet the men who were to be its victims had not the least presentiment of this; they nursed the foolish hope that a sudden, radical transformation of a very ancient, highly intricate social system could be effected almost painlessly, under the auspices of reason and by its efficacy alone. Theirs was a rude awakening! They would have done better to recall an ancient dictum formulated by their ancestors, four centuries before, in the rather crabbed language of the day: "Claim too great freedom, too much licence, and too great subjection shall befall you!"

Given their long exclusion from any form of public life, it is not surprising that the nobility and bourgeoisie should have developed this singular obtuseness. But it is decidedly surprising that those who were at the helm of public affairs—statesmen, Intendants, the magistrates—should have displayed little more foresight. No doubt many of these men had proved themselves highly competent in the exercise of their functions and had a good grasp of all the details of public administration; yet, as for true statecraft—that is to say clear perception of the way society is evolving, an awareness of the trends of mass opinion and an ability to forecast the future—they were as much at sea as any ordinary citizen. For it is only in an atmosphere of freedom that the qualities of mind indispensable to true statesmanship can mature and fructify.

In this context a memorandum submitted by Turgot to the King in 1775 is enlightening. In it he advises the King, amongst other things, to convoke yearly a "representative assembly" for a six-week session at which he (the King) would be present; but at the same time he counsels him against granting the assembly any effective power. It was to be concerned with administration, not with government, its business would be to make suggestions rather than to legislate, and its function that of discussing laws, not making them. "Thus Your Majesty will be kept posted as to popular feeling without being trammelled by it, and public opinion satisfied without any peril to the State. For these assemblies will have no right to vote against necessary measures, and, even should they overstep their powers, Your Majesty will always have the last word." This blindness to the certain consequences of such a measure and this incomprehension of the spirit of the age are singularly revealing. Often, towards the close of revolutions it has been possible to do what Turgot proposed; that is to say to give the people the shadow of liberty without its substance. The Emperor Augustus brought this off successfully. A nation that is weary of internecine conflict is quite ready to be duped provided it is given peace, and history tells us that at such times all that is needed to satisfy public opinion is to gather together from all

parts of the country a number of obscure or pliable men and to
have them play the part of a national assembly at a fixed salary.
There have been several instances of this. But at the early stage
of a revolution such methods always fail; all they do is to whet
the appetite of the masses, and nobody is satisfied. This is
known to even the humblest citizen of a free country; but,
great administrator though he was, Turgot was unaware of it.

When we remember also that the French nation, excluded
as it was from the conduct of its own affairs, lacking in political
experience, shackled by ancient institutions and powerless to
reform them—when we remember that this was the most literary-
minded of all nations and intellectually quickest in the uptake,
it is easy to understand why our authors became a power in
the land and ended up as its political leaders.

In England writers on the theory of government and those
who actually governed co-operated with each other, the former
setting forth their new theories, the latter amending or circum-
scribing these in the light of practical experience. In France,
however, precept and practice were kept quite distinct and remained in the hands of two quite independent groups. One of
these carried on the actual administration while the other set
forth the abstract principles on which good government should,
they said, be based; one took the routine measures appropriate
to the needs of the moment, the other propounded general
laws without a thought for their practical application; one group
shaped the course of public affairs, the other that of public
opinion.

Thus alongside the traditional and confused, not to say chaotic, social system of the day there was gradually built up in men's
minds an imaginary ideal society in which all was simple, uniform, coherent, equitable, and rational in the full sense of the
term. It was this vision of the perfect State that fired the
imagination of the masses and little by little estranged them
from the here-and-now. Turning away from the real world
around them, they indulged in dreams of a far better one and
ended up by living, spiritually, in the ideal world thought up by
the writers.

The French Revolution has often been regarded as a consequence of the American and there is no denying that the latter

had considerable influence on it. But it was due less to what actually took place in the United States than to ideas then prevalent in France. To the rest of Europe the American Revolution seemed merely a novel and remarkable historical event; whereas the French saw in it a brilliant confirmation of theories already familiar to them. Elsewhere it merely shocked and startled; for the French it was conclusive proof that they were in the right. Indeed, the Americans seemed only to be putting into practice ideas which had been sponsored by our writers, and to be making our dreams their realities. It is, as if Fénelon had suddenly found himself in Salente. Never before had the entire political education of a great nation been the work of its men of letters and it was this peculiarity that perhaps did most to give the French Revolution its exceptional character and the régime that followed it the form we are familiar with.

Our men of letters did not merely impart their revolutionary ideas to the French nation; they also shaped the national temperament and outlook on life. In the long process of moulding men's minds to their ideal pattern their task was all the easier since the French had had no training in the field of politics, and they thus had a clear field. The result was that our writers ended up by giving the Frenchman the instincts, the turn of mind, the tastes, and even the eccentricities characteristic of the literary man. And when the time came for action, these literary propensities were imported into the political arena.

When we closely study the French Revolution we find that it was conducted in precisely the same spirit as that which gave rise to so many books expounding theories of government in the abstract. Our revolutionaries had the same fondness for broad generalisations, cut-and-dried legislative systems, and a pedantic symmetry; the same contempt for hard facts; the same taste for reshaping institutions on novel, ingenious, original lines; the same desire to reconstruct the entire constitution according to the rules of logic and a preconceived system instead of trying to rectify its faulty parts. The result was nothing short of disastrous; for what is a merit in the writer may well be a vice in the statesman and the very qualities which go to make great literature can lead to catastrophic revolutions.

Even the politicians' phraseology was borrowed largely from the books they read; it was cluttered up with abstract words, gaudy flowers of speech, sonorous clichés, and literary turns of phrase. Fostered by the political passions that it voiced, this style made its way into all classes, being adopted with remarkable facility even by the lowest. Long before the Revolution, King Louis XIV in his edicts had often spoken of natural law and the rights of man. I have found peasants calling their neighbours "fellow citizens" in their petitions, the Intendant "our honourable magistrate", the village priest "the guardian of our altars", the God "the Supreme Being". All they needed, in fact, to become literary men in a small way was a better knowledge of spelling.

These habits have become so much ingrained in the French character that, recent though they are and due solely to a very special type of education, many seem to regard them as inborn. I have heard it said that the penchant, not to say the passion, of our politicians during the last sixty years for general ideas, systems, and high-flown verbiage stems from a national trait, the so-called "French spirit"—the idea presumably being that this alleged propensity suddenly came to the fore at the end of the last century after lying dormant throughout the rest of our history!

What seems particularly odd is that while retaining habits thus derived from books, we have almost completely lost our former love of literature. In the course of my public career I have often been struck by the fact that those who reproduce most faithfully some of the chief defects of the literary style prevailing in the previous generation are men who rarely, if ever, read our eighteenth-century books or, for that matter, any books at all.

CHAPTER TWO

*How vehement and widespread anti-religious feeling
had become in eighteenth-century France and its influence on the nature of the Revolution*

Ever since the sixteenth century when, with the great awakening of the spirit of inquiry, thinkers of the age were led to
investigate which were true, which false, among the various
Christian traditions, there had been no lack of more adven-
turous-minded men who boldly challenged these traditions,
sometimes rejecting them *in toto*. For the selfsame spirit that
in Luther's day had led several million Catholics to break
away from the mother church incited others, year by year, to
go still further and to repudiate Christianity altogether; thus
after heresy came unbelief.

Generally speaking, it may be said that by the eighteenth
century Christianity had lost much of its hold on men's minds
throughout the continent of Europe. However, in most countries it was by-passed rather than frontally attacked and even
those who abandoned it left the fold regretfully. Scepticism was
in fashion in the royal courts and among the intellectuals, but
the middle class and the masses were relatively impervious to it.
In short, it was the foible of an elite, and by no means generalised. "An idea is current in Germany," Mirabeau observed in
1787, "that the Prussian provinces teem with atheists. Actually,
however, though one comes across some free-thinkers, the mass
of the people is no less religious-minded in Germany than in
the most God-fearing countries; there are indeed many religious
fanatics among them." And he finds it "most regrettable" that
Frederick II did not think fit that Catholic priests should marry
and, above all, that he refused to allow those who married to
keep the emoluments of their benefices, "a measure that, we venture to think, would have been worthy of this great monarch."
Nowhere except in France had irreligion become as yet an all-
prevailing passion, fierce, intolerant, and predatory.

For something was taking place in France that the world had never seen before. In earlier ages established religions had been violently attacked, but this had always been due to the rise of a new type of religion and the fanaticism of its adherents. False and objectionable as they may have been, the religions of antiquity never encountered vigorous or widespread antagonism before they were challenged by Christianity. Until then they had been gradually dying out in an atmosphere of scepticism and indifference—that sort of senile decay which is the lot of so many religions. In France, however, though Christianity was attacked with almost frenzied violence, there was no question of replacing it with another religion. Passionate and persistent efforts were made to wean men away from the faith of their fathers, but once they had lost it, nothing was supplied to fill the void within. A host of zealots devoted all their energies to this thankless task. The total rejection of any religious belief, so contrary to man's natural instincts and so destructive of his peace of mind, came to be regarded by the masses as desirable. And what had previously induced merely a sort of wasting malady now inspired fanaticism and propagandist zeal.

The coincidence that several famous writers simultaneously proclaimed their disbelief in Christianity is hardly enough to account for this strange phenomenon, and in any case why was it that all these writers without exception took up arms against religion and none was found to champion it? Why this singular unanimity? And, finally, why was it that our men of letters caught the ear of the public at large so much more easily than any of their predecessors and found an audience so ready to accept their views? Their unanimous attack on religion and its prompt success can be explained only in terms of the very special climate of the age. True, for some time past Voltairian ideas had everywhere been "in the air", yet even Voltaire could hardly have triumphed as he did elsewhere than in France or in any period other than the eighteenth century.

As a matter of fact, the Church was no more open to attack in France than in any other country; the vices and abuses which had crept into its constitution were in fact less serious than in most Catholic kingdoms. It was much more tolerant in the past and than it still was in other lands. Thus it is less to religious than to social conditions that we must look when we seek to trace the causes of the events that now took place in France.

To understand them it is well to bear in mind a fact to which we drew attention in a previous chapter: the fact that, being unable to find any outlet in action, the discontent caused by the malpractices of the government found expression in the literature of the day and in this alone. Our men of letters were in fact the leaders of the vast movement whose aim it was to demolish the entire social and political structure of the kingdom. Thus the problem we are now considering assumes a different aspect. It is not a question of analysing the shortcomings of the Church as a religious institution, but one of perceiving in what manner it obstructed the revolution that was getting under way and in particular why the political-minded writers who were its chief promoters showed such animosity towards the Church.

It is obvious that the very principles on which the Church was founded were incompatible with those our writers wished to embody in the new, ideal system of administration they had set their hearts on. Tradition was fundamental to the whole conception of the Church, whereas our men of letters professed the utmost contempt for all such institutions as owed their prestige to the past. The Church acknowledged an authority superior to human reason and was based on a hierarchy; whereas the writers deified reason and were for levelling out all differences between men. To come to an understanding both parties would have needed to recognise the fact that there is a difference in kind between a system of a purely religious order and one that is political, i.e. materialist, and the same principles could not hold good for both. But in those days such an idea never crossed the minds of the votaries of reason; they were convinced that in order to overthrow the institutions of the existing social order they must begin by destroying those of the Church, on which these were modelled and from which, indeed, they derived.

Moreover, at this time the Church was, if not the most oppressive, the chief of all the powers in the land, and though neither her vocation nor her nature called for this, co-operated with the secular authority, often condoning vice in it that in other spheres she would have reprobated. Almost it seemed that she was bent on investing it with her aura of sanctity and making it as infallible and eternal as herself. Thus anyone attacking the Church could count on popular support.

But aside from these reasons of a general order our eighteenth-century writers had special, almost personal reasons for making the State religion the first target of their attack. The Church represented that part of the government which was at once in closest contact with themselves and irritated them most. For whereas the other authorities interfered with them but rarely, the Church, one of whose duties it was to keep watch on contemporary trends of thought and exercise a sort of censorship of literature, was frequently in conflict with our *littérateurs*. In championing freedom of thought for all against the Church they were fighting their own battle, and their first step was to do away with a control that handicapped them personally.

Furthermore, it seemed to them that the Church represented the most vulnerable and least defended side of the vast fortress they were attacking. For the powers of the Church had diminished in proportion as those of the temporal authorities increased.[65] After dominating them, then being on an equal footing, it had been reduced to the rank of a dependent. Nevertheless, there still was a sort of give-and-take between Church and State, the former giving the latter its moral support, and the latter seconding the Church on the material side. Thus the secular power insisted on obedience to the ecclesiastical authorities and the Church saw to it that the King's authority was respected. But now, with the spread of the revolutionary movement, this alliance was fraught with peril for the Church since such associations are always dangerous to a power founded not on constraint but on belief.

Though the French Kings still described themselves as "the eldest sons" of the Church, they performed their filial duties slackly and showed much less zeal for defending the Church than for safeguarding their own ascendancy. True, they prohibited the launching of frontal attacks on the Church, but they allowed her to be harassed by a sort of guerrilla warfare, carried on at long range. And these half measures, far from weakening the power of the enemies of the Church, added fuel to the

fire. For if there are periods of history when the state control of
writers succeeds in checking all progressive thought, there are
others when it has exactly the opposite effect. But never has a
policy of restrictions on the freedom of the press such as then
prevailed failed to augment its influence a hundredfold.

Authors were harried to an extent that won them sympathy,
but not enough to inspire them with any real fear. They were,
in fact, subjected to the petty persecutions that spur men to
revolt, but not to the steady pressure that breaks their spirit.
The legal proceedings taken against our writers were almost
always dilatory, widely publicised but ineffective; indeed, they
seemed less calculated to deter them from writing than to incite
them to persist. In short, total freedom of the press would not
have been so injurious to the Church as these half measures.

"You think," wrote Diderot to David Hume in 1768, "that
our intolerance is more favourable to the progress of thought
than your unbounded liberty? Helvétius, D'Holbach, Morellet,
and Suard do not share this view." Nonetheless, it was the
Scotsman who was right. Living in a free country, he had practical experience of freedom; Diderot's was the viewpoint of a
man of letters, Hume's that of a statesman.

I have sometimes asked Americans whom I chanced to meet
in their own country or in Europe whether in their opinion
religion contributes to the stability of the State and the maintenance of law and order. They always answered, without a
moment's hesitation, that a civilised community, especially one
that enjoys the benefits of freedom, cannot exist without religion. In fact, an American sees in religion the surest guarantee
of the stability of the State and the safety of individuals. This
much is evident even to those least versed in political science.
Yet there is no country in the world in which the boldest political theories of the eighteenth-century philosophers are put so
effectively into practice as in America. Only their anti-religious
doctrines have never made any headway in that country, and
this despite the unlimited freedom of the press.

Much the same may be said of the English. Our anti-religious
ideas had found exponents in England before our famous
French philosophers were born; Voltaire took his cue from
Bolingbroke. Throughout the eighteenth century great sceptics

made their voices heard in England, and brilliant writers and profound thinkers sponsored the views we now associate with Voltaire. Yet they never caused unbelief to triumph in England as it did in France for the good reason that all who had anything to fear from a revolution made haste to come to the rescue of the established faith. Even those Englishmen who were in close touch with contemporary French thought and were inclined to share the views of our philosophers repudiated them as being a danger to the State. As always happens in free countries, great political parties found it in their interest to join forces with the Church; even Bolingbroke allied himself with the bishops when it served his turn. Experience having taught them that they would never lack supporters, the clergy vigorously defended their positions, and the Church of England, despite the flaws in its constitution and malpractices of various kinds it countenanced within itself, never lacked orators and writers among its members to champion with wit and zeal the Christian cause. All such theories as were adverse to the Christian faith were rejected (after discussion and refutation) by the general public on its own initiative and there was never occasion for the government to intervene.

But why look to other countries when much the same thing has been happening in France? What Frenchman of today would dream of writing books like those of Diderot and Helvétius, and, supposing anyone were to do so, who would read them? Even the names of the books written by those two once-famous authors are all but forgotten. Our experience of public life during the last sixty years, incomplete though it has been, has been enough to give us a distaste for this subversive literature. Trained in the hard school of successive revolutions, all the various classes of the French nation have gradually regained that feeling of respect for religious faith which once seemed lost forever. The old nobility, which before 1789 had been the most irreligious class, became after 1793 the most pious; first to be infected with disbelief, it was also the first to be "converted." Once the bourgeoisie woke to the fact that its seeming triumph was likely to prove fatal to it, it, too, developed leanings towards religion. Thus little by little religion regained its hold on all who had anything to lose in a social upheaval and unbelief died out, or anyhow hid its head the more these men became alive to the perils of revolution.

This was not the case, however, in the last phase of the old order, when the French had completely lost touch with practical politics and had no inkling of the part played by religion in the government of nations. Indeed, agnosticism found its first addicts in that very class of the community which had the most urgent and immediate interest in the maintenance of law and order and in keeping the populace in hand. For impiety became modish, a new hobby to occupy their idle lives, and not satisfied with cultivating it between themselves, they propagated their ideas among the lower classes.

Once so well provided with eloquent spokesmen, the Church of France, finding herself deserted by just those people whom common interests should have made her allies, relapsed into silence. There was even a time when one might have thought that, provided she were allowed to keep her wealth and high position, the Church was quite ready to repudiate the faith for which she stood.

What with the loquacity of the opponents of Christianity and the silence of those who were still believers, there ensued a state of affairs that has often since been seen in France, not only as regards religion but also in quite different spheres of human behaviour. Those who retained their belief in the doctrines of the Church became afraid of being alone in their allegiance and, dreading isolation more than the stigma of heresy, professed to share the sentiments of the majority. So what was in reality the opinion of only a part (though a large one) of the nation came to be regarded as the will of all and for this reason seemed irresistible even to those who had given it this false appearance.

There is no question that the nation-wide discredit of all forms of religious belief which prevailed at the end of the eighteenth century had a preponderant influence on the course of the French Revolution. This was, in fact, its most salient characteristic, and nothing did more to shock contemporary observers.

The anti-religious spirit of the age had very various consequences, but it seems to me that what led the French to commit such singular excesses was not so much that it made them, callous or debased their moral standards as that it tended to upset their mental equilibrium. When religion was expelled from their souls, the effect was not to create a vacuum or a state of apathy; it was promptly, if but momentarily, replaced by a host of new loyalties and secular ideals that not only filled the void but (to begin with) fired the popular imagination.

For though the men who made the Revolution were more sceptical than our contemporaries as regards the Christian verities, they had anyhow one belief, and an admirable one, that we to-day have not; they believed in themselves. Firmly convinced of the perfectibility of man, they had faith in his innate virtue, placed him on a pedestal, and set no bounds to their devotion to his cause. They had that arrogant self-confidence which often points the way to disaster yet, lacking which, a nation can but relapse into a servile state. In short, they had a fanatical faith in their vocation—that of transforming the social system, root and branch, and regenerating the whole human race. Of this passionate idealism was born what was in fact a new religion, giving rise to some of those vast changes in human conduct that religion has produced in other ages. It weaned them away from self-regarding emotions, stimulated them to heroic deeds and altruistic sacrifices, and often made them indifferent to all those petty amenities of life which mean so much to us today.

Much of my life has been devoted to the study of history and I have no hesitation in affirming that never in the course of my studies have I discovered a revolution in which, anyhow to begin with, so many men displayed a patriotism so intense, such unselfishness, such real greatness of mind. In those days of hope the French nation manifested the chief defect but, likewise, the chief virtue of youth: inexperience, but generous enthusiasm.

Nevertheless, the attack that then was launched on all religious faith had disastrous effects. In most of the great political revolutions of earlier times we find that those who overthrew a system of government respected the established faith, while in religious revolutions we find that those who attacked the State religion did not include in their programme any drastic changes in the government of the country and the existing constitution. Thus even in the most violent social upheavals people had anyhow something of the past to cling to.

In the French Revolution, however, both religious institutions and the whole system of government were thrown into the melting pot, with the result that men's minds were in a state of utter confusion; they knew neither what to hold on to, nor where to stop. Revolutionaries of a hitherto unknown breed came on the scene: men who carried audacity to the point of sheer insanity; who balked at no innovation and, unchecked by any scruples, acted with an unprecedented ruthlessness. Nor were these strange beings mere ephemera, born of a brief crisis and destined to pass away when it ended. They were, rather, the first of a new race of men who subsequently prospered and proliferated in all parts of the civilised world, everywhere retaining the same characteristics. They were already here when we were born, and they are still with us.

CHAPTER THREE

*How the desire for reforms took precedence of the desire for freedom*

It is a remarkable fact that of all the ideas and aspirations which led up to the Revolution the concept and desire of political liberty, in the full sense of the term, were the last to emerge, as they were also the first to pass away.

Though for some time past the entire edifice of government had been under fire and threatening to collapse, the issue of freedom had not yet been raised. Voltaire hardly gave it a thought; his three-year stay in England had familiarised him with political freedom, but failed to make him like it. What delighted him in that country was the sceptical philosophy so freely voiced there; the English political system appealed to him but little and he had a sharper eye for its defects than for its merits. In his letters about England, which rank among his finest works, Parliament is hardly mentioned. The truth was that he envied the English above all for their freedom to write as they liked, while their political freedom left him indifferent and he quite failed to realise that the former could not have survived for long without the latter.

Towards the middle of the eighteenth century a group of writers known as the "Physiocrats" or "Economists", who made the problems of public administration their special study, came on the scene. Though the Economists figure less prominently than our philosophers in histories of the period and perhaps did less than them towards bringing about the Revolution, I am inclined to think it is from their writings that we learn most of its true character. In dealing with the problems of government the philosophers confined themselves for the most part to general ideas and purely abstract theories; the Economists, while never losing sight of theory, paid more heed to practical politics. Whereas the philosophers depicted imaginary utopias, the Economists sometimes pointed out what could and should be done in the existing world. Their chief targets of attack were those institutions which the Revolution was destined to sweep away forever; not one of them found favour in their eyes. Those, on the other hand, which we now regard as creations of the Revolution were anticipated and warmly advocated by them. Indeed, the germinal ideas of practically all the permanent changes effected by the Revolution can be found in their works.

What is more, their writings had the democratic-revolutionary tenor characteristic of so much modern thought. For they attacked not only specific forms of privilege but any kind of diversity whatsoever; to their thinking all men should be equal even if equality spelled servitude, and every obstacle to the achievement of this end should be done away with immediately. For contractual engagements they had no respect, and no concern for private rights. Indeed, private rights were, in their eyes, negligible; only the public interest mattered. Though most of them were amiable, well-meaning persons, men of substance, conscientious public servants or able administrators, such was their enthusiasm for the cause they sponsored that they carried their theories to fanatical lengths.

Our Economists had a vast contempt for the past. "The nation has been governed," Letronne declared, "on wrong lines altogether; one has the impression that everything was left to chance." Starting out from this premise, they set to work, and there was no French institution, however venerable and well founded, for whose immediate suppression they did not clamour if it hampered them to even the slightest extent or did not fit in with their neatly ordered scheme of government. One Economist proposed the abolition of all the existing territorial divisions of France and the renaming of the provinces forty years before this was actually done by the Constituent Assembly.

It is a curious fact that when they envisaged all the social and administrative reforms subsequently carried out by our revolutionaries, the idea of free institutions never crossed their minds. True, they were all in favour of the free exchange of commodities and a system of *laissez faire* and *laissez passer* in commerce and industry; but political liberty in the full sense of the term was something that passed their imagination or was promptly dismissed from their thoughts if by any chance the idea of it occurred to them. To begin with, anyhow, the Economists were thoroughly hostile to deliberative assemblies, to secondary organisations vested with local powers and, generally speaking, to all those counterpoises which have been devised by free peoples at various stages of their history to curb the domination of a central authority. "Any system of opposing forces within a government," Quesnay wrote, "is highly objectionable." And a friend of his observed that "all theories of a 'balance of power' within the State are the merest moonshine."

The only safeguard against State oppression they could think of was universal education, and they endorsed Quesnay's opinion that "when a nation is fully educated, tyranny is automatically ruled out." "Alarmed by the evils caused by excessive authoritarianism," writes another of Quesnay's disciples, "men have invented hosts of quite useless remedies; but the only really efficacious one, that is to say a long schooling of the nation as a whole in the basic principles of justice and natural law, has been neglected."

For these worthy men fondly imagined that nostrums of this order, the vapourings of *littérateurs*, could take the place of solid political guarantees of the nation's freedom. Thus when Letronne declaims against the government's neglect of the welfare of the rural districts, the shocking state of the roads, the absence of any industries, and the ignorance of the countryfolk, it never occurs to him that if the residents of these districts were empowered to manage their own affairs, there might well be an improvement.

Even Turgot, a man of quite another stamp, endowed with quite exceptional insight and far-ranging vision, had as little liking for political freedom as the men of whom we have just been speaking. Or, rather, he developed a liking for it only later, when he sensed that public opinion was moving in that direction. Like most of the Economists he thought that the best way of ensuring the political welfare of the nation was for the State to provide education for all, conducted in a certain manner and indicating certain trends of thought. He had boundless faith in this "intellectual panacea", as a contemporary called it, and in an educational system "governed by sound principles". In a memorandum addressed to the King he outlined a plan of this order. "I venture to affirm that if this programme be adopted, our subjects will have changed out of all recognition within a mere decade, and their intelligence, good behaviour, and enlightened zeal in your service and their country's will place them far above all other modern nations. For by that time children now ten years old will have grown up into young men trained to do their duty by the State; patriotic and law-abiding, not from fear but on rational grounds, understanding and respecting justice, and prompt to help their fellow citizens in time of need."

Political freedom had been so long extinct in France that people had almost entirely forgotten what it meant and how it functioned. Indeed, its few surviving relics and the institutions seemingly created to substitute for it tended to give an unfavourable impression of the whole idea of political freedom and its corollaries. For most of the provincial assemblies that had survived were run on antiquated lines, still imbued with the medieval spirit, and, far from promoting social progress, impeded it. Likewise the parlements, the only representative political bodies that still existed, not only failed to check the evil practices of the central government but often prevented it from carrying out beneficial measures.

The Economists saw no hope of effecting the revolutionary changes they had in mind with this obsolete machinery, and the idea of recognising the nation as sole arbiter of its own destinies and entrusting to it the execution of their plans was little to their taste. For how could a whole nation be persuaded to accept and to put through a programme of reform so vast and so intricate? To their thinking the simplest, most practical solution was to enlist the support of the royal power.

This was a "new" power since it neither stemmed from the Middle Ages nor bore any mark of them, and despite its short-comings the Economists saw in it great possibilities. Like them it favoured equality among men and uniformity of law throughout the land. Again like them it had a strong aversion for all the ancient powers deriving from feudalism or associated with aristocracy. Nowhere else in Europe could they see a sys-tem of government so solidly established and so efficient, and it seemed to them a singularly happy chance that in France they had such an implement ready to their hand. In fact, had it been customary, as it is today, to see the hand of Providence in everything, they would have called it providential. "The present situation in France," Letronne observed complacently, "is vastly superior to that of England, for here reforms changing the whole social structure can be put through in the twinkling of an eye, whereas in England such reforms can always be blocked by the system of party government."

Thus there could be no question of destroying this absolute power; far better, turn it to account. "The State should govern in accordance with the rules basic to the maintenance of a well-organised society," was the opinion of Mercier de la Riviére, "and, this being so, it should be all-powerful." "We must see to it that the State rightly understands its duty," said another writer of the day, "and then give it a free hand." Indeed, all thinkers of the period, from Quesnay to the Abbé Bodeau, were of the same opinion. These men did not regard the mon-archy merely as a potential ally in their efforts to reform the social system; the new form of government contemplated by them was to be modelled to some extent on the monarchical government then in force, which bulked large in their vision of the ideal régime.

According to the Economists the function of the State was not merely one of ruling the nation, but also that of recasting it in a given mould, of shaping the mentality of the population as a whole in accordance with a predetermined model and instilling the ideas and sentiments they thought desirable into the minds of all. In short, they set no limit to its rights and powers; its duty was not merely to reform but to transform the French nation—a task of which the central power alone was capable. "The State makes men exactly what it wishes them to be." This remark of Bodeau's neatly sums up the Economists' approach to the subject.

But the all-controlling power of which they dreamed was not only far greater than the one with which they were familiar; its source and nature, too, were different. It did not derive immediately from God, nor was it rooted in tradition; it was impersonal and functioned under the aegis not of the King but of the State. It was not hereditary and confined to a single family but representative of the nation as a whole and as such entitled to subject the rights of individuals to the will of all.

The form of tyranny sometimes described as "democratic despotism" (it would have been unthinkable in the Middle Ages) was championed by the Economists well before the Revolution. They were for abolishing all hierarchies, all class distinction, all differences of rank, and the nation was to be composed of individuals almost exactly alike and unconditionally equal. In this undiscriminated mass was to reside, theoretically, the sovereign power; yet it was to be carefully deprived of any means of controlling or even supervising the activities of its own government. For above it was a single authority, its mandatory, which was entitled to do anything and everything in its name without consulting it. This authority could not be controlled by public opinion since public opinion had no means of making itself heard; the State was a law unto itself and nothing short of a revolution could break its tyranny. *De jure* it was a subordinate agent; *de facto,* a master.

Being unable to find anything in contemporary Europe corresponding to this ideal State they dreamed of, our Economists turned their eyes to the Far East, and it is no exaggeration to say that not one of them fails, in some part of his writings, to voice an immense enthusiasm for China and all things Chinese. As a matter of fact, China was an almost unknown country in those days, and what they wrote about it was absurd to a degree. That unenlightened, barbarian government which lets itself be manipulated at will by a handful of Europeans was held up by them as a model to the world. It was for them what England came to be for Frenchmen of a later date and, in our times, America has come to be. They went into ecstasies over a land whose ruler, absolute but free from prejudices, pays homage to the utilitarian arts by ploughing a field once a year; where candidates for government posts have to pass a competitive examination in literature; where philosophy does duty for religion, and the only aristocracy consists of men of letters.

It is commonly thought that the subversive theories of what today is known as socialism are of recent origin. This is not so; views of this kind were sponsored by the earliest Economists. But while the all-powerful government of which they dreamed was regarded by them merely as a means to changing the structure of the social order, their followers saw in it an instrument for undermining the very foundations of society.

In Morelly's *Code of Nature* may be found not only the ideas of the Economists regarding the unlimited rights of the State but also several of the alarming political theories which we were inclined to think had made their first appearance in our own generation; for example, community of property, the right to be provided with work, absolute equality, State control of all the activities of individuals, despotic legislation, and the total submerging of each citizen's personality in the group mind.

"Nothing shall be personally and exclusively owned by any member of the nation," we read in the First Article of Morelly's *Code*. "Private ownership of anything whatever is an abomination and anyone trying to reintroduce it shall be treated as a dangerous lunatic, an enemy of mankind, and imprisoned for life." From Article Two we learn that "every citizen shall be provided for and given employment at the public expense. All produce and manufactured goods shall be placed in public warehouses, with a view to being distributed to all citizens and utilised by them for their needs. All towns shall be laid out in the same manner and all dwelling houses alike. At the age of

five children shall be taken from their parents and educated
communally at government expense and on uniform lines."
We well might think these words were written only the other
day. Actually the *Code* made its appearance in 1755, at the
time when Quesnay was founding his school—so true it is
that socialism and centralisation thrive on the same soil; they
stand to each other as the cultivated to the wild species of a
fruit.

Of all the men of their age the Economists would be least
out of their element at the present day; indeed, so fervent was
their zeal for equality and so tepid their desire for liberty that
we well might think them our contemporaries. When reading
the speeches and writings of the men who made the Revolution
I am plunged into an unfamiliar world, a social climate
foreign to me; but when I read the works of the Economists I
am on familiar ground, I almost feel they are old acquaintances,
people with whom I have just been talking.

In the mid-eighteenth century the French people, if consulted,
would have shown no more enthusiasm than the Economists
for liberty; it was something they had quite lost touch with,
indeed the very idea of freedom meant nothing to them. What
they wanted was not so much a recognition of the "rights of
man" as reforms in the existing system, and had there then
been on the throne a monarch of the calibre and temperament
of Frederick the Great, he would certainly have initiated many
of the sweeping changes made by the Revolution in social conditions and the government of the country, and thus not only
have preserved his crown but greatly added to his power. We
have good authority for believing that one of Louis XV's ablest
Ministers, de Machault, glimpsed this possibility and even suggested it to the King. But such steps are rarely taken on another's advice; only a man who himself is capable of conceiving
such ideas is disposed to put them into practice.

Twenty years later things were very different. By now the
idea of freedom had found its way into the minds of Frenchmen
and was appealing to them more and more. There were many
symptoms of this change of heart. The provinces began to
show a desire to administer their own affairs once again and
the feeling that every French citizen had the right to take a

share in the government of his country was gaining ground. Memories of the old Estates-General were revived; this, in fact, was the only feature of its early history to which the nation looked back without repugnance. Aware of the trend of popular feeling, the Economists found themselves obliged to allow for some free institutions in their programme of nation-wide unification.

When the parlements were abolished in 1771, the self-same public which had so often suffered from their abuses of justice was much perturbed by their disappearance. For there was a general feeling that with them had fallen the last barrier still capable of holding in check the monarch's absolute power.

Voltaire was amazed, indeed shocked, by this outbreak of popular feeling. "Almost the whole kingdom," he wrote to his friends, "is in an uproar and feelings run as high in the provinces as in the capital itself. Nevertheless, the King's edict seems to me to embody a great number of excellent reforms. To abolish the sale of offices, to make justice free of charge, to save litigants the ruinous expense of having to come to Paris from all ends of the kingdom, and to require the King to shoulder the costs of proceedings in the seigneurial courts—surely these are benefactions which should be welcomed by every Frenchman. Moreover, have not the parlements often acted in a highhanded, vexatious, even barbarous manner? I am frankly astonished at the conduct of the ignoramuses who take sides with our self-assertive, unruly middle class. Personally I am convinced that the King is in the right and that since we needs must have a master it is better to serve a thoroughbred lion than two hundred rats—like myself!" And he adds, as if to excuse himself, "To be sure, I am personally grateful to the King for his kindness in defraying the expenses of our seigneurial courts."

Having been absent from Paris for some time, Voltaire was under the impression that public feeling had remained the same as when he left the capital. In this he was mistaken. The French now wanted something more than ameliorations in the existing system; they wished to get the administration into their own hands. And it was clear that the gigantic revolution that now was getting under way would be carried out not merely with the consent but with the active help of the populace at large.

I am convinced that from this moment the far-reaching political upheaval which was to sweep away without distinction both what was worst and what was best in the old system became inevitable. A nation so unused to acting for itself was bound to begin by wholesale destruction when it launched into a programme of wholesale reform. An absolute monarch would have been a far less dangerous innovator. Personally, indeed, when I reflect on the way the French Revolution, in destroying so many institutions, ideas, and customs inimical to freedom, abolished so many others which were indispensable to freedom, I cannot help feeling that had this revolution, instead of being carried out by the masses on behalf of the sovereignty of the people, been the work of an enlightened autocrat, it might well have left us better fitted to develop in due course into a free nation. In any case, what I have said above should, I think, be borne in mind by those who wish to understand the nature of the Revolution and the course it took.

By the time their ancient love of freedom reawakened in the hearts of the French, they had already been inoculated with a set of ideas as regards the way the country should be governed that were not merely hard to reconcile with free institutions but practically ruled them out. They had come to regard the ideal social system as one whose aristocracy consisted exclusively of government officials and in which an all-powerful bureaucracy not only took charge of affairs of State but controlled men's private lives. Desirous though they were of being free, they were unwilling to go back on the ideology described above and merely tried to adjust it to that of freedom.

This they proposed to do by combining a strong central administration with a paramount legislative assembly: the bureaucratic system with government by the electorate. The nation as a whole had sovereign rights, while the individual citizen was kept in strictest tutelage; the former was expected to display the sagacity and virtues of a free race, the latter to behave like an obedient servant.

It was this desire of grafting political liberty on to institutions and an ideology that were unsuited, indeed adverse to it, but to which the French had gradually become addicted—it was this desire of combining freedom with the servile state that led during the last sixty years to so many abortive essays of a free régime followed by disastrous revolutions. The result has been that, wearied of these vain attempts and the efforts involved, many Frenchmen have lost their taste for freedom and come to think that, after all, an autocratic government under which all men are equal has something to be said for it. This is why the political views of the modern Frenchman are far more similar to those of the Economists than to those of his forbears, the men of '89.

I have often wondered what lies behind that craving for political freedom which in all ages has spurred men to deeds that justly rank among the most momentous in human history; what are the feelings that engender and nurture it. It is quite understandable that when a nation is badly governed it should develop a wish to govern itself. But a desire for independence of this kind, stemming as it does from a specific, removable cause—the evil practices of a despotic government— is bound to be short-lived. Once the circumstances giving rise to it have passed away, it languishes and what at first seemed a genuine love of liberty proves to have been merely hatred of a tyrant. But what a nation with a real instinct for freedom cannot endure is the feeling of not being its own master.

Nor do I think that a genuine love of freedom is ever quickened by the prospect of material rewards; indeed, that prospect is often dubious, anyhow as regards the immediate future. True, in the long run freedom always brings to those who know how to retain it comfort and well-being, and often great prosperity. Nevertheless, for the moment it sometimes tells against amenities of this nature, and there are times, indeed, when despotism can best ensure a brief enjoyment of them. In fact, those who prize freedom only for the material benefits it offers have never kept it long.

What has made so many men, since untold ages, stake their all on liberty is its intrinsic glamour, a fascination it has in itself, apart from all "practical" considerations. For only in countries where it reigns can a man speak, live, and breathe freely, owing obedience to no authority save God and the laws of the land. The man who asks of freedom anything other than itself is born to be a slave.

Some nations have freedom in the blood and are ready to face the greatest perils and hardships in its defence. It is not for what it offers on the material plane that they love it; they regard freedom itself as something so precious, so needful to their happiness that no other boon could compensate for its loss, and its enjoyment consoles them even in their darkest hours. Other nations, once they have grown prosperous, lose interest in freedom and let it be snatched from them without lifting a hand to defend it, lest they should endanger thus the comforts that, in fact, they owe to it alone. It is easy to see that what is lacking in such nations is a genuine love of freedom, that lofty aspiration which (I confess) defies analysis. For it is something one must *feel* and logic has no part in it. It is a privilege of noble minds which God has fitted to receive it, and it inspires them with a generous fervour. But to meaner souls, untouched by the sacred flame, it may well seem incomprehensible.

CHAPTER FOUR

*How, though the reign of Louis XVI was the most prosperous period of the monarchy, this very prosperity hastened the outbreak of the Revolution*

There can be no question that the exhaustion of the kingdom under Louis XVI began at the very time when that monarch's arms were triumphant throughout Europe. Indeed, the first symptoms of an economic decline made their appearance in the years of his most spectacular successes; France was ruined long before she had ceased to be victorious. The gloomy picture of "administrative statistics" given by Vauban is familiar to all students of the period. In memoranda addressed to the Duke of Burgundy at the close of the seventeenth century, even before that ill-fated War of the Spanish Succession had begun, all the Intendants without exception drew attention to the progressive decline of our national prosperity; nor do they regard this as a new phenomenon. "In this district," one Intendant writes, "the population has been diminishing for a number of years"; another reports that "in this once rich and flourishing town all the old industries have died out"; a third that "there once were many factories in this province, all are derelict today"; a fourth that "our cultivators used to get much bigger crops from their land than they do now, indeed, agriculture was in a vastly better state twenty years ago." And an Intendant stationed at Orléans reported that both population and production had declined twenty per cent during the past thirty years. Any of my readers who are still enamoured of absolutism and warlike monarchs would do well to peruse these records.

Since these calamities were chiefly due to defects inherent in the constitution, the death of Louis XIV and the coming of peace did nothing to restore prosperity. When discussing the administration and the social economy of France, all contemporary writers agree that there were no signs of recovery in the provinces, some going so far as to say that things were going from bad to worse. Paris alone, according to them, was growing more populous and wealthier. Intendants, ex-Ministers, and businessmen were at one, on this point, with our men of letters.

Personally I must confess I do not share the view that there was a continuous decline in the prosperity of France during the first half of the eighteenth century. Nonetheless, the fact that this opinion was so widespread and expressed by such well-informed observers proves that, anyhow, no visible progress was being made. From all the administrative records of the period that have come under my notice I gather that at this time the whole social system was the prey of a curious lethargy. The government did little more than keep to the beaten track of the old routine without ever striking out in new directions; municipal authorities did hardly anything to make living conditions in the towns healthier or more agreeable; even private enterprise was in the doldrums.

Some thirty or forty years before the Revolution, however, a change came over the scene. There were strings of a kind hitherto unknown throughout the social system, at first so faint as to be almost imperceptible, but steadily becoming more and more apparent. Year by year these movements spread, at an increasing tempo, until the whole nation seemed to be in the throes of a rebirth. But a rebirth in no literal sense, for what was coming to life was not the France of long ago, and the new spirit animating the nation made short work of all that it resuscitated. For the minds of men were in a ferment, every Frenchman was dissatisfied with his lot and quite decided to better it. And this rankling discontent made him at once impatient and fiercely hostile to the past; nothing would content him but a new world utterly different from the world around him.

Before long the government itself was infected by this spirit; to all appearances the administrative system remained as it had always been but within there was a change of heart. The laws were not altered but differently enforced.

I have already pointed out that the Controller-General and Intendants of 1740 were quite unlike the Controller-General and Intendants of 1780. Factual evidence of the difference can be found in the official correspondence of the two periods. True, the Intendant of 1780 had the same functions, the same subordinates, the same despotic power as his predecessor, but his aims were not the same. The Intendant of an earlier day busied himself chiefly with keeping his province well in hand, levying the militia, and, above all, collecting the *taille*. The 1780 Intendant had quite other interests; he was always trying to think up plans for increasing the wealth of his province. Roads, canals, industries, and commerce were his chief preoccupation, and that famous financial expert of the past, the Duc de Sully, was regarded by our executive officers as a paragon of wisdom.

It was in this period that the agricultural societies, of which I have already spoken, arose, organised competitions, and awarded prizes. Some of the Controller-General's publications read more like treatises on agriculture than official circulars. This change in the mentality of the central administration was most apparent in the new methods adopted for collecting taxes. The laws on the subject were as unjust, harsh, and arbitrary as ever, but they were now more leniently handled.

"When I began to study our fiscal legislation," writes Mollien in his *Memoirs*, "I was shocked by what I found there: fines, imprisonment, even corporal punishment could be inflicted by special courts for mere remissness on the taxpayer's part, while the local employees of the tax farmers, by means of their 'decisive oath', could exercise tyrannical control over almost all estates and persons. Fortunately I did not confine myself to a mere perusal of the code, and I soon discovered that the same difference existed between its clauses and their application as between the methods of the old financiers and the new. The courts always tended to treat such offences less seriously, and to impose light sentences."

In 1787 the Provincial Assembly of Lower Normandy, while deploring the malpractices of the fiscal authorities, went on to say: "We must admit, however, that during the last few years they have been showing much less harshness and a willingness to consider cases on their merits."

This is confirmed when we turn to the records of the period; they often evince a genuine respect for civic freedom and the rights of individuals. Particularly striking is a real concern for the hardships of the poor, which was far to seek in the earlier records. Rarely do we find the fiscal authorities harassing people who are not in a position to pay their taxes; remissions of taxation are more frequent, poor relief is more liberally granted. During this period the King increased the sums bespoken for the establishment of "charity workshops" in rural areas, and for the assistance of the poor, and time and again he sanctioned new grants of this order. I find that over 80,000 *livres* were distributed in poor relief in a single province, Upper Guienne, in 1779; 40,000 *livres* in Tours in 1784: 48,000 in Normandy, in 1787. Louis XVI took a personal interest in these benefactions and did not leave them solely to the discretion of his Ministers. Thus when in 1776 an Order in Council fixed the compensation to be paid to certain peasants whose lands were in the neighbourhood of royal game preserves and whose crops had suffered for this reason, the King drew up the preamble with his own hand. Turgot records that when handing him the document that kindly, ill-starred monarch said, "You see, I, too, do my share of work." If the old order were depicted under its final aspect, the picture would, in fact, be flattering—but sadly far from the truth.

Parallel with these changes in the mentality of the rulers

and the ruled there was an advance as rapid as it was unprecedented in the prosperity of the nation. This took the usual forms: an increase in the population and an even more spectacular increase in the wealth of individuals. The American war did not check this upward movement; though the State fell yet more heavily in debt, private persons went on making fortunes; also, they worked harder than in the past, showed more initiative and resourcefulness.

"Since 1774," wrote a member of the government, "the general expansion of industry has been bringing in more money by way of taxes on commodities." When we compare the contracts made at successive periods of the reign of Louis XVI between the State and the finance companies to which the taxes were farmed out by the Crown, we find that the sums paid by these companies shot up every year. The payments made by the tax farmers in 1786 exceeded those of 1780 by fourteen million *livres*. "We reckon that the revenue from taxes on commodities"—thus Necker in the 1781 budget—"rises by two millions yearly."

Arthur Young declared that in 1788 Bordeaux was a busier commercial centre than Liverpool, and added that in recent times the progress of overseas commerce had been more rapid in France than even in England, and French trade had doubled in volume during the past twenty years.

A study of comparative statistics makes it clear that in none of the decades immediately following the Revolution did our national prosperity make such rapid forward strides as in the two preceding it.[66] Only the thirty-seven years of constitutional monarchy, which were for us a time of peace and plenty, are in any way comparable in this respect with the reign of Louis XVI.

At first sight it seems hard to account for this steady increase in the wealth of the country despite the as yet unremedied shortcomings of the administration and the obstacles with which industry still had to contend. Indeed, many of our politicians, being unable to explain it, have followed the example of Molière's physician, who declared that no sick man could recover "against the rules of medicine"—and simply denied its existence. That France could prosper and grow rich, given the inequality of taxation, the vagaries of local laws, internal customs barriers, feudal rights, the trade corporations, the sales of offices, and all the rest, may well seem hardly credible. Yet the fact remains that the country did grow richer and living conditions improved throughout the land, and the reason was that though the machinery of government was ramshackle, ill-regulated, inefficient, and though it tended to hinder rather than to further social progress, it had two redeeming features which sufficed to make it function and made for national prosperity. Firstly, though the government was no longer despotic, it still was powerful and capable of maintaining order everywhere; and secondly, the nation possessed an upper class that was the freest, most enlightened of the day and a social system under which every man could get rich if he set his mind to it and keep intact the wealth he had acquired.

The King still used the language of a master but in actual fact he always deferred to public opinion and was guided by it in his handling of day-to-day affairs. Indeed, he made a point of consulting it, feared it, and bowed to it invariably. Absolute according to the letter of the law, the monarchy was limited in practice. In 1784 Necker frankly recognised this as an accepted fact in an official declaration. ''Few foreigners have any notion of the authority with which public opinion is invested in present-day France, and they have much difficulty in understanding the nature of this invisible power behind the throne. Yet it most certainly exists.''

The belief that the greatness and power of a nation are products of its administrative machinery alone is, to say the least, shortsighted; however perfect that machinery, the driving force behind it is what counts. We have only to look at England, where the constitutional system is vastly more complicated, unwieldy, and erratic than that of France today. Yet is there any other European country whose national wealth is greater; where private ownership is more extensive, takes so many forms, and is so secure; where individual prosperity and a stable social system are so well allied? This is not due to the merits of any special laws but to the spirit animating the English constitution as a whole. That certain organs may be faulty matters little when the life force of the body politic has such vigour.[67]

It is a singular fact that this steadily increasing prosperity, far from tranquillising the population, everywhere promoted a spirit of unrest. The general public became more and more hostile to every ancient institution, more and more discontented; indeed, it was increasingly obvious that the nation was heading for a revolution.

Moreover, those parts of France in which the improvement in the standard of living was most pronounced were the chief centres of the revolutionary movement. Such records of the Ile-de-France region as have survived prove clearly that it was in the districts in the vicinity of Paris that the old order was soonest and most drastically superseded. In these parts the freedom and wealth of the peasants had long been better assured than in any other *pays d'élection*.[68] Well before 1789 the system of forced labour (as applied to individuals) had disappeared in this region. The *taille* had become less onerous and was more equitably assessed than elsewhere. The Order in amendment of this tax must be studied if we wish to understand how much an Intendant of the time could do by way of improving—or worsening—the lot of an entire province. As set forth in this Order the impost in question assumes a very different aspect from that with which we are familiar. Tax commissioners were to be sent by the government yearly to each parish and all the inhabitants were to be summoned to appear before them. The value of all property subject to tax was to be assessed in public, the means of each taxpayer to be determined after hearing both parties, and finally, the incidence of the *taille* was to be fixed by the authorities in concert with all the taxpayers. The arbitrary powers of the Syndic and uncalled-for measures of coercion were abolished. No doubt the vices inherent in the whole system of the *taille* could not be eradicated; whatever improvements were made in the manner of collecting it, it affected only one class of taxpayers and was levied not only on their chattels but on the industries they carried on. Nevertheless, the *taille* as levied in the Ile-de-France was very different from the tax which still bore that name in nearby revenue subdivisions of the country.

Around the Loire estuary, in the Poitou fenlands, and the *landes* of Brittany the methods of the past were kept to more tenaciously than in any other part of France. Yet it was in these regions that civil war blazed up after the outbreak of the Revolution and the inhabitants put up the most passionate and stubborn resistance to it.

Thus it was precisely in those parts of France where there had been most improvement that popular discontent ran highest. This may seem illogical—but history is full of such paradoxes. For it is not always when things are going from bad to worse that revolutions break out. On the contrary, it oftener happens that when a people which has put up with an oppressive rule over a long period without protest suddenly finds the government relaxing its pressure, it takes up arms against it. Thus the social order overthrown by a revolution is almost always better than the one immediately preceding it, and experience teaches us that, generally speaking, the most perilous moment for a bad government is one when it seeks to mend its ways. Only consummate statecraft can enable a King to save his throne when after a long spell of oppressive rule he sets to improving the lot of his subjects. Patiently endured so long as it seemed beyond redress, a grievance comes to appear intolerable once the possibility of removing it crosses men's minds. For the mere fact that certain abuses have been remedied draws attention to the others and they now appear more galling; people may suffer less, but their sensibility is exacerbated. At the height of its power feudalism did not inspire so much hatred as it did on the eve of its eclipse.[69] In the reign of Louis XVI the most trivial pinpricks of arbitrary power caused more resentment than the throughgoing despotism of Louis XIV. The brief imprisonment of Beaumarchais shocked Paris more than the *dragonnades* of 1685.

In 1780 there could no longer be any talk of France's being on the downgrade; on the contrary, it seemed that no limit could be set to her advance. And it was now that theories of the perfectibility of man and continuous progress came into fashion. Twenty years earlier there had been no hope for the future; in 1780 no anxiety was felt about it. Dazzled by the prospect of a felicity undreamed of hitherto and now within their grasp, people were blind to the very real improvement that had taken place and eager to precipitate events.

Aside from such considerations of a general order there were specific and no less potent reasons for this changed mentality. Though, like all other government departments, the financial administration had been thoroughly overhauled, it still had the vices inherent in all despotic systems, and since the Treasury accounts were never audited or published, some of the worst practices of the reigns of Louis XIV and Louis XV still prevailed. Moreover, the very efforts of the government to increase national prosperity, the reliefs and bounties it distributed, constantly imposed new burdens on the budget with which incoming revenue did not keep pace. Thus Louis XVI was involved in financial difficulties even worse than those of his predecessors. Like them he persistently kept his creditors waiting, like them he borrowed money right and left, without publicity and without stint, and his creditors were never sure of being paid the interest due on loans; indeed, even their capital was always at the mercy of the monarch's good will.

An eyewitness whom we have every reason to trust, since he was better placed than any other to see what was going on, tells us that "the French of those days were exposed to constant risks in their dealings with their own government. If they invested capital in government securities they could never feel certain that the interest would be forthcoming on the due dates; if they built ships, repaired roads, or supplied clothing to the army they had no guaranty for the sums disbursed and were reduced to assessing the risks involved in taking up a government contract as one calculates them for some highly speculative venture. During this period," he adds with much good sense, "when owing to the rapid progress of industry a larger number of people than ever before had acquired the possessive instinct and a taste for easy living, those who had entrusted the State with a portion of their capital were all the more irritated by the frequent breaches of contract committed by a debtor who, more than any other, should have made a point of keeping faith."

There was nothing new in these delinquencies on the part of the administration; what was new was the indignation they aroused. The vices of the financial system had been far more glaring in the past, but a great change had supervened in both the methods of government and in the structure of society, a change which made the French far more acutely conscious of these vices than they had been hitherto.

During the last twenty years the government had become more energetic, had launched out into a host of activities to which until then it had never given a thought, and as a result had become the greatest consumer of industrial products and the chief employer of labour in the kingdom. The number of persons having monetary dealings with it, subscribing to its loans, living on wages paid by it, and speculating in government-sponsored enterprises had enormously increased. Never before had the interests and fortunes of private individuals been so closely bound up with those of the State. Thus the mismanagement of the State finances, which formerly had affected only the administration, now brought ruin to many homes. In 1789 the State owed nearly six hundred million *livres* to its creditors, who themselves were for the most part deep in debt and made common cause with all who likewise were being victimised by the remissness of the government in punctually fulfilling its obligations. As the number of malcontents increased, they became ever more loud-spoken in their protests; for the habit of speculation, the passion for money-making, and the taste for comfortable living that had developed along with the expansion of commerce and industry made such grievances seem intolerable to those very persons who, thirty years earlier, would have endured them without a murmur.

Thus it was that *rentiers,* merchants, manufacturers, businessmen, and financiers—the section of the community usually most averse to violent political changes, warm supporters of the existing government, whatever it may be, and essentially law-abiding even when they despise or dislike the laws—now proved to be the most strenuous and determined advocates of reform. What they demanded most vociferously was nothing short of a radical change in the entire financial administration of the country, and they failed to realise that a change so revolutionary would spell the downfall of the constitution as a whole. It is hard to see how a catastrophe could have been averted. On the one hand was a nation in which the love of wealth and luxury was daily spreading; on the other a government that while constantly fomenting this new passion, at the same time frustrated it—and by this fatal inconsistency was sealing its own doom.

CHAPTER FIVE

*How the spirit of revolt was promoted by well-intentioned efforts to improve the people's lot*

For a hundred and forty years the French people had played no part on the political stage and this had led to a general belief that they could never figure there. So inert did the working class appear that it was assumed to be not only dumb but hard of hearing, with the result that when at long last the authorities began to take an interest in the masses, they talked about them in their presence, as if they were not there. Indeed, there seems to have been an impression that only the upper classes could use their ears and the sole danger was that of failing to make oneself understood by them.

Thus the very men who had most to fear from the anger of the masses had no qualms about publicly condemning the gross injustice with which they had always been treated. They drew attention to the monstrous vices of the institutions which pressed most heavily on the common people and indulged in highly coloured descriptions of the living conditions of the working class and the starvation wages it received. And by thus championing the cause of the underprivileged they made them acutely conscious of their wrongs. The people of whom I now am speaking, be it noted, were not our literary men but members of the government, high officials, the privileged few.

When thirteen years before the Revolution the King attempted to abolish forced labour, his preamble to the measure ran as follows: "Outside a few provinces (the *pays d'états*) almost all the roads in the kingdom have been made by the unpaid labour of the poorest of our subjects. Thus the whole burden has fallen on those who till the soil and make relatively little use of the highways; it is the landed proprietors, nearly all of them privileged persons, who stand to gain, since the value of their estates is enhanced by the making of these roads. When the poor man is constrained to bear the brunt, unaided of keeping the roads in order and forced to give his time and toil without remuneration, the one and only means he has of avoiding poverty and hunger is being taken from him and he is being forced to work for the benefit of the rich."

When an attempt was made at the same time to do away with the injustices and restrictions of the guild system, the King issued a declaration to the effect that "the right to work is a man's most sacred possession and any law that tampers with it violates a natural right and should be treated as null and void. The existing trade and craft corporations are unnatural and oppressive organisations stemming from self-regarding motives, greed, and a desire to domineer." It was indiscreet enough to utter such words, but positively dangerous to utter them in vain. For some months later the guild system and forced labour were reinstated.

It was Turgot, we are told, who put these words into the mouth of the King. And most of Turgot's successors followed his example. When in 1780 the King announced that notice would be given by publication in the register offices of any increases in the *taille* he made a point of referring to the hardships of those subject to this tax. "Already aggrieved by the inconsiderate manner in which the *taille* is collected, the taxpayer until now has often had to face quite unexpected increases in the sum demanded; indeed, the taxes imposed on the poorest of our subjects have risen out of all proportion to other forms of taxation." Though the King did not venture as yet to level out the incidence of taxation in general, he attempted, anyhow, to apply the same methods of collection to all taxpayers, great and small. "His Majesty trusts that the rich will not feel aggrieved if they are treated on an equal footing with the rest of his subjects. After all, they will only be shouldering a burden that for a long time past they should have shared more equally with others."

But it was especially in times of scarcity that it almost seemed as though the authorities were aiming less at providing relief for the poor than fuel for their passions. Wishing to encourage the rich to show more generosity, an Intendant denounced the lack of human feeling and any sense of justice on the part of landowners, "who owe all that they possess to the poor man's toil, yet are quite ready to let him die of starvation at the very time when he is working his hardest to keep their estates productive." The King spoke to much the same effect on a similar occasion. "His Majesty is doing his utmost to protect the worker from malpractices that deprive him even of the bare necessities of life by forcing him to work at any wage, however small, that his rich employer thinks fit to give him. The King will not tolerate rapacity of this sort and the exploitation of one class of his subjects by another."

As long as the monarchy lasted, the hostility between the various administrative authorities gave rise to declarations of this order, in which each party blamed the other for the sufferings of the labouring class. A good example is the conflict which arose in 1772 between the parlement of Toulouse and the King. According to the spokesman of the former "our poor folk are on the brink of starvation as a result of the ill-conceived measures taken by the government." To which the King retorted that the arrogance of the parlement of Toulouse and the greed of the rich were responsible for the misfortunes of the people. On one point, it will be noticed, both parties concurred: on giving the public to understand that their superiors were to blame for the evils that befell them.

It should be borne in mind that these opinions were expressed not in private letters but in official documents which the government and parlements caused to be printed by thousands and widely circulated. In some the King takes his predecessors and even himself severely to task, nor does he mince his words. "The extravagance of certain reigns has burdened our finances with a heavy load of debt. Concessions of our inalienable domains have been granted in many cases for a mere pittance." "The trade guilds," he was led to remark on another occasion, with more justice than discretion, "owe their existence chiefly to our Kings' appetite for new forms of taxation." And he goes on to say that "the reason why needless expenditure was so often indulged in and the *taille* increased out of all reason was that our Finance Ministry found that the easiest way of raising money was to increase the *taille,* owing to the secrecy surrounding its operations, and took advantage of this; nonetheless, there were several other forms of taxation which would have been less irksome to our subjects.''[70]

Such remarks were addressed to the more enlightened section of the nation and intended to convince them of the expediency of reforms which, *prima facie,* told against their interests. As for the uneducated classes it was assumed that if they heard them at all, they would fail to grasp their purport.

We must admit, moreover, that notwithstanding these expressions of good will and despite a genuine desire to better the condition of the poorer classes, the feelings of the elite towards them were strongly tinctured with contempt. We are reminded of the conduct of Mme. Duchâtelet, as reported by Voltaire's secretary; this good lady, it seems, had no scruples about undressing in the presence of her manservants, being unable to convince herself that these lackeys were real flesh-and-blood men!

It must not be thought that Louis XVI and his Ministers were alone in voicing the dangerous opinions cited above; members of the privileged class, immediate object of the underlings' resentment, expressed similar sentiments in the hearing of all and sundry. For it is a proven fact that the upper classes in France were beginning to show a philanthropic concern for the lot of the poor before the latter threatened them in any way, and took an active interest in improving their condition at a time when the thought that these people they befriended might one day cause their downfall had never entered their heads. This is particularly evident in the decade preceding '89; much compassion was shown for the poor, there was constant talk about their wrongs, and frequent attempts were made to find remedies for them. In particular the fiscal system, that ancient bugbear of the unprivileged class, came under fire. And as a rule the terms in which these new, charitable sentiments were expressed were as ill advised as the callousness displayed in former years.

When we read the minutes of the provincial assemblies convoked in 1779 in certain parts of France (and subsequently

throughout the kingdom) and such other records of their proceedings as have survived, we cannot but be struck both by
the benevolent intentions of all concerned and by the extraordinary rashness of the terms in which they voiced them.

"There have been far too many cases"—thus the Assembly
of Lower Normandy—"in which sums earmarked by the
King for the upkeep of roads have been used to the advantage
of the rich, without benefiting the general public in any way.
For example, money that should have been expended on mend-
ing the roads to a town or village has often been spent on
improving the approaches to some château." At this same assembly the Orders of the nobility and clergy, after denouncing
the evils of forced labour, offered to contribute fifty thousand
*livres* for road repairs. The object of this voluntary contribu-
tion, they said, was to improve the local roads without imposing any burden on the public. It might have cost these privileged classes less to replace the forced-labour system by a tax
falling on all alike and to pay their share of it; but though they
were prepared to forego the advantages they got from inequality
of taxation, they were not prepared to put a stop to it. Thus,
while relinquishing the financial benefits due to their privileged
position, they were careful to retain its most objectionable
feature.

Other assemblies, composed almost entirely of land-owners
who were exempted from the *taille* and had every intention of
remaining so, depicted in no less lurid colours the injustices
and hardships the *taille* inflicted on the poor. What is more,
they saw to it that copies of these pronouncements were widely
distributed. But what seems stranger still is that alongside
demonstrations of their sympathy with the lower classes they
sometimes gave publicity to expressions of contempt. For
though they had learned to sympathise with their "inferiors"
they still despised them.

The Provincial Assembly of Upper Guienne, while warmly
pleading the peasants' cause, described them as "uncouth
yokels, boors with no respect for law and order, no sense of
discipline." Even Turgot, who did so much for the people,
spoke of them in much the same way.[71]

More amazing still, expressions of this kind figured in reports to which the utmost publicity was given and which were intended to be read by the peasants themselves. One has a feeling that people who behaved in this way imagined they were living in some such backward country as Galicia, where the aristocracy speak a language different from that of the lower classes and cannot be understood by them. In the eighteenth century our feudal-minded nobility, while treating their peasants and others owing allegiance to them with a kindness, justice, and considerateness that would have much surprised their forbears, still referred to them on occasion as "churls". Indeed, contemptuous expressions of this kind seem to have been quite "in order"—as our lawyers say.

The sympathy shown for the sufferings of the poor became more and more active, and more and more indiscreet in its manifestations, as the Revolution drew near. I have read circulars sent out by provincial assemblies at the beginning of 1788 to the inhabitants of parishes inviting them to give a detailed account of their grievances. The signatories of one of these circular letters are a priest, a great lord, three noblemen, and a bourgeois, all members of the assembly and acting in its name. They instructed the Syndic of each parish to convene a meeting of all the peasants and to ask what they had to say against the manner in which the taxes they paid were assessed and collected. "We know in a general way that most taxes, especially the *gabelle* [salt-tax] and the *taille,* cause much hardship to the cultivator, and we wish to know, in detail, exactly what is amiss."

But this was only one item of the programme these delegates of the assembly set themselves. They also called for a report giving the number of persons in each parish—nobles, clergy, and commoners—who enjoyed any special privileges as regards taxation, and in what these privileges consisted; what was the value of the property owned by these privileged persons; whether or not they resided on their estates; if there was in the parish much Church-owned property or, as it was then described, "property in mortmain", that is to say inalienable, and what was its value. This was not all; they also asked a question that struck deeper. Supposing, they said, equality of taxation came into practice and exempted persons were required

to pay their share, at what figure might be assessed the sums
they would contribute under the heads of the *taille* and its acces-
sories, poll tax, and forced-labour dues?

The effect of all this on the peasant can be easily imagined.
Now that his grievances were ventilated, now that the men
responsible for them were pointed out to him and he realised
how small was their number, he was emboldened to take arms
against them, while in his heart were kindled the primitive
emotions of envy, malice, and cupidity. It would seem, indeed,
that the men responsible for thus enlightening him had completely forgotten the bloodthirsty uprisings of the past, the
Jacquerie, the Council of "the Sixteen", the Maillotins of 1382,
and failed to realise that though the French are the most good-
natured and docile nation in the ordinary way, they are capable
of the utmost savagery once their passions are aroused.

Unfortunately I have been unable to discover all the replies
sent in by the peasants to this fateful questionnaire, but I have
studied enough of them to glean an idea of their general tenor.
In these returns the name of each privileged person, noble or
bourgeois, is given in full; his way of living is sometimes
described and always adverted to. Great pains have obviously
been taken to find out the exact value of his property; the scope
and nature of his privileges are set forth at length, with special
emphasis on the injury they do to the other residents of the
village. The amount of wheat that has to be paid to him is
calculated down to the last bushel and his income is evaluated
with jealous minuteness, an income from which, as is carefully
pointed out, no one benefits except himself. The priest's emoluments (already called his "salary") are judged excessive and
resentment is expressed at the way in which the Church wants
fees for everything and the poor man cannot even get buried
free of charge. As for the taxes, all alike, they say, are wrongly
assessed and extortionate; not a single one finds favour in their
eyes and they trounce them in terms that are nothing if not
outspoken.

"The indirect taxes are detestable. The exciseman has no
respect for the privacy of our homes; he comes poking and
prying, laying his hands on everything, and nothing is sacred
in his eyes. Registration fees are much too heavy. The collector

of the *taille* is a rapacious harpy whose one idea is to squeeze the poor in every way he can. The bailiffs are no better; no cultivator, honest though he be, is safe from their extortions. The villagers charged with the collection of the taxes are compelled to ruin their neighbours so as not to be victimised themselves by the exorbitant demands of these petty despots."

In these reports there is more than a premonition of the Revolution; it is present in them, speaking its authentic tongue and showing its true colours.

Of the many differences between the religious revolution of the sixteenth century and the Great Revolution one is particularly revealing. In the sixteenth century most members of the ruling class were led to accept the new form of religion by motives of ambition or self-interest, whereas the common people adopted it out of genuine conviction and without any prospect of gain. In the eighteenth century, on the other hand, disinterested beliefs and human fellow feeling led the French elite to sponsor the revolutionary cause, while the masses were moved to action by the hardships of their lot and a passionate desire to better it. Thus the generous enthusiasm of the former took part in activating the rancour and cupidity of the populace and, indeed, touched off revolution.

CHAPTER SIX

*How certain practices of the central power completed the revolutionary education of the masses*

For some time past the government itself had been busily instilling into the minds of the populace at large what were later to be known as revolutionary ideas; ideas, that is to say, which, taking no account of individuals or private rights, encouraged acts of violence. And it was the King who took the lead in showing with what disdain the most venerable and seemingly most firmly established institutions could now be treated.

Louis XV did as much to weaken the monarchy and to speed up the Revolution by his innovations as by his personal defects, by his energy as by his indolence. The disappearance of the French parlement, an institution almost coeval with the monarchy, made the nation vaguely aware of standing on the threshold of an age of violence and instability, when anything might happen; an age in which, however ancient, few traditions of the past would be respected and scarcely any novelty, however startling, would not seem worth trying out.

During his entire reign Louis XVI was always talking about reform, and there were few institutions whose destruction he did not contemplate before the Revolution broke and made an end of them. But after eliminating from the constitution some of its worst features he made haste to reinstate them; in fact, he gave an impression of merely wanting to loosen its foundations and leaving to others the task of laying it low.

Some of the reforms he personally put through made over-hasty, ill-considered changes in ancient and respected usages, changes which in certain cases violated vested rights. They prepared the ground for the Revolution not so much because they removed obstacles in its way but more because they taught the nation how to set about it. Paradoxically enough what made things worse was that the King and his Ministers were inspired by purely altruistic ideals; for by showing that methods of violence can be employed with good intentions by people of good will, they set a dangerous precedent.

Long before this Louis XIV had publicised in his edicts the view that all the landed estates in the kingdom had in the first instance been granted to their occupants conditionally and that their true owner was the State and the State alone. Thus the title to his property of every landowner in France could be called in question and his tenure was precarious. The theory had its origin in feudal law; but in France it was put forward only at the time when feudalism was dying out, and it had never been endorsed by courts of justice. This idea is basic to our modern socialism, and it is odd to find it emerging for the first time in France under a despotic monarchy.[12]

During the following reigns the administration persistently instilled into the minds of Frenchmen, from a more practical angle and in a manner they could better understand, the notion that private ownership need not, indeed should not, invariably be respected. When, for example, in the second half of the eighteenth century, public works and road making were the order of the day, the government showed no compunction about seizing all the private land it needed and tearing down houses that stood in its way. For the Highways Department was as fascinated then as it seems to be today by the perfectly straight line and studiously avoided making use of existing roads if they showed the least deviation from this ideal rectitude. Rather than make a detour, however slight, our road makers hacked their way through ancient estates, defacing and destroying valuable parklands. Compensation for the damage done was arbitrarily assessed and often paid belatedly—if at all.[73]

When the Provincial Assembly of Lower Normandy took over the administration from the Intendant, it was found that the compensation due for land that had been seized during the past twenty years was still unpaid. The sum owed by the State to private owners in this one small French province was no less than 250,000 *livres*. Owing to the way the land had been subdivided in recent times, small landowners were the chief victims, while the owners of big estates came off relatively lightly. Thus every small holder had learned by personal experience how little heed was given to the rights of individuals when it was in the public interest to ride roughshod over them— a lesson he took care to keep in mind when it was a question of applying it to others and for his own benefit.

In a great many parishes there had once been charitable institutions which were intended by their founders to distribute poor relief in certain cases and in a manner specified in the bequest. During the last period of the monarchy most of these foundations were either abolished or diverted from their original purpose by Orders in Council, that is to say by purely arbitrary acts on the part of the government. Usually the funds that had been donated to villages for the relief of paupers were requisitioned on behalf of local hospitals. But at about the same time the property of the hospitals came under fire, being treated in a way that the original benefactors had never contemplated and of which they certainly would not have approved. By an edict of 1780 these institutions were authorised to dispose of the property that had been bequeathed to them on the understanding that they were to enjoy its usufruct in perpetuity, and to transfer the sums thus realised to the State in return for an annuity guaranteed by government. This was, the government spokesman pointed out, making a better use of our ancestors' charity than they had made themselves. It never seemed to cross anyone's mind that the surest way of training people to violate the rights of the living is to set at nought the wishes of the dead. None of the governments following the old order has gone further than it did in this direction. It had none of that almost over-scrupulous deference to a man's last wishes which we find among the British, and thanks to which every Englishman can feel assured that his fellow citizens will see to it that the provisions of his last will and testament are duly executed —that curious sentiment which leads them to show more deference to a dead man's memory than they did to the living man.

Requisitioning, compulsory sales of foodstuffs, and the fixing of maximum prices—all are practices which had their precedents under the old order. I have seen records showing that in times of scarcity officials fixed the prices of the produce offered for sale by the peasants and that if the latter, fearing this control, were reluctant to attend the public market, they were ordered to do so and threatened with fines if they failed to put in an appearance.

But there was no more dangerous precedent than the way criminal justice was administered where the common people were concerned. True, the poor man was much better protected than is generally thought against high-handed dealings on the part of richer or more influential members of the community. But if his adversary was the State, he came up (as mentioned in a previous chapter of this book) against "exceptional" tribunals, biased judges, summary procedure, a mere semblance of a trial, and execution of judgment was enforced peremptorily, there being no appeal against the orders of these courts. "The Provost and Lieutenant of the mounted constabulary are directed to deal with any unlawful assembly or disturbances in connection with the shortage of the wheat crop; trials of offenders shall take place in the provostal court and there shall be no appeal. His Majesty forbids all other courts to take cognisance of such offences." This Order in Council remained in force throughout the eighteenth century. We learn from records of the mounted constabulary that in such "states of emergency" a cordon was posted by night around villages which were thought likely to give trouble; that the police entered houses before dawn and were empowered to arrest without a warrant any person who had been informed against. Those who had been arrested in this manner were often kept in prison without trial over a long period, though it was laid down in the Order that the accused person should be brought before the judge for examination within twenty-four hours of his arrest. This provision of the law was as imperative, and disobeyed as often, as it is today.

Thus it was that a stable, well-intentioned government gradually accustomed the nation to a system of criminal procedure better suited to a revolutionary age or despotic rule, and, indeed, prepared men's minds for both. For the people were quick to learn the lesson taught them by their rulers. Even Turgot followed in the footsteps of his predecessors in this respect, and when his new corn laws encountered opposition in the parlement and led to riots in the rural districts, he persuaded the King to issue orders to the effect that such breaches of the peace should not be tried by ordinary courts of justice but by the provostal courts, "whose chief function it is to put a stop to insurrectionary movements when it is essential that examples should be made without the least delay." Worse still, all peasants who left their parishes without obtaining a certificate signed by the Syndic and their parish priest were to be arrested and summarily tried by the Provost's court as "vagabonds".

We must not forget, however, that while the letter of the law may seem brutally oppressive, sentences in practice were usually light. The laws were meant to be deterrent rather than to make people suffer. Though the authorities committed arbitrary, even violent acts, this was simply a matter of habit or indifference; at heart they were kindly disposed. Actually these summary methods of trial became more and more the general rule and the lighter was the penalty, the more there was a tendency to scamp the procedure leading up to it. Thus the mildness of the sentence blinded men's eyes to the iniquity of the system.

I have no hesitation in affirming, after a careful survey of the facts on record, that a great many of the practices we associate

with the Revolution had had precedents in the treatment of the
people by the government during the last two centuries of the
monarchy. The old order provided the Revolution with many
of its methods; all the Revolution added to these was a savagery
peculiar to itself.


CHAPTER SEVEN

*How revolutionary changes in the administrative sys-*
*tem preceded the political revolution and their con-*
*sequences*

Though most of the laws applicable to private persons and the
transaction of affairs had been either superseded or modified,
the structure of the constitution had not as yet been altered in
any way.

The suppression of the trade and craft corporations, followed
by their partial restoration, had entirely changed the old relations between worker and employer. But this relationship did
not merely take a different form; it now was ill defined and
irksome to all concerned. The employers' authority had been
undermined but the quasi-paternal control of the State was not
yet solidly established, and between the conflicting claims of the
government and his employer the artisan hardly knew where he
stood; from which of the two he should take orders, and which
could be counted on to protect his interests. This condition of
uncertainty, not to say anarchy, to which the working class in
all the towns of France had been reduced had far-reaching consequences when the people began once again to make their
voice heard in the political arena.

A year before the Revolution the King issued an edict over-
hauling the entire judicial system. Several new jurisdictions
were introduced, a number of others abolished, and all the rules
defining the powers of the various courts were altered. Now, as
I have already pointed out, the number of persons engaged in
trying cases or executing orders passed by the courts was at
this time immense; one might almost say that the whole middle
class was concerned in one way or another with the administra-

tion of justice. Thus the changes made in the judicial system of the country had a disturbing effect on both the social status and the pecuniary situation of thousands of families; they felt as if the ground had been cut from under their feet. The inconvenience caused to litigants by the edict was hardly less; as a result of these sweeping changes none could be sure what law applied to his special case and which court was competent to try it.

But it was above all the drastic reform of the administration (in the widest sense of the term) which took place in 1787 that not only threw public affairs into confusion but had repercussions on the private life of every Frenchman.

I have already drawn attention to the fact that in all *pays d'élection,* that is to say in nearly three quarters of France, the entire administration was in the hands of a single man, the Intendant, and that not only his will was law, but he came to his decisions alone, without seeking any outside advice. In 1787, however, a provincial assembly was associated with the Intendant and in effect it took over the entire administration of the district formerly under his sole charge. In the same way an elected municipal committee took over in the villages the functions of the parish council and, in most cases, of the Syndic.

Totally unlike the old system of administration and changing out of recognition both the manner in which public business was transacted and, more, the social status of private citizens, the new system (so the King decreed) was to come into force everywhere simultaneously and under practically the same form; that is to say without the least respect for ancient customs, local usages, or the particular conditions of each province. So deeply had this notion of standardised administration, destined to be a characteristic of the Revolution, already permeated the monarchical government which it was soon to sweep away.

It was easy then to see how large a part is played by habit in the functioning of political institutions and how much more easily a nation can cope with complicated, well-nigh unintelligible laws to which it is accustomed than with a simpler legal system that is new.

There had previously existed in France a host of authorities, widely varying from province to province and none of them with recognised, well-defined limits, the result being that their fields of action often overlapped. Nonetheless, the administration of the country under the old order had come to run relatively smoothly. The new authorities, however, who were fewer in number, with similar but carefully restricted powers, tended in practice to become entangled with each other, the result being a state of confusion often ending in a deadlock. Moreover, the new system had a grave defect which alone would have been enough (anyhow in its early days) to prevent its working efficiently. This was that all the powers it instituted were *collective*.

Under the monarchy there had existed only two methods of administration. In districts where a single man had all the power in his hands he carried on without the collaboration of an assembly of any kind. In those where there were assemblies —for example in the *pays d'états* and in towns—the executive power was not in the hands of any special person; the assembly not only supervised and controlled the administration, but also took a direct hand in it, either as a body or through temporary committees appointed by itself.

These being the only known forms of administration, when one was given up the other was adopted. It is a singular fact that in a nation so enlightened and one in which a central administration had so long played a vital part, nobody should have thought of trying to combine the two systems and distinguishing, without divorcing, the executive from the legislative, directive power. It was left to the nineteenth century to hit on this idea, self-evident though it seems to us today. Indeed, it is the only great discovery in the field of public administration for which we can claim credit. But the nation opted for the other alternative: the administrative methods of the past were transposed into the political sphere, and following the tradition of the old order, detested though it was, the system practised in the provincial Estates and small urban municipalities was adopted by the National Convention. Thus what had formerly been no more than an impediment to the proper handling of public affairs gave rise directly to the Reign of Terror.

Meanwhile, in 1787, the provincial assemblies were invested with most of the powers that had hitherto been the Intendants'. It was now their duty, subject to the orders of the central government, to assess the *taille* and supervise its collection; to decide what public works were to be undertaken and to have them duly carried out. All employees of the *Ponts et Chaussées*, from the Inspector down to the foreman of the labour gangs, were under their direct control. The assembly was responsible for seeing that these men carried out its orders, and was instructed to report on their work to the Minister and advise him as to suitable rates of pay. The administration of the villages was now transferred almost entirely to the assembly, which was to try as a court of first instance most of the suits which up to now had been heard by the Intendant. Some of these functions were obviously quite unsuitable for such a large and irresponsible body of men, complete novices, moreover, in such matters.

To make confusion worse confounded, the Intendant, while stripped of his powers, was continued in his post. But though unable to take action on his own initiative, he was instructed to keep an eye on the assembly and to aid it in every possible way, unlikely though it must have seemed that an official, under such circumstances, could enter into the spirit of the legislative body that had supplanted him, or wish to simplify its task.

The sub-delegate shared the fate of his Intendant. Alongside him and holding the position he had occupied there was now a "district assembly", which functioned under the aegis of the provincial assembly and on similar lines.

All that is known of the activities of the provincial assemblies created in 1787, and indeed their own records make it plain that no sooner were they in the saddle than they took the offensive, sometimes quite openly, sometimes furtively, against the Intendants, who retaliated by using their superior experience in administrative matters to make things difficult for their successors.[74] Thus in the records of some assemblies we find complaints that they have the utmost difficulty in getting the Intendant to make over documents of prime importance. Similarly, we find the Intendant accusing the assembly of trying to usurp the functions still left to him under the edicts. He appeals to the Minister to put a stop to this, but the Minister fails to acknowledge his letter or cannot make a ruling for the good

reason that his own ideas on the "new system" are as vague
as those of the parties directly concerned. Sometimes, too,
the assembly declares that the Intendant has been neglecting his
duties, that roads he has had made are badly planned or in a
state of disrepair; or that he has allowed villages under his
charge to come to rack and ruin. Often a provincial assembly
found the provisions of the new laws so baffling and obscure
that it sent letters to distant provinces requesting explanations;
indeed, the assemblies were constantly asking advice from each
other. The Intendent of Auch claimed to have the right of over-
ruling the provincial assembly's decision that a certain village
was to be allowed to assess its own taxes; the assembly took
the view that in such matters an Intendant could only give
advice, not orders, and applied to the Assembly of the Ile-de-
France for an opinion on the point.

As a result of all these bickerings and consultations the administration of the country slowed down, sometimes coming
to a standstill, and all public life lapsed into a state of suspended
animation. Thus the Provincial Assembly of Lorraine spoke of
"a total stagnation in the conduct of public affairs" (a lament
that was echoed by several other assemblies), adding that "all
good citizens are much distressed by this."

Sometimes, however, the new governing bodies erred in the
other direction, displaying an excess of zeal and misdirected
energy. In their eagerness for reform they sought to sweep away
the old system altogether or to amend long-standing defects in
the administration at a moment's notice. Alleging that the
management of the towns now devolved on them, they took
charge of all municipal affairs and, full of excellent intentions,
created total chaos.

When we reflect on the immense power that had been exercised for so long a time by the central government, the host of
private interests in which it had a hand, how many enterprises
linked up with it or needed its support; when we remember
that it was on the administration more than on his personal
efforts that the Frenchman relied for the success of his business
undertakings, for the regular supply of his daily needs, for the
upkeep of the roads he used, and in fact for everything that
could ensure his peace of mind and material well-being—when

we remember all this, we can easily realise the vast number of people whose personal interests were injuriously affected by the malady that had attacked the body politic.

It was in country villages that the shortcomings of the new administration were most conspicuous; for in them it not only involved a reshuffling of the public powers to which people were accustomed, but it also made abrupt changes in the relative positions of individuals and set one class against another.

When in 1775 Turgot submitted to the King a plan for re-modelling the administration of the rural districts, the greatest difficulty he encountered (we have his word for it) was the prevailing inequality of taxation. How, he asked, could one expect people who were liable to different kinds of taxation, and some of them wholly exempted, to put their heads together and discuss on an equal footing matters concerning the community as a whole—chief of which were the assessment and levy of taxes and the way they were to be expended? In each parish were members of the nobility and clergy who did not pay the *taille,* peasants who were wholly or partially exempt, and others who had to pay it in full. It was as if within each parish there were three distinct communities, each calling for an administration of its own. The problem was, in fact, insoluble.

For nowhere else was the unequal incidence of taxation so conspicuous as in the rural areas; nowhere else was the population so clearly split up into separate antagonistic groups. Obviously, if each village was to be given a small independent local government sponsored by the whole community, the first step should have been to make every member of it liable to the same taxes and to lower the barriers between classes.

But this course was not taken when the long-delayed reforms of 1787 were introduced. The old distinctions between the various Orders and the inequality of taxation, which was their chief sign, were maintained within the parishes despite the fact that the administration was now in the hands of elected representatives. And this inconsistency had some curious effects.

For example, when a parochial assembly was convened for the purpose of electing municipal officers, the curé and the seigneur were not allowed to figure in it. The reason given was that they belonged to the Orders of the clergy and the nobility respectively and it was principally the Third Estate that was choosing its representatives on such occasions. On the other hand, once the municipal council had been elected, the curé and seigneur were members of it by right; for the exclusion of two such prominent members of the community from the management of its affairs would have seemed unjustifiable. What is more, the seigneur presided at the meetings of the council in the election of whose members he had played no part. However, he had no say in most of its decisions; for example, when the assessment and collection of the *taille* were on the agenda, the curé and seigneur were debarred from voting, the argument being that both were exempted from this tax. As to the capitation tax the municipal council had no say; there were special procedures for its assessment and collection and the Intendant still took charge of these.

So as to make sure that the seigneur, isolated as he was from the body over which he nominally presided, should be unable to use his influence at second hand to the detriment of the Order of which he was not a member, it was proposed that the votes of his tenant farmers should not count. Consulted on the point, the provincial assemblies ruled that the proposal was quite in order and well justified. Other persons of noble birth were excluded from sitting in the municipal councils, which had thus become a preserve of commoners, unless they had been elected by the peasantry, in which case (as was laid down in the rules) their status was solely that of representatives of the Third Estate.

In short, when a seigneur attended these meetings he was entirely under the control of his former vassals, who had suddenly become the masters; he was their hostage rather than their leader. Indeed, it almost seemed that the object of bringing all these persons together was not so much to help them to fraternise as to make them yet more acutely conscious of their differences and conflicting interests.

The position of the Syndic now was something of an anomaly. Was the post still regarded as more of a nuisance to its holder than an honour, so much so that compulsion was needed to get a man to accept it[75] or had the Syndic's status been raised along with that of the community of which he was in a sense the "headman"? Opinions were divided on the answer to these questions. I have read a letter (written in 1788) from a village bailiff protesting against his election to the post of Syndic, incompatible, he said, with the dignity of his office. The Controller-General, to whom the letter was submitted, replied that the man must be shown the errors of this view. "Make him realise that he should be gratified at being thus honoured by his fellow citizens; and, furthermore, that the new Syndics will be very different from their predecessors and they can count on being treated with far more consideration by the government."

Another sign of the times was that persons of high social standing, even men of noble blood, now began to make overtures to the peasants, who had thus abruptly become a power in the land. We find a seigneur who held the post of "Lord Justice" in a village complaining that the new edict prevented him from taking part "as an ordinary resident" in the activities of the parish assembly. Others declared themselves "quite ready, out of a sense of public duty, even to accept the post of Syndic."

But it was too late. The more the members of the wealthy classes made advances to the peasants and tried to mix with them, the more the peasants clung to the isolation that had been their lot in earlier days, the more "exclusive" they became. In some parishes the municipal assemblies refused to allow the seigneur to attend their meetings; others put all kinds of obstacles in the way even of wealthy commoners seeking to take part in them. "We are informed"—thus the Provincial Assembly of Lower Normandy—"that several parish assemblies have excluded landowners of non-noble birth on the ground that they are not domiciled in the parish, though it is quite clear they are entitled to attend these meetings. In other parishes even ordinary farmers who have no land within their boundaries have been excluded."

Thus, though there had been as yet no changes in the constitutional law of the country and the structure of the State had not been tampered with, the innovations introduced in secondary laws had given rise to much confusion and ill-feeling. Even such as had remained intact were threatened, for the central power itself had announced the abolition of practically every existing law. Though this is hardly mentioned by present-day historians, the abrupt, wholesale remodelling of the entire administration which preceded the political revolution had already caused one of the greatest upheavals that have ever taken place in the life of a great nation. This first revolution had an incommensurable influence on the second, and, indeed, caused it to differ entirely from all the revolutions the world had known before or has witnessed during the last half century.

In England the first revolution made sweeping changes in the political constitution of the country and even overthrew the monarchy, but it hardly affected the secondary laws or the customs and habits of the nation. The judicature and administration kept their old forms and functioned as before. Even at the height of the civil war the twelve Justices of England continued making their Assize Circuits twice a year. Thus in England the upheaval was limited in scope and its effects on the social system were localised. The apex was shattered, but the substructure stood firm.

We have had several other revolutions in France since '89, revolutions which changed the whole structure of the government of the country from top to bottom. Most of them broke out suddenly and were carried through by force in flagrant violation of existing laws. All the same, the disturbances they caused never were widespread or lasted long; usually, in fact, the majority of the population was almost unaffected by them; sometimes it hardly knew a revolution was taking place.

The reason is that since '89 the administrative system has always stood firm and amid the debacles of political systems. There might be dynastic changes and alterations in the structure of the State machine, but the course of day-to-day affairs was neither interrupted nor deflected. Everyone kept to the rules and customs with which he was familiar in coping with the situations, trivial in themselves but of much personal import, which so frequently recur in the life of the ordinary citizen. He had to deal with and take orders from the same subaltern authorities as in the past and, oftener than not, the same officials. For though in each successive revolution the administration was, so to speak, decapitated, its body survived intact and active. The same duties were performed by the same civil servants, whose practical experience kept the nation on an even keel through the worst political storms. These men administered the country or rendered justice in the name of the King, then in that of the Republic, thereafter in the Emperor's. And when, with the changing tides of fortune, the cycle repeated itself in the present century, the same men continued administering and judging, first for the King, then for the Republic, then for the Emperor on exactly the same lines. Their business was less to be good citizens than good judges or administrators, and whenever the initial shock had spent its force, one might well have imagined that the nation had never swerved from the old groove.

When the Revolution broke out, that part of the government which, though subordinate, keeps every citizen constantly aware of its existence and affects his daily life at every turn, had just been thrown into confusion; the public administration had made a clean sweep of all its former representatives and embarked on a quite new programme. Radical as they were, these reforms did not seem to have jeopardised the State itself, but every Frenchman was affected by them, if only in a minor way. He felt that his life had somehow been disorganised, that he must cultivate new habits, and if a businessman, that his activities would now be handicapped. True, routine of a kind still prevailed in the conduct of affairs of vital importance to the nation, but already no one knew from whom he should take orders, to whom he should apply, or how to solve those small private problems which crop up almost daily in the life of every member of a social group.

Thus the nation as a whole was now in a state of unstable equilibrium, at the mercy of that final stroke of destiny which was to have such tremendous effects and to produce the most formidable social cataclysm the world had ever seen.

CHAPTER EIGHT

*How, given the facts set forth in the preceding chapters, the Revolution was a foregone conclusion*

My object in this final chapter is to bring together some of those aspects of the old order which were depicted piecemeal in the foregoing pages and to show how the Revolution was their natural, indeed inevitable, outcome.

When we remember that it was in France that the feudal system, while retaining the characteristics which made it so irksome to, and so much resented by, the masses, had most completely discarded all that could benefit or protect them, we may feel less surprise at the fact that France was the place of origin of the revolt destined so violently to sweep away the last vestiges of that ancient European institution.

Similarly, if we observe how the nobility after having lost their political rights and ceased, to a greater extent than in any other land of feudal Europe, to act as leaders of the people had nevertheless not only retained but greatly increased their fiscal immunities and the advantages accruing to them individually; and if we also note how, while ceasing to be the ruling class, they had remained a privileged, closed group, less and less (as I have pointed out) an aristocracy and more and more a caste —if we bear these facts in mind, it is easy to see why the privileges enjoyed by this small section of the community seemed so unwarranted and so odious to the French people and why they developed that intense jealousy of the "upper class" which rankles still today.

Finally, when we remember that the nobility had deliberately cut itself off both from the middle class and from the peasantry (whose former affection it had alienated) and had thus become like a foreign body in the State: ostensibly the high command of a great army, but actually a corps of officers without troops to follow them—when we keep this in mind, we can easily understand why the French nobility, after having so far weathered every storm, was stricken down in a single night.

I have shown how the monarchical government, after abolishing provincial independence and replacing local authorities by its nominees in three-quarters of the country, had brought under its direct management all public business, even the most trivial. I have also shown how, owing to the centralisation of power, Paris, which had until now been merely the capital city, had come to dominate France—or, rather, to embody in itself the whole kingdom. These two circumstances, peculiar to France, suffice to explain why it was that an uprising of the people could overwhelm so abruptly and decisively a monarchy that for so many centuries had successfully withstood so many onslaughts and, on the very eve of its downfall, seems inexpugnable even to the men who were about to destroy it.

In no other country of Europe had all political thought been so thoroughly and for so long stifled as in France; in no other country had the private citizen become so completely out of touch with public affairs and so unused to studying the course of events, so much so that not only had the average Frenchman no experience of "popular movements" but he hardly understood what "the people" meant. Bearing this in mind, we may find it easier to understand why the nation as a whole could launch out into a sanguinary revolution, with those very men who stood to lose most by it taking the lead and clearing the ground for it.

Since no free institutions and, as a result, no experienced and organised political parties existed any longer in France, and since in the absence of any political groups of this sort the guidance of public opinion, when its first stirrings made themselves felt, came entirely into the hands of the philosophers, that is to say the intellectuals, it was only to be expected that the directives of the Revolution should take the form of abstract principles, highly generalised theories, and that political realities would be largely overlooked. Thus, instead of attacking only such laws as seemed objectionable, the idea developed that *all* laws indiscriminately must be abolished and a wholly new system of government, sponsored by these writers, should replace the ancient French constitution.

Moreover, since the Church was so closely bound up with the ancient institutions now to be swept away, it was inevitable that the Revolution, in overthrowing the civil power, should assail the established religion. As a result, the leaders of the movement, shaking off the controls that religion, law, and custom once had exercised, gave free rein to their imagination and indulged in acts of an outrageousness that took the whole world by surprise. Nevertheless, anyone who had closely studied the condition of the country at the time might well have guessed that there was no enormity, no form of violence from which these men would shrink.

In one of his eloquent pamphlets Burke made no secret of his consternation. What particularly surprised him was there was no one anywhere who could stand surety for the smallest group of his fellow citizens or even for a single man, the consequence being that anyone could be arrested in his home without protest or redress, whether the offence alleged against him were royalism, "moderatism", or any other political deviation.

Burke failed to realise how things were in the kingdom which the monarchy (whose downfall he deplored) had bequeathed to its new masters. Under the old order the government had long since deprived Frenchmen of the possibility, and even the desire, of coming to each other's aid. When the Revolution started, it would have been impossible to find, in most parts of France, even ten men used to acting in concert and defending their interests without appealing to the central power for aid. Thus once that central power had passed from the hands of the royal administration into those of irresponsible sovereign assemblies and a benevolent government had given place to a ruthless one, the latter found nothing to impede it or hold up its activities even momentarily. The same conditions which had precipitated the fall of the monarchy made for the absolutism of its successor.

Never had religious tolerance, the lenient use of power and kindness towards one's neighbour been preached so earnestly and, to all appearances, so generally practised as in the eighteenth century. Even the rules of war, last resort of the will to violence, had been humanised. Yet it was in this humanitarian climate that the most inhuman of revolutions took its rise. Nor must it be thought that these amiable sentiments were merely feigned; once the Revolution had run its headlong course, these same feelings came to the fore again and promptly made their presence felt not only in legislation but in all the doings of the new government.

This contrast between theory and practice, between good intentions and acts of savage violence, which was a salient feature of the French Revolution, becomes less startling when we remember that the Revolution, though sponsored by the most civilised classes of the nation, was carried out by its least educated and most unruly elements. For, since the members of the cultured elite had formed a habit of keeping to themselves, were unused to acting together, and had no hold on the masses, the latter became masters of the situation almost from the start. Even where the people did not govern *de facto* and directly, they set the tone of the administration. And in view of the conditions in which these men had been living under the old order, it was almost a foregone conclusion how they now would act.

Actually it was to these very conditions that our peasantry owed some of their outstanding qualities. Long enfranchised and owning some of the land he worked, the French peasant was largely independent and had developed a healthy pride and much common sense. Inured to hardships, he was indifferent to the amenities of life, intrepid in the face of danger, and faced misfortune stoically. It was from this simple, virile race of men that those great armies were raised which were to dominate for many years the European scene. But their very virtues made them dangerous masters. During the many centuries in which these men had borne the brunt of nation-wide misgovernment and lived as a class apart, they had nursed in secret their grievances, jealousies, and rancours and, having learned toughness in a hard school, had become capable of enduring or inflicting the very worst.

It was in this mood that gripping the reins of power, the French people undertook the task of seeing the Revolution through. Books had supplied them with the necessary theories, and they now put these into practice, adjusting the writers' ideas to their lust for revenge.

Readers of this book who have followed carefully my description of eighteenth-century France will have noticed the steady growth amongst the people of two ruling passions, not always simultaneous or having the same objectives. One of these, the more deeply rooted and long-standing, was an intense, indomitable hatred of inequality. This inequality forced itself on their attention, they saw signs of it at every turn; thus it is easy to understand why the French had for so many centuries felt a desire, inveterate and uncontrollable, utterly to destroy all such institutions as had survived from the Middle Ages and, having cleared the ground, to build up a new society in which men were as much alike and their status as equal as was possible, allowing for the innate differences between individuals. The other ruling passion, more recent and less deeply rooted, was a desire to live not only on an equal footing but also as free men.

Towards the end of the old order these two passions were equally sincerely felt and seemed equally operative. When the Revolution started, they came in contact, joined forces, coalesced, and reinforced each other, fanning the revolutionary ardour of the nation to a blaze. This was in '89, that rapturous year of bright enthusiasm, heroic courage, lofty ideals—untempered, we must grant, by the reality of experience: a historic date of glorious memory to which the thoughts of men will turn with admiration and respect long after those who witnessed its achievement, and we ourselves, have passed away. At the time the French had such proud confidence in the cause they were defending, and in themselves, that they believed they could reconcile freedom with equality and interspersed democratic institutions everywhere with free institutions. Not only did they shatter that ancient system under which men were divided into classes, corporations, and castes, and their rights were even more unequal than their social situations, but by the same token they did away with all the more recent legislation, instituted by the monarchy, whose effect was to put every Frenchman under official surveillance, with the government as his mentor, overseer, and, on occasion, his oppressor. Thus centralisation shared the fate of absolute government.

But when the virile generation which had launched the Revolution had perished or (as usually befalls a generation engaging in such ventures) its first fine energy had dwindled;

and when, as was but to be expected after a spell of anarchy and "popular" dictatorship, the ideal of freedom had lost much of its appeal and the nation, at a loss where to turn, began to cast round for a master—under these conditions the stage was set for a return to one-man government. Indeed, never had conditions been more favourable for its establishment and consolidation, and the man of genius destined at once to carry on and to abolish the Revolution was quick to turn them to account.

Actually there had existed under the old order a host of institutions which had quite a "modern" air and, not being incompatible with equality, could easily be embodied in the new social order—and all these institutions offered remarkable facilities to despotism. They were hunted for among the wreckage of the old order and duly salvaged. These institutions had formerly given rise to customs, usages, ideas, and prejudices tending to keep men apart, and thus make them easier to rule. They were revived and skilfully exploited; centralisation was built up anew, and in the process all that had once kept it within bounds was carefully eliminated. Thus there arose, within a nation that had but recently laid low its monarchy, a central authority with powers wider, stricter, and more absolute than those which any French King had ever wielded. Rash though this venture may have been, it was carried through with entire success for the good reason that people took into account only what was under their eyes and forgot what they had seen before. Napoleon fell but the more solid parts of his achievement lasted on; his government died, but his administration survived, and every time that an attempt is made to do away with absolutism the most that could be done has been to graft the head of Liberty onto a servile body.

On several occasions during the period extending from the outbreak of the Revolution up to our time we find the desire for freedom reviving, succumbing, then returning, only to die out once more and presently blaze up again. This presumably will be the lot for many years to come of a passion so undisciplined and untutored by experience; so easily discouraged, cowed and vanquished, so superficial and short-lived. Yet during this same period the passion for equality, first to entrench itself in the hearts of Frenchmen, has never given ground; for it links up with feelings basic to our very nature. For while the urge to freedom is forever assuming new forms, losing or gaining strength according to the march of events, our love of equality is constant and pursues the object of its desire with a zeal that is obstinate and often blind, ready to make every concession to those who give it satisfaction. Hence the fact that the French nation is prepared to tolerate in a government that favours and flatters its desire for equality practices and principles that are, in fact, the tools of despotism.

To those who study it as an isolated phenomenon the French Revolution can but seem a dark and sinister enigma; only when we view it in the light of the events preceding it can we grasp its true significance. And, similarly, without a clear idea of the old order, its laws, its vices, its prejudices, its shortcomings, and its greatness, it is impossible to comprehend the history of the sixty years following its fall. Yet even this is not enough; we need also to understand and bear in mind the peculiarities of the French temperament.

When I observe France from this angle I find the nation itself far more remarkable than any of the events in its long history. It hardly seems possible that there can ever have existed any other people so full of contrasts and so extreme in all their doings, so much guided by their emotions and so little by fixed principles, always behaving better, or worse, than one expected of them. At one time they rank above, at another below, the norm of humanity; their basic characteristics are so constant that we can recognise the France we know in portraits made of it two or three thousand years ago, and yet so changeful are its moods, so variable its tastes that the nation itself is often quite as much startled as any foreigner at the things it did only a few years before. Ordinarily the French are the most routine-bound of men, but once they are forced out of the rut and leave their homes, they travel to the ends of the earth and engage in the most reckless ventures. Undisciplined by temperament, the Frenchman is always readier to put up with the arbitrary rule, however harsh, of an autocrat than with a free, well-ordered government by his fellow citizens, however worthy of respect they be. At one moment he is up in arms against authority and the next we find him serving the powers-that-be with a zeal such as the most servile races never display. So long as no one thinks of resisting, you can lead him on a thread, but once a revolutionary movement is afoot, nothing can restrain him from taking part in it. That is why our rulers are so often taken by surprise; they fear the nation either too much or not enough, for though it is never so free that the possibility of enslaving it is ruled out, its spirit can never be broken so completely as to prevent its shaking off the yoke of an oppressive government. The Frenchman can turn his hand to anything, but he excels in war alone and he prefers fighting against odds, preferring dazzling feats of arms and spectacular successes to achievements of the more solid kind. He is more prone to heroism than to humdrum virtue, apter for genius than for good sense, more inclined to think up grandiose schemes than to carry through great enterprises. Thus the French are at once the most brilliant and the most dangerous of all European nations, and the best qualified to become, in the eyes of other peoples, an object of admiration, of hatred, of compassion, or alarm—never of indifference.

France alone could have given birth to revolution so sudden, so frantic, and so thoroughgoing, yet so full of unexpected changes of direction, of anomalies and inconsistencies. But for the antecedent circumstances described in this book, the French would never have embarked on it; yet we must recognise that though their effect was cumulative and overwhelming, they would not have sufficed to lead to such a drastic revolution elsewhere than in France.

Thus I have brought my readers to the threshold of this memorable revolution; for the present I shall halt at this point, though I may perhaps go further in a subsequent work and study not its causes but the French Revolution itself and endeavour to appraise the new social order which issued from it.

# APPENDIX

## *The* pays d'états, *with special reference to Languedoc*

It is not my purpose here to give a detailed account of the conditions prevailing in each of the various *pays d'états* which
were still in existence at the time of the Revolution. I merely
wish to state their number, to draw attention to those which
had kept their "local colour", to show what were their relations
with the central administration, that is to say how far they
diverged from the governmental pattern obtaining in the rest
of France and how far they conformed to it, and finally, taking
one as an example, to suggest the lines on which all *pays
d'états* might well have developed under favourable conditions.

In early days there had been "Estates" (*états*) in most
French provinces; in other words, these provinces had been
administered (under the royal government) by the "Men of
the Three Estates"—*les gens des trois états*—as they were called:
an assembly composed of representatives of the clergy, nobility,
and commons. Like so many medieval institutions this form of
provincial government was once to be found in almost all the
civilised parts of Europe; anyhow, all those in which Germanic
ideas and customs had taken root. In many German provinces
the Estates survived up to the time of the French Revolution,
and even where they then no longer existed had lasted on as
late as the seventeenth and eighteenth centuries. For two centuries Kings and Princes everywhere in Europe had been attacking them, sometimes openly, sometimes indirectly, always with
persistence. It never occurred to them to try to improve the
working of this institution or to modernise it; their one idea
was to suppress it altogether or, failing that, to whittle down
its powers whenever an opportunity arose.

In 1789 Estates survived only in five fairly large provinces
of France and in some small, unimportant districts. True provincial self-government, however, existed only in two provinces, Brittany and Languedoc. Elsewhere the Estates had become
mere shadows of their former selves, ineffectual and inert.

I propose to examine in some detail the system of free government prevailing in Languedoc, largest and most thickly populated of all our *pays d'états*.

Languedoc contained over two thousand townships or, as they then were called, "communities", and had a population of more than two millions. Moreover, besides being the largest of all the *pays d'états*, it was by far the best organised and most prosperous. Thus it provides the best illustration of the nature of provincial self-government under the old order and of the extent to which, even in those parts of France where it seemed most to flourish, it had become subordinated to the royal power.

In Languedoc the Estates could meet only under express orders from the King and a writ of summons was addressed by him to each of the persons who were to sit in the assembly. Hence the ironical remark of a contemporary malcontent: "Of the three bodies composing our Estates, one, the clergy, is beholden to the King since it is he who bestows bishoprics and benefices; the other two are in much the same position since the Court can prevent any member of whom it disapproves from attending. So there is no need to persecute or exile undesirables; all that is needed is not to convoke them."

The King not only fixed the opening date of each session but also that of its termination. Under an Order in Council the normal duration was fixed at forty days. The King was represented in the assembly by commissioners, who were always given admission to its sittings when they so desired and whose function it was to make known to the assembly in session the wishes of the government. Moreover, the Estates were under strict control. They could not pass a resolution of any importance or enact any measure touching on finance without authorisation from the Council. When a tax, a loan, or a lawsuit was in question, express permission from the King was needed. None of their rules of procedure, even those relating to the conduct of their sessions, could come into force unless and until they had been sanctioned by the central power. The balance sheet of receipts and expenditure (their budget, as we would call it today) had likewise to be "passed" by it each year.

Furthermore, the Royal Council exercised in Languedoc the

same political rights as those it exercised in other parts of France; the laws it enacted and the "general regulations" it was constantly issuing applied to Languedoc no less than to the *pays d'élection*. All normal activities of government were carried on by the central power; it had the same representatives, the same police force in Languedoc as elsewhere. What was more, it created from time to time new official posts which this province, like the others, was forced to repurchase at considerable expense.

Like the other provinces, again, Languedoc was governed by an Intendant who had sub-delegates in each district, their function being to keep in contact with the local authorities and to supervise their activities. In short, the Intendant kept quite as firm a hold on Languedoc as on any *pays d'élection*. The smallest hamlet in the backwoods of the Cévennes could not embark on any expenditure, however trifling, without an authorisation of the Royal Council. That special category of civil suits known today as *le contentieux administratif*, i.e. suits to which the government is a party, covered as wide a field in Languedoc as in the rest of France; indeed, its scope was wider. Cases relating to public highways were decided by the Intendant sitting as a court of first instance; he tried all suits concerning the roads and, generally speaking, gave decisions in all proceedings in which the government was, or thought itself, involved. Moreover, the representatives of the government were no less immune in Languedoc than elsewhere from prosecutions instituted by private parties who, rightly or wrongly, claimed to have been unjustly treated by them.

This being so, what was it that differentiated Languedoc from other provinces and led them to envy its lot? There were three respects in which its administration differed totally from that of other parts of France.

Firstly, Languedoc possessed an assembly composed of men of substance, which was looked up to by the people and respected by the royal power, and of which no official employed by the central government, none of the "King's men" in the parlance of the day, could be a member. In the assembly all matters specially concerning the province were freely and conscientiously debated, and such was the prestige of this enlightened body of men that the royal administration exercised its privileges discreetly and, though employing the same representatives and being guided by the same principles, behaved quite otherwise in Languedoc than in other provinces.

Secondly, there was the fact that though a good many public works in Languedoc were paid for by the King, through his representatives, while for some others the central government provided a portion of the cost and supervised to a large extent their execution, the majority were carried out and paid for by the province alone. Once the King had signified his approval of the plans and the proposed expenditure, these works were put through by officials nominated by the Estates and under the supervision of delegates chosen among the members of the assembly.

. Finally, the province had the right of levying on its own initiative and in the manner it thought fit some of the royal taxes as well as all the taxes it was entitled to impose for its own requirements.

The way in which the province of Languedoc turned these privileges to account is rich in interest for every student of French history.

What strikes him most when he examines the fiscal procedures in a *pays d'élection* is the fact that there were few, if any, local taxes. The imposts levied by the government were often exorbitant, but the province spent next to nothing on itself. In Languedoc, on the other hand, the sums expended on works of public utility were very large; by 1780 they amounted to over two million *livres* per annum.

The central government sometimes demurred at the amount of money thus expended, fearing that the province, drained of its resources, would be unable to contribute its quota to the national revenue. I have read a statement made by the assembly in reply to the charge of "extravagance", and some extracts from this document will reveal better than any general description the spirit by which this small, self-contained government was animated.

The signatories begin by frankly admitting that the province had engaged in and was still carrying out large-scale public works; but, far from seeking to exonerate themselves, they declared that (unless the King should veto this) they proposed to carry on with, and even to enlarge, their programme. They pointed out that the beds of the chief rivers running through the province had been deepened or straightened out, and that they were now making extensions to the old Languedoc canal constructed in the reign of Louis XIV and quite inadequate for present-day requirements, with a view to linking the canal, by way of Cette and Agde, with the Rhone. Moreover, the port of Cette had now been opened up to sea-borne commerce and was being maintained in good order at considerable expense. These undertakings, they insisted, were of national rather than provincial interest; nevertheless, the province of Languedoc, which stood to gain most by them, would foot the bill. They were also engaged in draining the Aiguesmortes marshes, with a view to rendering the land suitable for cultivation. But it was on road improvement that they had concentrated especially, and they had cleared or reconditioned all the highways traversing the province and communicating with the rest of the kingdom. Local roads, too, between towns and villages had been repaired. All these were now in excellent condition and kept open even in the depths of winter; they were, in fact, infinitely superior to the rugged, ill-kept roads in the neighbouring provinces of Dauphiné, Quercy, and the Bordeaux *généralité* (all three *pays d'élection,* be it noted). The favourable opinions of businessmen and travellers were quoted—opinions endorsed ten years later by Arthur Young, who noted under the heading, *Languedoc, pays d'états,* "good roads, made without forced labour."

"Subject to His Majesty's approval," the memorandum continues, "the Estates will develop their programme of public works still further and improve the roads inside villages, which are no less important than the highways. For it is quite as desirable that the farmer should be able to take his merchandise from his barns to the village market as that he should be able to cart it to distant places. As regards public works, our criterion has always been that these should be useful rather than grandiose. Rivers, canals, and roads add value to all the produce of the soil and of industry since they facilitate its transport, at all seasons and at little cost, to places where these goods are wanted, and thanks to them all parts of the province are accessible to trade and commerce. Thus public works of this kind are good investments, whatever be their cost. Moreover, such works, if judiciously distributed throughout the province, keep up the wage level and benefit the poorer classes. Thus the King has no need to set up 'charity workshops' in Languedoc as he has done in the rest of France." And the memorialists conclude with justifiable pride: "We do not ask for favours of that order; the works of public utility we take in hand each year provide full and fructuous employment for everyone, so we can dispense with charity."

The more I studied the rules and regulations issued by the Estates of Languedoc with the King's permission (but seldom on his initiative) as regards such departments of the public administration as were left under their control, the more did I admire their wisdom, equity, and, indeed, benevolence; and the more superior did I find the methods of this local government to those prevailing in districts administered by the King exclusively.

The province was divided into "communities" (townships and villages), into administrative districts known as "dioceses", and finally, into three large areas named "*sénéchaussées*". Each of these divisions and subdivisions had its own representatives and a small governing body that functioned under the supervision of either the Estates or the King. When there was any question of public works in which the local interests of one of the small political units were involved, they were undertaken only at its request. If, however, it appeared that these undertakings might be of benefit to the large unit, the "diocese", the latter was called on to bear a portion of the expense. And when the *sénéchaussée* was an interested party, it had likewise to contribute. Finally the "diocese", the *sénéchaussée*, and the province as a whole were expected to come to the financial aid of a village whenever public works beyond its means were deemed necessary, though it was only the village itself that benefited by them. This was in accordance with the declared policy of the Estates. "Basic to our constitution is the principle that Languedoc forms an organic whole and each part of the province must co-operate for the general good."

The plans for public works to be carried out by the province were drawn up well in advance so that all the local administrative bodies expected to take part could study them at leisure. Only paid workers were employed; forced labour did not exist in Languedoc. I have already mentioned that in the *pays d'élection* land acquired from private owners for public purposes was paid for meagrely and belatedly; sometimes not at all. This was one of the chief grievances voiced by the provincial assemblies when they met in 1787. Some of them pointed out that since the value of the property acquired was often assessed after it had been damaged or completely ruined, they were unable to pay the sums that should properly have accrued to the original owners. In Languedoc, however, it was the rule that the value of each piece of land thus requisitioned was determined *before* work started on it, and that its owner received payment during the first year's operations.

The merits of the system adopted by the Estates of Languedoc as regards public works were not unnoticed by the central government, but it did not follow their example. After sanctioning the regulations drawn up by the Estates, the Royal Council had them printed at the King's press and directed that copies should be circulated to all Intendants "for reference and guidance".

What has been said above regarding public works applies even more strongly to that other equally important branch of the administration, the collection of taxes. It is above all in this respect that on moving from the kingdom to the provinces of Languedoc one can hardly believe that one is still in the same country. The subject has already been fully discussed and I confine myself here to mentioning that the Estates of Languedoc were so convinced of the superiority of their methods that whenever the King instituted new taxes, they never hesitated about purchasing, however much it cost, the right to levy them in their own manner and through their own officials.

Despite a heavy outlay on public services, Languedoc was so efficiently administered, so prosperous, and its credit so well assured that the central government often had recourse to it and borrowed under its name sums of money that could not have been raised on such good terms. Thus in the period immediately preceding the Revolution the province took out loans of no less than 73,200,000 *livres* nominally for itself but entirely on the King's behalf.

The government and its Ministers, however, looked with much disfavour on the exceptional freedom enjoyed by Languedoc; Richelieu began by truncating it and finally abolished it altogether. That indolent, morose, and ineffectual monarch, Louis XIII, so keenly resented the privileges accorded to certain provinces (so Boulainvilliers tells us) that he flew into a rage when he heard them mentioned. We often fail to realise what energy a weakling can develop in his hatred of anything calling for an effort on his part; such little virility as he possesses is canalised, as it were, into a display of strength on these occasions, however feeble he may prove himself on others. Happily Languedoc regained its ancient constitution during the minority of Louis XIV, who, regarding it as his own work, let it stand. And after suspending it for two years, Louis XV allowed it to be restored.

The creation of municipal offices staffed by governmental nominees exposed the province to dangers less direct but no less great. It was not only the local autonomy of towns that was wiped out by this obnoxious practice, it tended to undermine that of the provincial government as well. I do not know if representatives of the Third Estate in the provincial assemblies had ever been elected in this capacity; one thing is certain, that for a long time past they had not been so elected and municipal officials were the only representatives *de jure* of the middle and lower classes in the assemblies. This lack of a precise mandate given for a special purpose attracted little attention so long as the towns elected their officials freely, all citizens being entitled to cast their votes and the officials thus elected holding their posts for only a very limited period. For under these circumstances mayors, town councillors, and Syndics spoke in the name of the people and represented its interests no less effectively than if they had been elected by it expressly with that object. But for obvious reasons this ceased to be the case with a man who had obtained by purchase the right to administer the affairs of his fellow citizens, townsmen, or villagers. Such a person represented nobody but himself or, at best, the interests and ambitions of a clique. Nevertheless, the man who had bought his post had exactly the same powers as the man who in the past had been elected to it. The result was a drastic change in the whole nature of the provincial assemblies. The nobility and clergy no longer sat with, and had to reckon with, representatives of the people. The new men were self-regarding members of the middle class who, lacking both cohesion and authority, played for safety. Thus at the very time when the Third Estate was rapidly growing wealthier and becoming more and more a power in the land, it was relegated to an ever more subordinate role in the administration. In Languedoc, however, this was not the case, since whenever new posts were created, the province made a point of buying them in, no matter what the cost. In the one year 1773 the province contracted loans of over four million *livres* for this purpose.

But there were other respects in which the Estates of Languedoc could claim to be more progressive than any others and readier to infuse into those venerable institutions, the provincial assemblies, something of the new spirit of the age. Here, as in most of the South of France, the *taille* was "real", not "personal"; that is to say a man was taxed on the value of his land, not on his income. True, some private estates still carried with them immunity from such taxation. They had originally belonged to members of the nobility but subsequently, with the rapid advance of industry and the rise of a new-rich class, had passed into the hands of commoners. On the other hand, many estates subject to the *taille* had been acquired by noblemen. The transfer of privilege from persons to property, irrational though it might seem, had something to commend it, since it led to less ill-feeling; while still equally offensive to those who did not gain by it, it was not humiliating, as the old system had been. Since it did not involve any idea of class distinction or cause the interests of one section of the population to clash with another's, it no longer hindered the co-operation of all citizens in the management of public affairs. And more in Languedoc than in any other part of France the various classes did, in fact, co-operate on a footing of real equality.

In Brittany the nobles had the right of attending en masse the meetings of the Estates—a circumstance which often gave these assemblies the peculiar appearance we associate with the Polish "diets". In Languedoc, however, all the nobles did not attend in person; only twenty-three of them sat in the assembly, as representatives of their Order. Similarly the clergy were represented by twenty-three bishops of the province and—a notable point—the towns had as many votes as the two senior Orders.

Since the assembly functioned as a single chamber and debates were not conducted as between representatives of parties but as between individuals, the Third Estate came to play an important part and gradually impregnated the whole body with its very special ideology. Moreover, the executive officers who under the name of Syndics-General managed current affairs on behalf of the Estates were always lawyers, that is to say commoners. Though they still could count on being treated with due deference, the nobles were no longer strong enough to keep the reins of power in their hands alone. The clergy, on the other hand, though in many cases men of noble birth, were on excellent terms with the representatives of the Third Estate, warmly supported most of their projects, and joined forces with them in their attempts to better the living conditions of the poorer classes and to encourage trade and industry. Thus they often put their wide knowledge of human nature and their exceptional skill in handling difficult situations at the disposal of the people. It was usually a member of the clergy whom the assembly deputed to negotiate with the Minister of State at Versailles when differences of opinion arose between it and the central power. In short, it may be said that during the eighteenth century Languedoc was administered by commoners assisted by the bishops and supervised by the nobility.

Owing to the special characteristics of the constitution of Languedoc, as described above, it could adjust itself without any difficulty to the new spirit of the age, which, while modifying everything, destroyed nothing in that ancient institution. The same thing might have happened in the rest of France had our Kings devoted even a tithe of the energy and obstinacy they displayed in their efforts to weaken or destroy the provincial Estates to improving them on the lines of Languedoc and adapting them to modern needs. Unhappily our Kings' one desire was to keep power in their own hands at all costs and they turned a blind eye to the needs of modern civilisation.

# NOTES

1 (page 45) *Influence of the Roman law in Germany—how it had replaced the Germanic law*

At the close of the Middle Ages the Roman law became the chief and almost the only study of the German lawyers, most of whom, at this time, were educated abroad at the Italian universities. These lawyers exercised no political power, but it devolved on them to expound and apply the laws. They were unable to abolish the Germanic law, but they did their best to distort it so as to fit the Roman mould. To every German institution that seemed to bear the most distant analogy to Justinian's legislation they applied Roman law. Hence a new spirit and new customs gradually invaded the national legislation, until its original shape was lost, and by the seventeenth century it was almost forgotten. Its place had been usurped by a medley that was Germanic in name, but Roman in fact.

I have reason to believe that this innovation of the lawyers had a tendency to aggravate the condition of more than one class of Germans, the peasantry especially. Persons who had up to that time succeeded in preserving the whole or a part of their liberty or their property, were ingeniously assimilated to the slaves or emphyteutic tenants of the Roman law, and lost rights and possessions together.

This gradual transformation of the national law, and the efforts which were made to prevent its accomplishment, were plainly seen in the history of Wurtemberg.

From the rise of the county of this name in 1250 to the creation of the duchy in 1495, the whole legislation of Wurtemberg was indigenous in character. It consisted of customs, local city laws, ordinances of seigneurial courts, or statutes of the Estates. Ecclesiastical affairs alone were regulated by foreign, that is to say, by canon law.

But from the year 1495 a change took place. Roman law began to penetrate the legislations of the duchy. The *doctors*, as they were called—that is to say, the individuals who had studied at foreign schools—connected themselves with the government, and took the management of the high courts. From the commencement to the middle of the fifteenth century, a struggle between them and the politicians of the day was carried on, similar in character, though different in result from the struggle that took place in England at the very same time. At the Diet of Tubingen in 1514 and the following Diets, the lawyers were attacked violently by the representatives of feudal institutions and the city deputies; they were loudly charged with invading all the courts of justice, and altering the spirit or the letter of all the laws and customs. At first, victory seemed to rest with the assailants. They obtained of the government a promise that honourable and enlightened persons, chosen from the nobility and the Estates of the duchy—not doctors—should be set over the higher courts, and that a commission, consisting of government agents and representatives of the Estates, should be appointed to draft a bill for a code to have force throughout the country. Useless effort! The Roman law soon expelled the national law from a large section of the legislative sphere, and even planted its roots in the section where the latter was allowed to subsist.

German historians ascribe this triumph of foreign over domestic law to two causes: first, the attraction exercised over the public mind by ancient literature, which necessarily led to a contempt for the intellectual products of the national genius; and, secondly, the idea—with which the Germans of the Middle Ages, and even their laws, were imbued—that the Holy Empire was a continuation of the Roman Empire, and hence that the legislation of the latter was an heirloom of the former.

These causes do not suffice to explain the simultaneous introduction of Roman law into every Continental country. I think that the singular availability of the Roman law—which was a slave-law—for the purposes of monarchs, who were just then establishing their absolute power upon the ruins of the old liberties of Europe, was the true cause of the phenomenon.

The Roman law carried civil society to perfection, but it invariably degraded political society, because it was the work of a highly civilised and thoroughly enslaved people. Kings naturally embraced it with enthusiasm, and established it wher-

ever they could throughout Europe; its interpreters became
their Ministers or their chief agents. Lawyers furnished them
at need with legal warrant for violating the law. They have
often done so since. Monarchs who have trampled the laws
have almost always found a lawyer ready to prove the lawful-
ness of their acts—to establish learnedly that violence was just,
and that the oppressed were in the wrong.

2 (page 47)  *Transition from feudal to democratic monarchy*

As all European monarchies became absolute about the same
time, it is not probable that the constitutional change was due
to accidental circumstances which occurred simultaneously in
every country. The natural supposition is that the general
change was the fruit of a general cause operating on every country
at the same moment.

That general cause was the transition from one social state
to another, from feudal inequality to democratic equality. The
nobility was prostrate; the people had not yet risen up; the one
was too low, the other not high enough to embarrass the movements of the supreme power. For a period of a hundred and fifty
years Kings enjoyed a golden age. They were all-powerful, and
their thrones were stable, advantages usually inconsistent with
each other. They were as sacred as the hereditary chiefs of a
feudal monarchy, and as absolute as the masters of a democracy.

3 (page 47)  *Decline of free German cities—imperial cities*
(Reichstadten)

According to the German historians, these cities reached their
highest point of prosperity during the fourteenth and fifteenth
centuries. They were then the refuge of the wealth, of the arts,
of the learning of Europe, the mistress of commerce, and the
centre of civilisation. They ended, especially in northern and
southern Germany, by forming, with the surrounding nobility,
independent confederations, as the Swiss cities had done with
the peasantry.

They were still prosperous in the sixteenth century; but their
decline had begun. The Thirty Years' War hastened their downfall; they were nearly all destroyed or ruined during that period.
The Treaty of Westphalia, however, made special mention of

them, and maintained their condition as "immediate states", that is to say, communities independent of all control but the Emperor. But neighbouring monarchs on one side, and on the other the Emperor himself, whose power, after the Thirty Years' War, was nearly confined in its exercise to these small vassals of the Empire, constantly encroached on their sovereignity. They still numbered fifty-one in the eighteenth century. They occupied two benches at the Diet, and had a separate vote. But, practically, their influence over the direction of public affairs was gone.

At home they were overloaded with debts, chiefly arising from the fact that they were still taxed in proportion to their past splendour, and also, in some degree, from their defective administration. It is not a little remarkable that this maladministration appeared to flow from some secret disease that was common to all of them, whatever their constitution happened to be. Aristocratic and democratic forms of government provoked equal discontent. Aristocracies were said to be mere family coteries, in which favour and private interest controlled the government. Democracies were said to be under the sway of intrigue and corruption. Both forms of government were accused of dishonesty and profligacy. The Emperor was constantly obliged to interfere in their affairs to restore order. Their population was falling off, their wealth vanishing. They were no longer the centres of German civilisation; the arts had fled from them to take refuge in new cities created by Kings, and representing the modern era. Trade had deserted them. Their former energy, their patriotic vigour, had disappeared. Hamburg alone continued to be a great centre of wealth and learning; but this flowed from causes peculiar to itself.

(page 52)  *Date of the abolition of serfdom in Germany*
It will be seen from the following table that serfdom has only been very recently abolished in the greater part of Germany. Serfdom was abolished:

1. In Baden not till 1783;
2. In Hohenzollern in 1789;
3. Schleswig and Holstein in 1804;
4. Nassau in 1808;

5. Prussia. Frederick William I abolished serfdom in his domains in 1717. The code of Frederick the Great, as has been observed, pretended to abolish it throughout the kingdom, but in reality it only abolished its hardest form, *leibeigenschaft*; it preserved the milder form, called *erbunterthänigkeit*. It did not cease entirely till 1809.

6. In Bavaria serfdom disappeared in 1808.

7. A decree of Napoleon's, dated Madrid, 1808, abolished it in the Grand-duchy of Berg, and in several small territories, such as Erfurth, Baireuth, etc.

8. In the kingdom of Westphalia its destruction dates from 1808 and 1809.

9. In the principality of Lippe-Detmold from 1809.

10. In Schomberg-Lippe from 1810.

11. In Swedish Pomerania from 1810.

12. In Hesse-Darmstadt from 1809 and 1811.

13. In Wurtemberg from 1817.

14. In Mecklenburg from 1820 .

15. In Oldenburgh from 1814.

16. In Saxony for Lusatia from 1832.

17. In Hohenzollern-Sigmaringen from 1833 only.

18. In Austria from 1811. In 1782, Joseph II had abolished the *leibeigenschaft*; but serfdom in its mild form— *erbunterthänigkeit*—lasted till 1811.


5 (page 52)
A portion of Germany, such as Brandenburg, old Prussia, and Silesia, was originally peopled by the Slavic race, and was conquered and partly occupied by Germans. In those countries serfdom was always much harsher than in the rest of Germany, and left much plainer traces at the close of the eighteenth century.


6 (page 53)   *Code of Frederick the Great*
Of all the works of Frederick the Great, the least known, even in his own country, and the least brilliant, is the code drawn up by his orders, and promulgated by his successor. Yet I doubt whether any of his other works throws as much light on the mind of the man or on the times in which he lived, or shows

as plainly the influence which they exercised one upon the other.

This code was a real constitution in the ordinary sense of the word. It regulated not only the mutual relations of citizens, but also their relations to the State. It was a civil code, a criminal code, and a charter all in one.

It rests, or appears to rest, on a certain number of general principles, expressed in a highly philosophical and abstract form, and which bear a strong resemblance in many respects to those which are embodied in the Declaration of the Rights of Man in the Constitution of 1791.

It proclaims that the welfare of the commonwealth and of its inhabitants is the aim of society and the limit of law; that laws cannot restrain the freedom and the rights of the citizen save for public utility; that every member of the commonwealth ought to labour for the public good in proportion to his position and his means; that the rights of individuals ought to give way to those of the public.

It makes no allusion to any hereditary rights of the sovereign, nor to his family, nor even to any particular right as distinguished from that of the State. The royal power was already designated by no other name than that of the State.

On the other hand, it alludes to the rights of man, which are founded on the natural right of everyone to pursue his own happiness without treading on the rights of others. All acts not forbidden by natural law, or a positive state law, are allowable. Every citizen is entitled to claim the protection of the State for himself and his property, and may defend himself by using force if the State does not come to his defence.

These great principles established, the legislator, instead of evolving from them, as the constitution of 1791 did, the doctrine of popular sovereignty, and the organisation of a democratic government in a free society, turns sharp round and arrives at another conclusion, democratic enough, but not liberal. He considers the sovereign the sole representative of the State, and invests him with all the rights which he has stated belong to society. The sovereign does not figure in the code as the representative of God; he is the representative, the agent, the servant of society, as Frederick stated at full length in his works; but he is its sole representative, he wields its whole authority alone. The head of the State, on whom the duty of securing the public welfare—which is the sole object of society—devolves, is authorised to direct and regulate all the actions of individuals in this view.

Among the chief duties of this all-powerful agent of society, I find such as these mentioned: maintaining order and public safety at home, so that every citizen shall be guaranteed against violence; making peace and war; establishing all laws and police regulations; granting pardons; annulling criminal prosecutions.

Every association in the country, and every public establishment, is subject to his inspection and superintendence in the interest of the general peace and security. In order that the head of the State may be able to perform his duties, he must have certain revenues and lucrative rights; hence he is allowed to tax private fortunes, persons, professions, commerce, industry, articles of consumption. Public functionaries acting in his name must be obeyed as he is in all matters within the scope of their duties.

Under this very modern head we shall now see a thoroughly Gothic body placed. Frederick has taken away nothing but what might impede the action of his own power, and the whole will form a monstrous thing, which looks like a compromise between two creations. In this strange production Frederick evinces as much contempt for logic as care for his own power, and anxiety not to create useless difficulties in attacking what was still capable of defence.

With the exception of a few districts and certain localities, the inhabitants of the rural districts are placed in a state of hereditary serfdom; not only is the land clogged with *corvées* and inherent services, but, as has been seen already, similar burdens attach to the persons of the peasants.

Most of the privileges of landholders are recognised anew by the code—or, it might be said, in contradiction to the code; for it is expressly stated that wherever the new legislation clashes with local customs, the latter must prevail. It is formally declared that the State cannot abolish any of these privileges except by purchase, according to the legal forms.

True, the code states that serfdom, properly so called

(*leibeigenschaft*), is abolished in so far as it interferes with personal liberty; but the hereditary subjection which takes its place (*erbunterthänigkeit*) is, after all, a species of serfdom, as the text shows.

According to the code, the burgher remains wholly distinct from the peasant. Between the noble and the burgher, an intermediate class, consisting of high functionaries who are not noble, ecclesiastics, and professors of learned schools, gymnasia, and universities, is placed.

Superior to the burghers, these personages were not to be confounded with the nobility, to whom they were clearly understood to be inferior. They could not purchase equestrian estates, or fill the highest posts in the civil service. Nor were they *hoffähig*; that is to say they could but rarely appear at Court, and never with their families. As was the case in France, these distinctions became more insulting in proportion to the increasing knowledge and influence of this class, which, though excluded from the most brilliant posts, filled all those where business of importance was transacted. The privileges of the nobility necessarily gave birth to irritation, which mainly contributed to cause the revolution here, and make it popular in Germany. The principal author of the code was a burgher, but no doubt he merely obeyed the instructions of his master.

The old constitution of Europe is not in such ruin in this part of Germany that Frederick thinks it safe to allow his contempt for it to lead him to destroy its relics. Generally speaking, he deprives the nobility of the right of assemblage and corporate action; leaving to each nobleman his privileges, he limits and regulates their use. Hence it happens that this code, drawn up by the orders of a disciple of one of our philosophers, and put in force after the outbreak of the French Revolution, is the most authentic and latest legislative document which gives a legal warrant for the feudal inequalities which the Revolution was about to abolish throughout Europe.

The nobility is declared to be the first body in the State. Men of rank, it states, are to be preferred to all others for posts of honour, if they are capable of filling them. None but they are to possess noble estates, create substitutions, enjoy rights of chase, justiciary rights inherent to noble estates, and rights of presentation to clerical livings; none but they can assume the name of their estates. Burghers, specially authorised to acquire noble estates, can only enjoy the rights and honours attached to such possessions within these limits. A burgher owning a noble estate cannot leave it to an heir burgher unless he be heir in the first degree. When there are no such heirs and no heirs noble, the property must be sold at auction.

One of the most characteristic portions of the Code of Frederick the Great is its criminal provision for political offences.

Frederick's successor, Frederick William II, who, notwith-standing the feudal and absolutist provisions above noted, fancied he detected revolutionary tendencies in this work of his uncle's, and refrained from promulgating it till 1794, was only reconciled to it by the excellent penal provisions which served to counteract its bad principles. Nor has there ever been anything since devised more complete of the kind. Not only are revolts and conspiracies punished with the greatest rigour, but disrespectful criticisms of government are repressed with equal severity. It is forbidden to purchase or to distribute dangerous writings; printer, publisher, and vendor are all responsible for the act of the author. Public balls and masquerades are declared to be public meetings, which cannot take place without the authority of the police. Similar rules govern dinners in public places. Liberty of the press and of speech are under close and arbitrary supervision. It is forbidden to carry fire-arms.

By the side of this work, which was more than half borrowed from the Middle Ages, are provisions whose spirit borders on socialism. Thus it is declared that it devolves on the State to provide food, work, and wages for all who cannot support themselves, and have no claim for support on the lord or the community; they must be provided with work suited to their strength and capacity. The State is bound to provide establishments for relieving the poor. It is authorised to abolish establishments which tend to encourage idleness, and to distribute personally to the poor the money by which these establishments were supported.

Boldness and novelty in point of theory, and timidity in practice characterise every portion of this work of Frederick the

Great. On the one side, that great principle of modern society
—that all are equally subject to taxes—is loudly proclaimed; on
another, provincial laws containing exemptions to this rule are
allowed to subsist. It is affirmed that all lawsuits between the
sovereign and the State must be tried in the same forms and
according to the same rules as all other cases; but, in fact, this
rule was never carried into effect when the interests or passions
of the King were opposed to it. The mill of St. Souci was osten-
tatiously shown to the people, and justice was quietly made
subject to royal convenience in other cases.

What proves that this code, which assumed to be such a
novelty, really made but few changes, and is therefore a curious
study of German society in this section of country at the close
of the eighteenth century, is that the Prussian nation hardly
noticed its publication. Lawyers were the only persons who
studied it; and even in our time there are many enlightened
men who have never read it.

7 (page 55)   *Property of the German peasants*

Many families among the peasantry were not only free and
landholders, their property constituted a species of perpetual
*majorat*. Their estate was indivisible, and passed by descent to
one of the sons—usually the youngest—as was the case in some
English customs. He was expected to endow his brothers and
sisters.

The *erbgütter* of the peasantry were spread more or less over
the whole of Germany, for the land was nowhere absorbed by
the feudal tenures. Even in Silesia, where the nobility owned
immense estates comprising most of the villages, other villages
were possessed by the inhabitants, and were wholly free. In certain parts of Germany, such as the Tyrol and Frisia, the rule
was that the peasantry owned the land by *erbgütter*.

But in the greater part of the German countries this kind of
property was an exception rarely met with. In the villages where
it occurred, landholders of this kind constituted a sort of aristocracy among the peasantry.

8 (page 55)   *Position of the nobility and division of land along the Rhine*

From information obtained on the spot, and from persons who lived under the old order, it appears that in the electorate of Cologne, for instance, there were a great number of villages without seigneurs, and governed by agents of the King; that in the places where the nobility lived, their administrative powers were very limited; that their position (individually at all events) was rather brilliant than powerful; that they possessed honours and offices, but no direct control over the people. I also ascertained that in the same electorate property was much divided, and that many of the peasants owned the land they occupied. The fact was ascribed to the poverty that had long oppressed many of the noble families, and obliged them to sell their estates to the peasants for an annual rent or a sum of money. I have had in my hands a schedule of the population and estates within the Bishopric of Cologne at the beginning of the eighteenth century: it indicated that, at that time, one third of the soil belonged to the peasantry. From this fact arose sentiments and ideas which predisposed these people to a far greater extent than the inhabitants of other parts of Germany to welcome a revolution.

9 (page 55)   *How the usury laws favoured subdivision of land*

At the close of the eighteenth century it was still illegal to lend money on interest, whatever was the rate charged. Turgot says that this law was observed in many places as late as 1769. These laws are still in force, says he, but they are often violated. Consular judges allow interest on loans, while the ordinary courts condemn the practice. Dishonest debtors still prosecute their creditors criminally for having lent money without alienating the capital.

Independently of the effects which such laws as these must have had on commerce, industry, and the morals of businessmen, they affected the division and tenure of lands to a very great extent. They caused an immense increase of perpetual rents, ground rents (*foncières*) as well as others. They compelled the old landowners, instead of borrowing in times of need, to sell small portions of their domains, partly for a given sum, partly for a rent; hence leading, first, to the infinite subdivision of estates, and, secondly, to the creation of a multitude of perpetual rents on their little properties.

10 (page 58) *Example of the irritation caused by tithes ten years before the Revolution*

In 1779, a petty lawyer of Lucé complains in a bitter and revolutionary tone that curés and other large titheholders are selling at exorbitant prices to farmers the straw which has been paid them by way of tithes, and which the farmers need for manure.

11 (page 58) *Example of the manner in which the privileges of the clergy alienated the affection of the people from them*

In 1780, the prior and canons of the priory of Laval complain of being made to pay duty on articles of consumption, and on the materials required for the repair of their buildings. They argue that the duty is an accessory of the *taille*, and that being exempt from the one, they ought not to be liable for the other. The Minister tells them to apply to the *election,* with recourse to the Court of Aides.

12 (page 59) *Feudal rights exercised by priests—one example out of a thousand*

The Abbey of Cherbourg, in 1753, possessed seigneurial rents, payable in money or produce, in almost all the villages in the neighbourhood of Cherbourg: one village alone paid 306 bushels of wheat. It owned the barony of Ste. Geneviève, the barony and seigneurial mill of Bas du Roule, and the barony of Neuville au Plein, at least ten leagues distant. It received, moreover, tithes from twelve parishes on the peninsula, some of which were at a great distance from the abbey.

13 (page 61) *Irritation among the peasantry proceeding from the feudal rights, especially those of the Church*

Letter written shortly before the Revolution by a peasant to the Intendant. It is no authority for the facts it states, but indicates admirably the state of feeling in the class to which the writer belonged:

"Though we have but few nobles in this part of the country," it says, "it must not be supposed that real estate is free from rents; on the contrary, nearly all the fiefs belong to the Cathedral, or the archbishopric, or the collegiate church of St. Martin, or the Benedictines of Noirmontiers, of St. Julien, or some other ecclesiastics, against whom no prescription runs, and who are constantly bringing to light old musty parchments whose date God only knows!

"The whole country is infected with rents. Most of the farm-lands pay every year a seventh of a bushel of wheat per acre, others wine; one pays the seigneur a fourth of all fruits, another a fifth, another a twelfth, another a thirteenth—the tithes being always paid on the gross. These rights are so singular that they vary from a fourth part of the produce to a fortieth.

"What must be thought of these rents in kind—in vegetables, money, poultry, labour, wood, fruit, candles? I am acquainted with rents which are paid in bread, in wax, in eggs, in head-less pigs, in rose shoulder-knots, in bouquets of violets, in golden spurs, etc.; and there are a host of seigneurial dues besides these. Why has France not been freed from all these extravagant rents? Men's eyes are at last being opened; one may hope everything from the wisdom of the present government. It will stretch a kindly hand to the poor victims of the exactions of the old fiscal system, called seigneurial rights, which could not be alienated or sold.

"What must be thought of this tyranny of *lods et ventes*? A purchaser exhausts his means in acquiring a property, and is obliged to pay besides in expenses to secure his title, contracts, actual entry, *procés-verbaux*, stamp, registry, *centième denier*, eight *sous* per *livre*; after which he must exhibit his title to his seigneur, who will exact the *lods et ventes* on the gross price of his purchase, now a twelfth, and now a tenth. Some claim a fifth, others a fifth and a twenty-fifth besides. All rates are demanded; I know some who charge a third of the price paid. No, the most ferocious and the most barbarous nations of the known world have never invented such or so many exactions as our tyrants heaped on the heads of our forefathers." (This literary and philosophical tirade is sadly defective in orthography.)

"What! the late King permitted the commutation of ground rents on city property, but excluded those on farms! He should have begun with the latter. Why not permit poor farmers to break their chains, to pay off and get rid of the hosts of seigneurial dues and ground rents, which are such an injury to the vassal and so small a gain to the seigneur? No distinction should have been made between town and country, seigneurs and private individuals.

"The stewards of the owners of ecclesiastical estates rob and plunder the farmers at every transfer. We have seen a recent example of the practice. The steward of our new archbishop gave notice to quit to all the farmers holding under leases from M. de Fleury, his predecessor, declared all their leases null and void, and turned out every man who refused to submit to his rent being doubled, and to pay a large bonus besides, though they had already paid a bonus to M. de Fleury's steward. They have thus been deprived of seven or eight years' holding, though their leases were executed in due form, and have been driven out upon the world on Christmas eve, the most critical period of the year, owing to the difficulty of feeding cattle. The King of Prussia could have done nothing worse."

It appears, in fact, that, with regard to Church property, leases granted by one titulary did not bind his successor. The writer of the letter states what is true when he says that feudal rents were redeemable in cities, but not in the country; a new proof of the neglect in which the peasantry lived, and of the manner in which all who were placed above them contrived to provide for their own interest.

## 14 (page 61)

Every institution that has long been dominant, after establishing itself in its natural sphere, extends itself, and ends by exercising a large influence over those branches of legislation which it does not govern. The feudal system, though essentially political, had transformed the civil law, and greatly modified the condition of persons and property in all the relations of private life. It had operated upon successions by creating unequal divisions of property—a principle carried out in certain provinces even among the middle classes (as witness Normandy). It had affected all real estate, for there were but few tracts of land that were wholly freed from its effects, or whose possessors felt none of the consequences of its laws. It affected the property of *communes* as well as that of individuals. It affected labour by the impositions it laid upon it. It affected incomes by the inequality of taxation, and, in general, the pecuniary interest of every man in every business: land-owners, by dues, rents, *corvées*; farmers in a thousand ways among others by rights of banality, ground rents, *lods et ventes,* etc.; traders, by market dues; merchants, by tolls, etc. In striking it down, the Revolution made itself perceived and felt at the same time at all points by every private interest.

15 (page 69)  *Public charities granted by the State—favouritism*

In 1748—a year of great famine and misery, such as often occurred in the eighteenth century—the King granted twenty thousand pounds of rice. The Archbishop of Tours claimed that he alone had obtained the gift, and that it ought to be distributed by him alone, and in his diocese. The Intendant argued that the gift was made to the whole province, and should be distributed by him to all the parishes. After a long contest, the King, to settle the quarrel, doubled the quantity of rice given to the province, so that the Archbishop and the Intendant might each distribute half. Both agreed that it ought to be distributed by the curés. No one thought of the seigneurs or the Syndics. It appears from the correspondence between the Intendant and the Controller-General that the former accused the Archbishop of wishing to give the rice to his favourites, and especially to the parishes which belonged to the Duchess of Rochechouart. The collection also contains letters from noblemen which demand aid for their parishes in particular, and letters from the Controller-General which make reference to the parishes of certain individuals.

Public charities are always liable to abuses under every system; but when distributed from a distance, without publicity, by the central government, they are actually futile.

16 (page 69)  *Example of the manner in which these public charities were distributed*

A report, made in 1780 to the Provincial Assembly of Upper Guienne, states, "Out of the sum of 385,000 *livres* which His Majesty has granted to this province from the year 1773, when workhouses were established, to the year 1779 inclusive, the *election* of Montauban, capital and place of residence of the Intendant, has alone had more than 240,000 *livres,* most of which has been spent in the *commune* of Montauban."

17 (page 70)  *Powers of the Intendant for the regulation of manufactures*

The archives of the Intendants' offices are full of papers which refer to the regulation of industrial enterprises by the Intendants.

Not only is labour subject to the inconvenience of trade-companies, guilds, etc., it is liable to be affected by every whim of government, that is to say of the Council in great matters, of the Intendants in small ones. The latter are constantly giving directions about the length of woofs, the kind of thread to use, the pattern to prefer, errors to avoid. Independently of the sub-delegates, they have local inspectors of manufactures under their orders. In this particular centralisation had gone farther than it now does; it was more capricious, more arbitrary; it created a swarm of public functionaries, and gave rise to general habits of submission and dependence.

Note also that these habits were imparted to the middle classes, merchants, and traders, who were about to triumph, to a far greater extent than to the classes that were on the point of defeat. Hence, instead of destroying, the Revolution tended to confirm and spread them.

The preceding remarks have been suggested by the perusal of a quantity of correspondence and documents taken from the Intendant's office of the Ile-de-France, and endorsed, "Manufactures and Fabrics", "Drapery", "Drugs". I have found in the same place reports from the inspectors to the Intendant giving full and detailed accounts of their visits of inspection to factories; moreover, various Orders in Council, passed on reports of the Intendant, prohibiting or permitting manufactures of certain stuffs, or in certain places, or in certain methods.

The dominant idea in the intercourse of these inspectors with the manufacturer—who, by the way, is treated very cavalierly—seems to be that their duty and the rights of the State compel them to see that the manufacturer not only acts fairly towards the public, but looks after his own interest. They consequently feel bound to make him adopt the best methods, and admonish him on the most trifling details of his business, larding the whole with a profusion of penalties and heavy fines.

18 (page 71)  *Spirit of the government of Louis XI*

Nothing indicates more clearly the spirit of the government of Louis XI than the constitutions he gave to towns. I have had occasion to study very closely those which he gave to most of the towns of Anjou, Maine, and Touraine.

All these constitutions are framed on the same plan, and all reveal the same designs. Louis XI appears in a new light in these charters. He is generally regarded as the enemy of the nobility, but the sincere though somewhat brutal friend of the people. They reveal him as a hater alike of the political rights of the people and of those of the nobility. He uses the middle-classes to lower the nobility and keep down the people: he is both anti-aristocratic and anti-democratic—the model of the *bourgeois* King. He loads town notables with privileges with the aim of increasing their importance, grants them titles of nobility in order to cheapen rank, and thus destroys the popular and democratic town governments, and places the whole authority in the hands of a few families, attached to his policy, and pledged to his support by every tie of gratitude.

19 (page 72)  *A city government in the eighteenth century*

I select from the Inquiry into City Governments, made in 1764, the papers which relate to Angers; they contain an analysis, attacks upon, and defences of the constitution of this city, emanating from the presidial, the city corporation, the sub-delegate, and the Intendant. As the same facts occurred in many other places, the picture must not be regarded as a solitary example.

*Memorial of the presidial on the present state of the municipal constitution of Angers, and on the reforms that it needs*

"The Corporation of Angers never consults the people at large even on the most important occasions, unless it is compelled to do so; hence its policy is unknown to everyone but its own members. Even the removable aldermen have only a superficial acquaintance with its mode of proceeding."

(The tendency of all these little *bourgeois* oligarchies was, in truth, to consult the people at large as little as possible.)

The corporation is composed of twenty-one officers, in virtue of a decree of 29th March, 1681, to wit:

A Mayor, who becomes noble *ex officio*, and whose term is four years;

Four removable aldermen, who hold office for two years;

Twelve consulting aldermen, who are elected and hold office for life;

Two city counsel;

One counsel holding the reversion of the office;

A clerk.

They enjoy many privileges: among others, their capitation tax is fixed at a moderate sum; they are exempt from lodging soldiers, arms, or baggage; they are exempt from dues *de cloison double et triple*, from the old and new excise, from the accessory dues on articles of consumption, even from benevolences, "from which latter they have asserted their own freedom," says the presidial. They enjoy, moreover, allowances in the shape of lights, and in some cases salaries and lodgings.

We see from this that a post of perpetual alderman at Angers was not to be despised in those days. Note here, as everywhere else, the contrivances to secure exemptions from taxes for the rich. The memorial goes on to say that "these offices are eagerly sought by the richest citizens, who desire them in order to reduce their capitation tax, and increase that of their fellow citizens in proportion. There are at this moment several municipal officials who pay 30 *livres* of capitation, and ought to pay 250 to 300 *livres*; one, among others, ought, in proportion to his fortune, to pay 1000 *livres* at least." In another part of the memorial it is said that among the richest inhabitants of the place are more than forty officials, or widows of officials, whose rank exempts them from the heavy capitation tax paid by the city. The tax consequently falls upon an infinite number of poor mechanics, who, believing themselves overtaxed constantly, complain of the amount of their tax—unjustly so, for there are no inequalities in the division of the burden laid upon the city.

The General Assembly is composed of seventy-six persons:
The Mayor;
Two deputies of the chapter;
A Syndic of the clerks;
Two deputies of the presidial;
A deputy of the university;
A lieutenant-general of police;
Four aldermen;
Twelve consulting aldermen;
A King's attorney at the presidial;
A city counsel;
Two deputies of the woods and forests;
Two of the *election*;
Two of the salt warehouse;
Two of the *traites*;
Two of the mint;
Two of the advocates and attorneys;
Two of the consular judges;
Two of the notaries;
Two of the shopkeepers;
And, lastly, two deputies from each of the sixteen parishes.

These latter are understood to be the special representatives of the people; they are, in fact, the representatives of industrial corporations, and the council is so arranged, as the reader has seen, that they are sure to be in a minority.

When posts in the corporation become vacant, the General Assembly chooses three candidates for each vacancy.

Most of the posts in the city government are free to persons of all professions; the Assembly is not—as others which I have noticed—obliged to choose a magistrate or a lawyer to fill a vacancy. To this the presidial objects strongly.

According to the same presidial, which seems terribly jealous of the town corporation, and whose main objection to the constitution was, I suspect, that it did not confer privileges enough on the presidial, "the General Assembly is too numerous, and composed of persons too devoid of intelligence to be consulted on any matters but sales of the town property; the negotiation of loans, the establishment of town dues, and the election of municipal officials. All other business should be transacted by a smaller body, wholly composed of notables. No one should be a member of this assembly but the lieutenant-general of the *sénéchaussée,* the King's attorney, and twelve other notables chosen out of the six bodies, the clergy, the magistracy, the nobility, the university, the merchants, and the *bourgeoisie,* and no others who do not belong to any of these six classes. The first choice of notables should be made by the Assembly, and future elections by the assembly of notables or the body from which each notable is chosen."

A resemblance existed between these public functionaries, who thus became members of municipal bodies as officeholders or notables, and the functionaries of the same title and character in our day. But their position was very different from that of modern officeholders—a fact which cannot be safely overlooked; for nearly all these old functionaries were city notables before they obtained office, or only sought office in order to become notables. They had no notion of either resigning their rank or being promoted; this alone creates a vast difference between them and their successors in office.

### *Memorial of the municipal officials*

This document shows that the town corporation was created in 1474 by Louis XI upon the ruins of the old democratic constitution of the town, and that its principle was of the nature explained above; that is to say nearly all political power was vested in the middle classes; the people were kept at a distance, or weakened; a vast number of municipal officials were created in order to muster partisans for the scheme; hereditary titles of nobility were granted in profusion, and all sorts of privileges were secured to the *bourgeois* administrators.

The same paper also contains letters patent from successors of Louis XI, which recognise this new constitution and curtail still further the power of the people. It mentions that in 1485 the letters patent granted with this view by Charles VIII were assailed by the people of Angers before the parlement, just as, in England, disputes relative to the charter of a town would have been carried before the courts. In 1601 a decree of parlement again fixed the political rights which were authorised by the royal charter. From thenceforth, no other controlling authority appears but the Royal Council.

It appears from the same memorial that Mayors, like all other town officials, were selected by the King out of a list of three names presented by the General Assembly; this was in virtue of an order in Council of 22nd June, 1708. It also appears that, in virtue of Orders in Council of 1733 and 1741, the small traders were entitled to one alderman (perpetual) or councillor. Finally, the memorial shows that at the time the corporation was entrusted with the distribution of the sums raised for the capitation, equipment, quartering, support of the poor, of the troops, of the revenue service, of foundlings.

Then follows an enumeration of the great labours which devolve upon municipal officials. They fully justify, in the opinion of the memorialists, the privileges and the permanent rank which they enjoy, and which, it is plain, they are much afraid of losing. Many of the reasons which they assign for the severity of their office-labours are curious, such as the following: "Their financial duties have been much increased by the extensions which are constantly being made to the aid dues, the salt-tax, the stamp and registry dues, and the unlawful exactions of registry dues and freehold duties. They have been involved, on the town's behalf, in perpetual lawsuits with the financial companies in reference to these taxes; they have had to go from court to court, from the parlement to the Council, in order to resist the oppression under which they are groaning. An experience and a public-service of thirty years enable them to state that the life of man is hardly long enough to defend oneself against the stratagems and the traps which the agents of the revenue farmers are constantly laying for the citizen, in order to preserve their commissions."

Curiously enough, it is to the Controller-General that these things are said, and said with the view of winning his support for the privileges of the class that expresses these views. So deeply rooted was the habit of viewing the companies which farmed the taxes as an adversary that might be abused on all sides without objection from anyone. This habit steadily spread and gained strength; men learned to view the Treasury as an odious tyrant, hateful to all: the common enemy instead of the common agent.

"All offices were first united with the corporation," adds the same memorial, "by an Order in Council of the 4th September, 1694, in consideration of a sum of 22,000 *livres*;" that is to say the offices were redeemed that year for that sum. By an order of 26th April, 1723, the offices created by the edict of 24th May, 1722, were also united to the corporation, or, in other words, the town was permitted to redeem them. By another order of 24th May, 1723, the town was authorised to borrow 120,000 *livres* for the acquisition of the said offices. Another, of 26th July, 1728, authorised it to borrow 50,000 *livres* to redeem the office of clerk-secretary of the City Hall. "The town," says the memorial, "has paid its money to preserve the freedom of its elections, and to secure to the officers it elects for one or two years, or for life, the various prerogatives attached to their offices." Some of the municipal offices were re-established by the edict of November, 1733; an order was subsequently obtained at the instance of the Mayor and aldermen, allowing the city to purchase an extension of its rights, for a term of fifteen years, for a sum of 170,000 *livres*.

This is a fair criterion of the policy of the government of the old régime, as regards towns. It compelled them to contract debts, then authorised them to establish extraordinary taxes to liquidate them. And to this it must be added that afterwards many of these taxes, which were naturally temporary, were made perpetual, and then the government got its share.

The memorial continues: "The municipal officials were never deprived of their judicial functions till the establishment of royal courts. Until 1669, they had sole cognisance of disputes between masters and servants. The accounts of the town dues are rendered before the Intendant, in obedience to the decrees establishing or continuing the said dues."

The memorial makes it plain that the representatives of the

sixteen parishes, who, as above mentioned, had seats in the General Assembly, were chosen by companies, corporate bodies, or commonalties, and were the mere organs of these bodies. They were bound by their instructions on all points.

In fine, this memorial shows that, at Angers as elsewhere, no expenses could be incurred by the town without the concurrence of the Intendant and the Council. And it must be acknowledged that, when the government of a town is entrusted to certain men to be used as their private property, and when these men receive no salary, but enjoy in lieu thereof privileges which exonerate them from all responsibility to their fellow citizens for maladministration, an over-seeing central government may seem a necessity.

The whole of this memorial, which is clumsily drawn up, indicates a state of great alarm on the part of these officials lest the existing state of things should be changed. All kinds of reasons, good and bad, are accumulated together, and pressed into the service of the *status quo*.

### Memorial of the sub-delegate

The Intendant, having received these two contradictory memorials, asks for the opinion of his sub-delegate. He gives it:

"The memorial of the municipal councillors," says he, "does not deserve attention; its only aim is to subserve their own privileges. That of the presidial may be beneficially consulted, but there is no reason for granting them all the prerogatives they desire."

He admits that the constitution of the civic body has long needed reform. Besides the immunities already mentioned, which were enjoyed by all the municipal officials of Angers, he states that the Mayor, during his term of service, was lodged at a cost of at least six hundred francs; that he received fifty francs salary, and one hundred francs for expenses of his office, besides vouchers. The Attorney-Syndic was also lodged, and so was the clerk. In order to escape aid and town dues, the municipal officials had fixed upon a presumed amount of consumption by each of them; and by accounting for this, they could introduce into the town as many casks of wine or other merchandise as they pleased.

The sub-delegate does not propose to deprive the councillors of their exemption from taxes; but he thinks their capitation tax, which is now fixed at a very low figure, should be settled every year by the Intendant. He also advises that these officials should be made to contribute with everyone else to the "free gift", their exemption from which is without authority or precedent.

The municipal officials, says the memorial, are intrusted with the preparation of the capitation-rolls for the people. They perform this duty carelessly and arbitrarily, whence the Intendant is regularly overwhelmed every year with petitions and reclamations. It would be desirable that this tax should be distributed hereafter, in the interest of each commonalty or company, by its members, in a general and stable manner; and that municipal officials should in future fix the capitation of *bourgeois* only, and of persons belonging to no public body, such as certain workmen and the servants of privileged persons.

The memorial of the sub-delegate confirms what the municipal officials have already stated in regard to the redemption, in 1735, of the municipal offices, for the sum of 170,000 *livres*.

### Letter from the Intendant to the Controller-General

Armed with these various documents, the Intendant writes to the Minister. "The public interest and that of the citizens," he says, "require a reduction in the number of municipal officials, whose privileges have become a heavy burden on the public.

"I am struck," he adds, "with the enormous amount of money that has been repeatedly paid for the redemption of municipal offices at Angers. A similar sum, employed usefully, would have done the town much good; as it is, it has only made people feel the weight of the authority and of the privileges of these officials.

"The internal abuses of this government fully deserve the attention of the Council. Independently of vouchers and lights, which consume the annual appropriation of 2127 *livres* (this was the sum set apart for this class of expeditures in the normal budget, which was occasionally imposed on towns by the King), the public money is squandered and employed for clandestine purposes by these officials. The King's attorney, who has held his office for thirty or forty years, has obtained such a mastery over the administration, of which he alone understands the details, that the citizens have been unable to obtain the least information with regard to the employment of their money." In consequence, the Intendant proposes to the Minister to reduce the corporation to a Mayor serving for four years, six aldermen serving for six years, one King's attorney serving for eight, and a perpetual clerk and receiver.

In other respects the Constitution which he proposes for Angers is precisely the same as the one he elsewhere proposed for Tours. In his opinion,

1st. The government should preserve the General Assembly, but merely as an electoral body for the election of municipal officials.

2nd. It should create an extraordinary Council of Notables, whose functions should be those with which the edict of 1764 appeared to invest the General Assembly. This council to be composed of twelve persons, holding office for six years, and elected, not by the General Assembly, but by the twelve bodies esteemed notable, each body electing one. He designates as notable bodies,

The presidial,
The university,
The *election*,
The office of woods and forests,
The salt warehouse,
The office of the *traites*,
The mint,
The advocates and attorneys,
The consular judges,
The notaries,
The traders (*marchands*),
The *bourgeois*.

As will be remarked, nearly all these notables were public functionaries, and all the public functionaries were notables. From this, as from a thousand other papers in these collections, it may be inferred that the middle classes were then as great place-hunters and as destitute of independent ambition as they are now. The only difference is, as I remarked in the text, that formerly the petty importance afforded by these places was bought, whereas now candidates beg the government to grant them the charity of a place for nothing.

It is here seen that the whole real power in the municipality is vested in the extraordinary council, and the administration of the town is thus further confined to a small circle of *bourgeois*. The only assembly in which the people continue to exercise the least interference is now confined to the electing of municipal officials whom it cannot instruct. It is to be remarked, also, that the Intendant is more unbending and anti-popular in his principles than the King, who seemed in his edict to have transferred most of the public authority to the General Assembly, and again, that the Intendant is far more liberal and democratic than the *bourgeoisie*. This last inference is at all events a fair one from the memorial I have quoted in the text, from which it appears that the notables of another town were desirous of excluding the people from the election of municipal officials in opposition to the views of the Intendant and the King.

It may be noticed that the Intendant recognises two distinct classes of notables under the names of *bourgeois* and *marchands*. It may not be useless to give an exact definition of these words, in order to show into how many small fragments the *bourgeoisie* was divided, and by how many petty vanities it was actuated.

The word *bourgeois* had a general and also a particular meaning; it meant the members of the middle classes at large, and it also meant a certain number of men within those classes. "*Bourgeois*," says a memorial filed at the inquiry of 1764, "are individuals whose birth and fortune enable them to live without engaging in lucrative pursuits." Other portions of the memorial show that the word *bourgeois* does not apply to persons who belong to companies or industrial corporations; it is not so easy to say to whom it does apply. "For," as the same memorial says, "many persons assume the title of *bourgeois* whose only claim to it is their idleness, who have no fortune, and lead a rude, obscure life. The *bourgeois* should, on the contrary, always be distinguished by their fortune, their birth, their talents, manners, and mode of life. Mechanics composing trade-companies have never been classed in the rank of notables."

Traders (*marchands*) were another class of individuals who, like the *bourgeois*, belonged to no company or corporation: but where were the limits of this little class? "Must we," says the same memorial, "confound small, lowborn dealers with wholesale merchants?" To overcome the difficulty, the memorial proposes to have the aldermen draw up every year a table of notable traders (*marchands*), to be handed to their chief or Syndic, who shall invite to the deliberations at the city hall none but those who are thereon inscribed. Care will be taken to inscribe on this table no traders who may have been domestics, porters, wagoners, or followers of other low trades.

20 (page 74)

One of the most striking features of the administration of towns in the eighteenth century is not the absence of all representation and intervention of the public in business, but the extreme variability of the rules governing such administration. Civic rights were constantly bestowed, taken away, restored, increased, diminished, modified in a thousand ways, and unceasingly. No better indication of the contempt into which all local liberties had fallen can be found than these eternal changes of laws which no one seemed to notice. This mobility would alone have sufficed to destroy all initiative or recuperative energy, and all local patriotism in the institution which is best adapted to it. It helped to prepare the great work of destruction which was to be effected by the Revolution.

21 (page 75)

The pretext which Louis XIV put forward for destroying the municipal liberty of towns was the maladministration of their finances; yet the evil, according to Turgot, continued to exist, and even assumed large proportions after the reform of this monarch. He adds that most towns are heavily in debt at the present time, partly for moneys lent to government, and partly for expenses or decorations which municipal officials—who dispose of other people's money, who render no account, and receive no instructions—are constantly incurring, in order to increase the splendour or the profit of their position.

22 (page 76)  *A village government in the eighteenth century (taken from the papers of the Intendant's office in the Ile-de-France)*

The affair which I am about to relate is one instance out of a thousand which illustrates the forms and the dilatory methods used by parochial governments, and shows what a general parochial assembly really was in the eighteenth century.

The parsonage house and steeple of a rural parish—that of Ivry, Ile-de-France—required repair. To whom was application to be made to make the repairs? Who was to pay for them? How was the money to be procured?

1st. Petition from the curé to the Intendant, setting forth that the parsonage house and steeple need immediate repairs; that his predecessor had caused useless buildings to be erected adjoining the parsonage house, and had thus altered and deformed the character of the spot; and that the inhabitants, having permitted him to do this, ought to bear the expense of all needful repairs, having their recourse on the late curé's heirs for the expense.

2nd. Ordinance of Monseigneur the Intendant (29th August, 1747), ordering the Syndic diligently to convene an assembly to deliberate on the necessity of the repairs.

3rd. Deliberation of the inhabitants, by which they declare that they do not object to the parsonage house being repaired, but as for the steeple, they hold that, as it is built on the choir, which the curé, as a large tithe-holder, is bound to repair, he must pay for any repairs it may need. (An Order in Council of April, 1695, had, in fact, imposed the duty of keeping the choir in repair upon the tithe-holder, leaving the tithe-payers to look after the nave.)

4th. New ordinance of the Intendant, which, in view of the conflict of statements, orders an architect, the Sieur Cordier, to visit and examine the parsonage house and steeple, hear evidence, and make estimates of the works.

5th. Minutes of all these proceedings, testifying that a certain number of landholders of Ivry, apparently men of rank, *bourgeois*, and peasants, appeared before the Intendant's commissioner, and gave evidence for or against the pretensions of the curé.

6th. New ordinance of the Intendant, directing that the estimates prepared by his architect be laid before the landholders and inhabitants in a general assembly convoked with due diligence by the Syndic for the purpose.

7th. New parochial assembly in pursuance of the ordinance, in which the people declare that they adhere to their expressed opinions.

8th. Ordinance of the Intendant, directing, first, that in presence of his sub-delegate at Corbeil, the curé, Syndic, and principal inhabitants of the parish being also present, the contracts for the work according to the estimates shall be given out; and, secondly, that, whereas the want of repairs involves absolute danger, the whole cost shall be levied upon the inhabitants, without prejudice to the legal rights of those who conceive that the cost of repairing the steeple should be borne by the curé as tithe-holder.

9th. Notice to all parties to be present at the office of the sub-delegate at Corbeil, where the contracts are to be given out.

10th. Petition of the curé and several inhabitants, praying that the costs of the preliminary proceedings be not charged, as usual, against the contractor, lest they should deter bidders from coming forward.

11th. Ordinance of the Intendant, directing that all expenses incurred in order to bring the affair to issue be settled by the sub-delegate, added to the contract, and included in the imposition.

12th. Authority from several notables of the parish to the Sieur X. to be present on their behalf at the execution of the contract, and confirm it according to the architect's estimates.

13th. Certificate of the Syndic, stating that the usual notices and advertisements have been made.

14th. Official report of the contract:

Expenses of repairs .............................487*l.*
Legal expenses pertaining thereto............237*l.* 18s. 6d.

724  18  6

15th. Lastly, Order in Council (23rd July, 1748), authorising an impost to raise this sum.

It may have been noticed that frequent allusions are here made to the parochial assembly. The following report of one of these assemblies will show how matters were usually managed on these occasions.

NOTARISED MINUTE: "This day, at the close of the parochial mass, at the usual and customary place, was present at the assembly held by the inhabitants of the said parish before X., notary at Corbeil undersigned, and the witnesses hereinafter mentioned, the Sieur Michaud, vine-dresser, Syndic of the said parish, who presented the ordinance of the Intendant authorising the assembly, read the same, and applied for an official certificate of his due diligence in the premises:

"And then and there appeared an inhabitant of the said parish, who stated that the steeple was upon the choir, and, consequently, that its repairs should be charged to the curé; did furthermore appear —— (here follow the names of various parishioners, who, on the contrary, consent to the request of the curé); and thereafter appeared fifteen peasants, mechanics, masons, and vine-dressers, who declare themselves of the same mind as the preceding persons. Did also appear the Sieur Raimbaud, vine-dresser, who declared that he would agree to whatever Monseigneur the Intendant decided. Did also appear the Sieur X., doctor of the Sorbonne, curé, who persists in the allegations and conclusions of his request.

"Whereof the said parties have required of us official certificate.

"Done and passed at the said place of Ivry, in front of the burial-ground of the said parish, before the undersigned; and the meeting aforesaid lasted from eleven o'clock in the morning till two."

It will be noticed that this parish assembly was a mere administrative inquiry, in the same form and as costly as judicial inquiries; that it never led to a vote or other clear expression of the will of the parish; that it was merely an expression of individual opinions, and constituted no check upon government. Many other documents indicate that the only object of parish assemblies was to afford information to the Intendant, and not to influence his decision even in cases where no other interest but that of the parish was concerned.

It may be remarked, also, that this affair gives rise to three separate inquiries; one before the notary, another before the architect, and a third before two notaries, to ascertain whether the people have not changed their minds.

The impost of 724 *livres* 18 *sous*, authorised by the Order of 23rd July, 1748, bears upon all landholders, whether privileged or not. This was generally the case in affairs of this kind; but the share of the various rate-payers was not fixed on uniform principles. Persons who paid the *taille* were taxed in proportion to their *taille*. Privileged individuals, on the other hand, were taxed in proportion to their assumed fortunes, which gave them a great advantage over the former class.

It appears, finally, that in this matter the distribution of the impost was made by two Collectors, inhabitants of the village; not elected, nor serving in their turn, as was usually the custom, but chosen and appointed by the Intendant's sub-delegate.

23 (page 79) *The State was guardian of convents as well as Communes; instance thereof*

The Controller-General, authorising the Intendant to pay over fifteen thousand *livres* to the Convent of Carmelites, to which certain indemnities were due, desires the Intendant to satisfy himself that the money, which represents a capital, is properly invested. Similar instances abound.

24 (page 85) *How the administrative centralisation of the old order can be best judged in Canada*

The physiognomy of governments can be best detected in their colonies, for there their features are magnified, and rendered more conspicuous. When I want to discover the spirit and vices of the government of Louis XIV, I must go to Canada. Its deformities are seen there as through a microscope.

A number of obstacles, created by previous occurrences or old social forms, which hindered the development of the true tendencies of government at home, did not exist in Canada. There was no nobility, or, at least, none had taken deep root. The Church was not dominant. Feudal traditions were lost or obscured. The power of the judiciary was not interwoven with old institutions or popular customs. There was, therefore, no hindrance to the free play of the central power. It could shape all laws according to its views. And in Canada, therefore, there was not a shadow of municipal or provincial institutions; and no collective or individual action was tolerated. An Intendant far more powerful than his colleagues in France; a government managing far more matters than it did at home, and desiring to manage everything from Paris, notwithstanding the intervening eighteen hundred leagues; never adopting the great principles which can render a colony populous and prosperous, but, instead, employing all sorts of petty, artificial methods, and small devices of tyranny to increase and spread population; forced cultivation of lands; all lawsuits growing out of the concession of land removed from the jurisdiction of the courts and referred to the local administration; compulsory regulations respecting farming and the selection of land—such was the system devised for Canada under Louis XIV: it was Colbert who signed the edicts. One might fancy oneself in the midst of modern centralisation and in Algeria. Canada is, in fact, the true model of what has always been seen there. In both places the government numbers as many heads as the people; it preponderates, acts, regulates, controls, undertakes everything, provides for everything, knows far more about the subject's business than he does himself—is, in short, incessantly active and sterile.

In the United States, on the contrary, the English anti-centralisation system was carried to an extreme. Parishes became independent municipalities, almost democratic republics. The republican element, which forms, so to say, the foundation of the English constitution and English habits, shows itself and develops without hindrance. Government proper does little in England, and individuals do a great deal; in America, government never interferes, so to speak, and individuals do everything. The absence of an upper class, which renders the Canadian more defenceless against the government than his equals were in France, renders the citizen of the English colonies still more independent of the home power.

In both colonies society ultimately resolved itself into a democratic form. But in Canada, so long as it was a French possession at least, equality was an accessory of absolutism; in the British colonies it was the companion of liberty. And, so far as the material consequences of the two colonial systems are concerned, it is well known that in 1763, at the conquest, the population of Canada was sixty thousand souls, that of the English provinces three million.

25 (page 86)  *An example, chosen at haphazard, of the general regulations which the Council of State was in the habit of making for the whole of France, and by which it created special misdemeanours of which the government courts had sole cognizance*

I take the first which I happen to find. Orders in Council of 29 April, 1779, which enacts that thereafter throughout the kingdom all sheep-growers and sheep-dealers shall mark their sheep in a peculiar manner, under penalty of three hundred *livres* fine. "His Majesty orders the Intendant to see this order obeyed," it says, whence it follows that it devolved upon the Intendant to pronounce penalties incurred. Another instance: An Order in Council of 21st December, 1778, forbids express companies and wagoners to warehouse the goods they have in charge, under pain of three hundred *livres* fine. "His Majesty enjoins upon his lieutenant-general of police and his Intendants to see to it."

26 (page 96)

The Provincial Assembly of Guienne cries aloud for new brigades of horse police, just as in our day the Council-General of the department of Aveyron or Lot no doubt demands new brigades of *gendarmerie*. Always the same idea—*gendarmerie* constitute order, and order cannot be had except with the gendarme of the government. The report adds: "Complaint is daily made that there is no police in the country." (How could there be? Noblemen take no concern for anything, the *bourgeois* live in town; and the community is represented by a rude peasant, and has no power in any case.) It must be admitted that, except in some cantons in which benevolent and just seigneurs use their influence over their vassals to prevent those appeals to violence to which the country people are prone, in consequence of the rudeness of their manners and the roughness of their character, there exists hardly anywhere any means of controlling these ignorant, rough, and hotheaded men."

Such was the manner in which the nobles of the Provincial

Assembly allowed themselves to be spoken of, and in which the Third Estate, comprising half the assembly, spoke of the people in public documents.

## 27 (page 97)

Tobacco licences were as eagerly sought after under the old régime as at present. The most distinguished people begged them for their dependents. Some, I find, were granted at the request of noble ladies, some to please archbishops.

## 28 (page 98)

Local life was more thoroughly extinguished than almost seems credible. One of the roads leading from Maine into Normandy had become impassable. Who calls for its repair? The district of Touraine, which it crosses? The province of Normandy, or that of Maine, both vitally interested in the cattle trade of which it is the outlet? Some canton particularly injured by the bad condition of the road? Neither district, nor province, nor canton utter a word. The duty of attracting the attention of government to the road is left to the traders who use it, and whose wagons stick in the mud. They write to Paris to the Controller-General, and beg him to come to their rescue.

## 29 (page 105) *Varying value of seigneurial rents and dues according to provinces*

Turgot says in his works: "I must remark that the importance of these dues is very different in most of the rich provinces, such as Normandy, Picardy, and the vicinity of Paris. In the latter, riches usually consist in the produce of land; the farms are large, close together, and bring high rents. The seigneurial rents of large farms form a very small portion of the income from them, and are regarded rather as honorary than lucrative. In poorer and worse-farmed provinces, seigneurs and men of rank possess but little land of their own; farms, which are much subdivided, are burdened with heavy rents in produce, and all the cotenants are jointly responsible for their payment. These rents eat up the clearest portion of the income of the land, and constitute the bulk of the seigneur's revenue."

30 (page 111)  *Discussion of public affairs antagonistic to the establishment of castes*

The unimportant labours of the agricultural societies of the eighteenth century show how the general discussion of public affairs militated against castes. Though these assemblages took place thirty years prior to the Revolution, in the midst of the old régime, the mere fact that they discussed questions in which all classes were interested, and that all classes mingled in the discussion, drew men together and effected a sort of fusion. Ideas of reasonable reform suggested themselves to the minds even of the privileged classes, and yet they were mere conversations about agriculture.

I am satisfied that only a government which relied wholly on its own strength, and invariably dealt with individuals singly, as that of the old order did, could have maintained the ridiculous and insane inequality which existed at the time of the Revolution. The least touch of self-government would have soon altered or destroyed it.

31 (page 111)

Provincial liberties may survive national liberty for a time, when they are of old standing, and interwoven with manners, customs, and recollections, and the despotism is new. But it is unreasonable to suppose that local liberties can be created at will, or maintained for any length of time, when general liberty is extinct.

32 (page 112)

Turgot gives a statement of the extent of the privileges of the nobility, in the matter of taxation, in a memorial to the King. It appears to me to be quite correct.

1st. Privileged persons may claim exemption from taxes for a farm which consumes the labour of four ploughs. Such a farm in the neighbourhood of Paris would usually pay two thousand francs of taxes.

2ndly. The same privileged persons pay nothing for woods, meadows, rivers, ponds, or enclosed lands near their châteaux, whatever be their extent. Some cantons are almost wholly laid out in meadow or vineyard; in these, seigneurs who have their

ands managed by a steward pay no impost whatever. All the
taxes fall on the *taille*-payers. The advantage of this is immense.

33 (page 112) *Indirect privilege in respect of taxes—difference
in the manner of collection when the tax is levied on all alike*

Turgot draws a picture of this, which I have reason to believe
is correct.

"The indirect advantages of the privileged classes with
regard to the capitation tax are very great. The capitation tax
is naturally an arbitrary impost; it is impossible to divide it
among the citizens at large otherwise than blindly. It was found
convenient to take the *taille* rolls, which were already made, as
a basis. A special roll was made for the privileged classes; but,
as the latter made objections, and the *taille*-payers had no one
to speak for them, it came about that the capitation of the
privileged classes was gradually reduced in the provinces to a
very small sum, while the *taille*-payers paid as much for capitation as the principal of the *taille*."

34 (page 112) *Another example of inequality in the collection
of a uniform tax*

It is known that local imposts were levied on all classes
equally; "which sums," say the Orders in Council authorising
these expenditures, "shall be levied on all persons without distinction, whether privileged or not, jointly with the capitation
tax, or in proportion thereto."

Note that, as the capitation tax of *taille*-payers, which was
assimilated to the *taille*, was always heavier than the capitation of privileged persons, the very plan which seemed to favour
uniformity kept up the inequality between the two.

35 (page 112) *Same subject*

I find a bill of 1764, which tended to render the taxes uniform, all sorts of provisions that were intended to preserve a
distinction in favour of the privileged classes in respect to the
tax levy. For instance, no property of theirs could be appraised
for taxation except in their presence or in the presence of their
attorney.

36 (page 112)  *How the government admitted that, even in the*
*case of taxes weighing alike on all classes, the tax ought to be*
*collected differently from the privileged and unprivileged classes*

"I see," said the Minister in 1766, "that the most difficult
taxes to collect are those which are due by nobles and privileged
persons, in consequence of the consideration which the tax collectors feel bound to pay to these persons. It has resulted from
this that they are heavily in arrears on their capitation tax and
*vingtièmes*" (the taxes which they paid in common with the
people).

37 (page 122)

Arthur Young, in his *Journey* in 1789, draws a picture in
which the condition of the two societies is so agreeably sketched
and so skilfully set that I cannot resist giving it here.

In travelling through France during the emotion caused by
the capture of the Bastille, Young was arrested in a village by
a mob, who, seeing no *cocarde* on his hat, were about to drag
him to jail. To get out of the scrape, Young improvises the
following little speech:

" 'Gentlemen, it has just been said that the taxes are to be
paid just as before. The taxes must be paid, certainly, but not
as before. They must be paid as they are in England. We have
many more taxes than you; but the Third Estate, the people,
pays none of them; they fall upon the rich. In my country,
windows pay a tax; but a man who has only six in his house
pays nothing. A seigneur pays his *vingtièmes* and the *taille*, but
the owner of a small garden escapes scot free. Rich men pay for
their horses, their carriages, their servants, for the right of
shooting their own partridges; but small landholders know
nothing of these taxes. More than this: we have, in England,
a tax that is levied on the rich for the maintenance of the poor.
If, then, taxes are still to be paid, they must be paid on a new
plan. The English plan is the best.'

"As my bad French," adds Young, "suited their patois well
enough, they understood what I said. They applauded every
word of this speech, and concluded that I might be a good
fellow—an impression which I confirmed by crying *Vive le
Tiers!* They then let me pass with a hurrah."

38 (page 124)

The church of X., election of Chollet, was falling into ruin. Measures were being taken to repair it, according to the plan indicated by the Order of 16th December, 1684, that is to say, by a tax on all the citizens. When the Collectors proceed to levy the tax, the Marquis of X., seigneur of the parish, declares that as he undertakes to repair the choir without assistance, he cannot be expected to contribute to the tax. The other inhabitants reply very reasonably that as seigneur and large tithe-holder (he possessed, no doubt, the tithes enfeoffed), he was bound to repair the choir, and that he was by no means, on that account, relieved from his obligation to contribute to the other repairs. On reference to the Intendant, he decides against the Marquis and in favour of the Collectors. The records of the affair contain more than ten letters of the Marquis, each more pressing than the last, begging that the other people of the parish be made to pay in his stead, and condescending to call the Intendant "monseigneur", and even to "supplicate him".

39 (page 125)   *Example of the manner in which the government of the old order respected acquired rights, formal contracts, and town or associate liberties*

Royal declaration "suspending, in time of war, repayment of all loans made to the crown by towns, bourgs, colleges, commonalties, hospitals, poorhouses, corporations of artisans and tradesmen, and others, for the payment of which town or other dues were pledged; interest to accrue on the same."

This was not only suspending payment at the time fixed, but laying hands on the security pledged for the payment of the loan. Similar measures were common under the government of the old régime; they could never have occurred in a country where a free press or free assemblies existed. Compare these proceedings with those which have taken place in England and America in the like circumstances. Here the contempt for right was not less flagrant than the contempt for local liberties.

40 (page 127)

The case cited in the text is not the only one in which the

privileged classes perceived that they were affected by the feudal dues which weighed upon the peasantry. An agricultural society, composed wholly of privileged persons, said, thirty years before the Revolution,

"Irredeemable rents, whether ground rents or feudal rents attaching upon land, become so onerous to the debtor when they are considerable, that they ruin him and the land too. He is forced to neglect his farm, for he cannot effect loans on a property so burdened, nor can he find a purchaser for it. If the rent were redeemable, he would soon find a lender to advance money to pay it off, or a purchaser to extinguish it. One is always glad to improve a property of which one believes oneself peaceable owner. It would be of infinite service to agriculture if a means could be found of rendering these rents redeemable. Many feudal seigneurs are convinced of this, and would gladly concur in any arrangement for the purpose. It would therefore be desirable to indicate a plan for redeeming all these ground rents."

41 (page 128)

All public functionaries, including the representative of the tax farmers, enjoyed exemptions from taxes. The privilege was granted them by the ordinance of 1681. An Intendant says, in a letter addressed to the Minister in 1782, "The most numerous class of privileged persons consists of clerks of the salt-tax, of *traites,* of the domain, of the post, of aids, and other excise of all kinds. One or more of these are to be found in every parish."

His object was to prevent the Ministers from proposing to the Council a measure to extend the exemption from taxes to the clerks and servants of these privileged officials. The farmers-general, says the Intendant, are always asking for extensions of the privilege in order to obtain clerks without paying them a salary.

42 (page 128)

Venal offices were not wholly unknown abroad. In Germany some small sovereigns had introduced the system; but they had applied it to but few offices, and these subordinate ones. The system was carried out on a grand scale in France only.

43 (page 133)

One must not be surprised—though it certainly seems surprising—to see functionaries of the old government, closely connected with the administration, go to law before the parlement about the limits of their respective powers. The fact is easily explained: the questions at issue were questions of public administration, but they were also questions of private property. What here appears to be an encroachment of the judiciary was, in fact, nothing but a consequence of the fault which the government committed in selling offices. All places being bought, and their incumbents being paid by fees, it was impossible to alter the functions of an office without injuring individual rights which had been purchased for a valuable consideration. One example out of a thousand: the lieutenant general of police of Le Mans institutes an action against the financial department of that city to claim the right of paving the streets, and obtaining fees thereon, that being, he says, part of the police of the streets, which devolves upon him. The department replies that the very title of its commission entrusts it with the paving of the streets. This time it is not the King's council which decides between them; as the point involved is chiefly the interest of the capital invested by the lieutenant in the purchase of his office, the case goes before the parlement. Instead of being a government question, it is a civil suit.

44 (page 134) *Analysis of the* cahiers *of the nobility in 1789*

The French Revolution is the only one, I believe, at the beginning of which the different classes of society were enabled to present an authentic account of the ideas they had conceived, and express the feelings which animated them, before the Revolution had distorted or modified those ideas and feelings. This authentic account was recorded, as is known, in the *cahiers* which the three Orders drew up in 1789. These *cahiers* or *mémoires* were drawn up in perfect freedom, in the midst of the widest publicity, by each of the three Orders; they were the fruit of long discussion by the parties in interest, and ripe deliberation by their authors; for in those days, when the government spoke to the nation, it did not undertake to answer its own questions. At the time the *cahiers* were composed, the principal parts of them were collected and published in three volumes, which are to be found in all libraries. The originals are deposited in the national archives, and with them the reports of the assemblies which drew them up, and a portion of the correspondence between M. Necker and his agents in reference to the subject. This collection forms a long series of folio volumes, and is the most precious document we have on the subject of ancient France. All who desire to become acquainted with the spirit of our forefathers at the time of the Revolution should consult it without delay.

I had imagined that perhaps the printed extract, in three volumes, which I have mentioned above, was a one-sided performance, and an unfaithful reflection of this immense collection; but I find, on comparing the two, that the smaller work is a correct miniature of the greater.

The following extract from the *cahiers* of the nobility shows the spirit which animated the majority of that body. It shows which of their old privileges the nobility desired at all hazards to keep, which they were half inclined to abandon, and which they proposed of their own accord to sacrifice. It discloses especially the views which pervaded the whole body on the subject of political liberty. Curious and melancholy spectacle!

INDIVIDUAL RIGHTS—The nobility demand, in the first place, that an explicit declaration of the rights of man be made, and that that declaration bear witness to the liberty and secure the safety of all men.

PERSONAL RIGHTS—They desire that the serfdom of the glebe be abolished wherever it may still exist, and that means be sought for the extinction of the slave-trade and Negro slavery; that all be free to travel withersoever they will, and to reside where they please, within or without the kingdom, without being liable to arbitrary arrest; that the police regulations be amended, and that the police be under control of the magistracy, even in case of riot; that no one be arrested and judged except by his natural judges; that, in consequence, state prisons and other illegal places of detention be suppressed. Some demand the destruction of the Bastille. The nobility of Paris insist warmly on this point.

All *lettres de cachet* should be prohibited. If the danger of the state requires the arrest of a citizen who cannot be handed over directly to the ordinary courts of justice, measures must be taken to prevent injustice, either by notifying the Council of State, or in some other way.

The nobility desire that all special commissions, irregular courts, privileges of *committimus*, reprieves, be abolished; that the most severe penalties be laid upon all who execute or order the execution of an arbitrary command; that the ordinary courts —which alone should be preserved—take all necessary measures to secure individual liberty, especially in criminal matters; that justice be administered gratuitously, and useless jurisdictions abolished. One *cahier* says, "Magistrates were made for the people, not the people for magistrates." They demand that an honorary counsel and advocates for the poor be established in every bailiwick; that all examinations be public, and prisoners be allowed to defend themselves; that in criminal matters the prisoner be provided with a counsel, and the judge assisted by a number of citizens of the same Order as the prisoner, who shall decide upon the fact of the crime or misdemeanour charged (reference is here made to the constitution of England; that penalties be proportioned to offences, and uniform; that capital punishment be employed more rarely, and all corporal punishments, torture, etc., be abolished; that the condition of prisoners be improved, especially those who are confined before their trial).

The *cahiers* demand that an effort be made to respect individual liberty in the recruiting service both of soldiers and sailors. It should be allowable to avoid military service by paying a sum of money. No lots should be drawn save in the presence of deputies of the three Orders. Finally, an attempt should be made to reconcile military discipline and subordination with the rights of the citizen and the freeman. Blows with the flat of the sword should be forbidden.

LIBERTY AND INVIOLABILITY OF PROPERTY—Property should be inviolable, and should never be molested save for the necessities of the public weal. In such cases the government should pay a high price, and that promptly. Confiscations should be abolished.

LIBERTY OF TRADE, LABOUR AND INDUSTRY—Freedom of labour

and trade should be secured. In consequence, all monopolies should be taken from trade-companies, as well as other privileges of the kind. No custom-houses should exist except on the frontier.

LIBERTY OF RELIGION—The Catholic faith should be the only dominant religion in France, but all other religions shall be tolerated, and persons who are not Catholics shall be reinstated in their properties and civil rights.

LIBERTY OF THE PRESS, INVIOLABILITY OF LETTERS IN THE POST OFFICE—The liberty of the press shall be secured, and a law shall fix beforehand the restrictions that may be established in the interest of the public. No works but such as treat of religious doctrine shall be liable to ecclesiastical censorship; in the case of all others, it shall be sufficient that the names of the author and printer are known. Many demand that charges against the press be tried before jury.

All the *cahiers* insist energetically on the inviolability of secrets confided to the post, so that private letters may never be brought in accusation against individuals. The opening of letters, say they, bluntly, is the most odious form of espionage, as it violates the public faith.

EDUCATION—The *cahiers* of the nobility confine themselves to recommending that all proper means be taken to spread education, both in towns and in the country, and that each boy be taught with a view to his future vocation. They insist on the necessity of teaching children the political rights and duties of the citizen, and suggest that a catechism on the principal points of the Constitution be used in schools. They do not, however, point out any means to be used to facilitate and spread education. They merely demand educational establishments for the children of the poor nobility.

CARE TO BE TAKEN OF THE PEOPLE—Many of the *cahiers* demand that the people be treated with more consideration. They exclaim against the police regulations, in virtue of which they say hosts of mechanics and useful citizens are daily thrust into prisons and jails without any regular commitment, and often on mere suspicions, a manifest violation of natural liberty. All the *cahiers* demand that *corvées* be definitely abolished. A majority of bailiwicks desire that rights of banality and toll be made redeemable. Many demand that the collection of various feudal dues be rendered less oppressive, and that the freehold duty be abolished. One *cahier* observes that the government is interested in facilitating the purchase and sale of lands. This is precisely the reason that will soon be urged for abolishing at a blow all seigneurial rights, and throwing all mainmortable lands into the market. Many *cahiers* ask that the right of pigeon-houses be rendered less prejudicial to agriculture. As for the establishments for the preservation of the King's game, known by the name of captainries, they demand their immediate abolition, as being subversive of the rights of property. They desire to see, in lieu of the present taxes, new ones established which shall be less onerous to the people.

The nobility demand that an effort be made to disseminate plenty and comfort throughout the rural districts; that looms and factories of coarse stuffs be established in the villages, so as to occupy the country people during the idle season; that in each bailiwick public storehouses be founded, under the inspection of the provincial governments, to provide for seasons of famine, and sustain the regularity of prices; that attempts be made to improve agriculture and better the condition of the country parts; that more public works be undertaken, and especially that marshes be drained, and means taken to guard against inundations, etc.; finally, that special encouragements be offered to agriculture and trade in all the provinces.

The *cahiers* suggest that, instead of the present hospitals, small establishments of the kind be founded in every district; that the poorhouses be abolished, and replaced by workhouses; that a charitable fund be placed at the disposal of the Provincial Estates; that surgeons, physicians, and midwives be appointed for every county to tend the poor gratuitously, and paid by the province; that the Courts of Justice should always be open to the poor, free of charge; that thought be taken for the establishment of blind, deaf and dumb asylums, foundling-hospitals, etc.

In all these matters the nobility express their general views as to what reforms are needed; they do not enter into details. It is easy to see that they have been less frequently brought into contact with the poor than the lower order of clergy, and that, having seen less of their sufferings, they have reflected less on the subject of a remedy.

OF ELIGIBILITY TO OFFICE, OF THE HIERARCHY OF RANKS, AND OF THE HONORARY PRIVILEGES OF THE NOBILITY—It is chiefly, or rather it is only when they come to deal with distinctions of rank and class divisions that the nobles turn their backs on the prevailing spirit of reform. They make important concessions, but, on the whole, they adhere to the spirit of the old order. They feel that they are fighting for life. Their *cahiers* thus demand energetically that the nobility and the clergy be maintained as distinct orders. They even desire that a method be devised for preserving the purity of the order of the nobility; that, for instance, the practice of selling titles or coupling them with certain offices be prohibited, and that rank be the reward of long and meritorious services rendered to the State. They wish that all the false nobles could be found out and prosecuted. All the *cahiers,* in short, demand that the nobility be maintained in all its honours. Some think it would be well for men of rank to wear a distinctive badge.

Nothing could be more characteristic than such a demand; nothing could indicate more plainly the similarity between the noble and the commoner. Generally speaking, the nobility, while abandoning many of their beneficial rights, cling with anxiety and warmth to those which are purely honorary. They want not only to preserve those which they possess, but also to invent new ones. So conscious were they that they were being dragged into the vortex of democracy: so terribly did they dread perishing there. Singular fact! Their instinct warned them of the danger, but they never perceived it.

As to the distribution of office, the nobility demand that posts in the magistracy be no longer sold, but that any citizen of suitable age and capacity be eligible as a candidate to be presented by the nation to the King. In respect to military rank, a majority of the *cahiers* are against excluding the Third Estate, and conceive that a man who has deserved well of his country ought to be able to attain the highest rank. Several *cahiers* say, "The order of the nobility disapproves all laws which close the door of military preferment to the Order of the Third Estate." Some few, however, suggest that noblemen alone should have the right of entering the army as officers without passing through the inferior grades. Nearly all the *cahiers* demand that uniform rules be established with regard to promotion, that advancement be not wholly obtained by favour, and that, with the exception of the highest posts, promotion proceed by seniority.

As for clerical functions, they demand that elections be re-established for the distribution of livings, or, at all events, that the King appoint a committee to guide him in distributing ecclesiastical preferment.

They say that henceforth pensions must be granted with more discrimination, and not accumulated in certain families; that no citizen must receive two pensions, or draw pay for two offices at once; that survivorships must be abolished.

CHURCH AND CLERGY—When they have done with their own rights and peculiar constitution, and turn to the privileges and constitution of the Church, the nobility are not so timid; they have a very sharp eye for abuses.

They demand that the clergy be deprived of all exemptions from taxes; that they pay their debts, and do not call upon the nation to pay them; that the monastic orders be thoroughly reformed. Most of the *cahiers* declare that these institutions have departed from the spirit of their founders.

Most of the bailiwicks desire that tithes be rendered less injurious to agriculture; several demand their entire abolition. One *cahier* says that "tithes are for the most part exacted by those curés who give themselves the least trouble to supply their flocks with spiritual food." The second Order, as is seen, handled the first unceremoniously. Nor was it more respectful in dealing with the Church itself. Many bailiwicks formally assert the right of the Estates-General to suppress certain religious orders, and apply their property to other uses. Seventeen bailiwicks declare that the Estates-General may regulate ecclesiastical discipline. Many say that there are too many fête days; that they injure agriculture, and favour drunkenness; that, in consequence, a great number of them must be suppressed, and Sundays kept instead.

POLITICAL RIGHTS—As to these, the *cahiers* recognise the right of all Frenchman to take part directly or indirectly in the government, that is to say to be electors and eligible. But this right is restricted by the distinction of ranks; that is to say no one can be elected but by and for his Order. This principle laid out, representation should be so devised as to secure to each Order an active share in the public affairs.

Opinions are divided as to the way of taking votes in the assembly of the Estates-General: a majority advocate voting by Order, others think this rule ought not to apply to questions of taxation, and others, again, object to it altogether. These latter say, "Each member shall have a vote, and all questions shall be decided by a majority of votes. This is the only rational plan, and the only one that can extinguish that *esprit de corps* which has been the only source of our misfortunes, draw men together, and lead them to the result which the nation is entitled to expect of an assembly in which patriotism and the virtues are enlightened by learning." Still, as this innovation might be fraught with danger if hastily introduced in the present state of the public mind, many are for postponing its adoption to subsequent assemblies of the Estates-General. In any event, the nobility demand that each Order preserve the dignity that is meet in Frenchmen; that, consequently, the old humiliating forms which were imposed on the Third Estate—such as bending the knee—be abolished. One *cahier* says that the "sight of one man on his knees before another is offensive to the dignity of man, and indicates an unnatural inequality among men whose essential rights are the same."

OF THE FORM OF GOVERNMENT AND ITS CONSTITUTIONAL PRINCIPLES —As to the form of government, the nobility demand the maintenance of royalty, the preservation of legislative, judicial, and executive powers in the hands of the King, but, at the same time, the establishment of fundamental laws for the purpose of guarding the rights of the nation against the exercise of arbitrary power.

Consequently, all the *cahiers* proclaim that the nation is entitled to be represented in the Estates-General, which body must be numerous enough to secure its independence. They desire that these Estates meet at periodical intervals, and at every change of monarch without special summons. Many bailiwicks express a wish to see this assembly permanent. If the

Estates-General are not convened at the time appointed, it ought to be lawful to refuse to pay taxes. Some *cahiers* propose that during the interval between the sessions of the Estates a small committee be entrusted with the duty of watching the administration; but the bulk oppose this scheme flatly, on the ground that such a committee would be unconstitutional. The reason they allege is curious. They say there would be reason to fear that so small a body could easily be seduced by government.

The nobility deny to Ministers the right of dissolving the assembly, and propose that they be prosecuted before the courts when they disturb it with their intrigues; they desire that no official, or person in any way dependent on government, shall be a deputy; that the persons of deputies shall be inviolable, and that they shall not be liable to account for opinions expressed in debate; finally, that all sittings of the assembly shall be public, and that the nation be made a spectator by printing the debates.

The nobility unanimously demand that the principles which must govern the State administration be applied to the administration of every portion of the national territory; hence, that in every province, district, and parish, assemblies be established composed of members freely elected for a limited period.

Many *cahiers* think that the offices of Intendant and receiver-general should be abolished; all are of opinion that thenceforth the business of distributing taxes, and managing provincial business, should be left to the provincial assemblies. They advise that a similar plan be adopted with regard to county and parochial assemblies, which henceforth should be under the control of the Provincial Estates.

DIVISION OF POWERS: LEGISLATIVE POWER—In dividing power between the assembled nation and the King, the nobility ask that no law shall take effect until it has been sanctioned by the Estates-General and the King, and recorded in the registers of the courts appointed to enforce it; that the business of establishing and fixing the quotas of taxes shall belong exclusively to the Estates-General; that subsidies voted shall only be considered as having been appropriated for the interval between one session of the Estates and another; that all taxes, established or levied without the consent of the Estates, shall be deemed illegal, and that all Ministers and Collectors who shall have ordered or levied such taxes shall be prosecuted for extortion; that, on the same principle, no loan shall be contracted without the consent of the Estates-General, but that a limited credit shall be opened by the Estates, to be used by government in case of war or sudden calamity, until a new session of the Estates can be called; that all the national treasuries shall be under the supervision of the Estates; that the expenses of each department shall be fixed by them, and that the most careful precautions shall be taken to prevent any appropriation being exceeded.

Most of the *cahiers* demand the suppression of those vexatious imposts known by the names of insinuation dues, *centiéme denier*, ratification dues, and comprised under the title of *régie* of the King's domains (one *cahier* says: "The word *régie* would alone suffice to condemn them, since it implies that property which actually belongs to citizens is owned by the King"); that all the public domains which are not sold shall be placed under the government of the Provincial Estates, and that no ordinance or edict for raising extraordinary taxes shall be issued, except with the consent of the three Orders of the nation.

The idea of the nobility obviously was to transfer the whole administration of the finances, including loans, taxes, and this class of imposts, to the nation as represented by the general and provincial assemblies.

JUDICIAL POWER—In the same way, the organisation of the judiciary tends to make the power of the judges largely dependent upon the assembled nation. Thus several *cahiers* declare:

"That magistrates shall be responsible for their acts to the assembled nation;" that they shall only be dismissed with the consent of the Estates-General; that no court shall, on any pretext whatever, be disturbed in the exercise of its functions without the consent of these Estates; that delinquencies of the Court of Cassation and of the parlements shall be judged by these Estates. Most of the *cahiers* recommend that no judges but such as the people present for office be appointed by the King.

EXECUTIVE POWER—This is wholly reserved to the King, but it is limited in order to prevent abuses.

Thus, as to the administration, the *cahiers* demand that the accounts of the various departments be printed and made public, and that the Ministers be responsible to the nation assembled; and in like manner, that the King be bound to communicate his intentions to the Estates-General before he can employ the troops on foreign service. At home, the troops shall not be used against the people without a requisition from the Estates-General. The standing army shall be limited; and in ordinary seasons, two thirds only shall be kept in effective service. As to the foreign troops which the King may have in his service, they must be kept away from the heart of the kingdom, and stationed on the frontier.

The most striking feature of the *cahiers* of the nobility—a feature which no extract can reproduce—is the perfect harmony which exists between these noblemen and their age. They are imbued with its spirit and speak its language. They speak of "the inalienable rights of man," "principles inherent to the social compact." In treating of individuals, they speak of their rights; in alluding to society they talk of its duties. Political principles seem to them "as absolute as moral truths, both the one and the other having reason for their basis." When they want to abolish the remains of serfdom, they say they must "efface the last traces of human degradation." They sometimes call Louis XVI a "citizen King," and constantly allude to the crime of "high treason against the nation," with which they are so soon themselves to be charged. In their eyes, as in those of everyone else, public education seems the grand panacea, and its director must be the State. One *cahier* says that "the Estates-General will give their attention to forming the national character by modifying the education of children." Like their contemporaries, they are fond of uniformity in legislative measures, always excepting everything that concerns the existence of the Orders. They seek a uniform administration, uniform laws, etc., as ardently as the Third Estate. They call for all kinds of reforms, and those radical enough. They are for abolishing or transforming all the taxes without exception, and the whole judicial system, with the exception of the seigneurial courts, which only need improvement. Like all other Frenchmen, they regard France as a trial field—a sort of political model farm—

in which everything should be tried, everything turned upside down, except the little spot in which their particular privileges grow. To their honour, it may even be said that they did not wholly spare that spot. In a word, it is seen from these *cahiers* that the only thing the nobles lacked to effect the Revolution was the rank of commoners.

45 (page 135) *Example of the religious government of an ec-clesiastical province in the middle of the eighteenth century*

1. The archbishop.
2. Seven vicars-general.
3. Two ecclesiastical courts called officialities: the one, known as the "metropolitan officiality", having cognisance of all sentences of the suffragans; the other, known as the "diocesan officiality", having cognisance, first, of all personal affairs among the clergy, and, secondly, of all disputes regarding the validity of marriages, in reference to the sacrament. This last tribunal is composed of two judges: there are attorneys and notaries attached to it.
4. Two fiscal courts: one, styled the diocesan office, has original jurisdiction over all disputes which may arise respecting the taxes of the clergy in the diocese (the clergy, as is known, imposed their own taxes). This tribunal consisted of the archbishop, presiding, and six other priests. The other court hears appeals from the other diocesan offices of the ecclesiastical province. All these courts admit lawyers, and hear cases pleaded in due form.

46 (page 136) *Spirit of the clergy in the Provincial Estates and assemblies*

What I say in the text of the Estates of Languedoc applies equally to the Provincial Estates which assembled in 1779 and 1787, especially those of Haute Guienne. The members of the clergy are distinguished in this assembly for their learning, their activity, their liberality. The proposition to make the reports of the assembly public comes from the Bishop of Rodez.

47 (page 137)

This liberal tendency of the clergy in political matters, which was evidenced in 1789, was not the fruit of the excitement of the moment; it was of old standing. It was witnessed in Berri in 1779, when the clergy offered 68,000 *livres* as a free gift if the provincial administration were allowed to subsist.

## 48 (page 139)

Note that political society was disjointed, but that civil society still held together. In the heart of the different classes individuals were linked together; there even subsisted some trace of the old bond of union between seigneurs and people. These peculiarities of civil society had their influence on politics; men thus united formed irregular and ill-organised masses, but bodies that were certain to be found refractory by government. The Revolution burst these ties, and substituted no political bonds in their stead; it thus paved the way for both equality and servitude.

## 49 (page 139) *Example of the tone in which the courts spoke of certain arbitrary measures*

It appears from a memorial laid before the Controller-General by the Intendant of the district of Paris, that it was the custom of that district that each parish should have two Syndics, one elected by the people in an assembly over which the sub-delegate presided, the other appointed by the Intendant, and directed to superintend his colleague. A quarrel took place between the two Syndics of the parish of Rueil, the one who was elected refusing to obey his colleague. The Intendant induced M. de Breteuil to imprison the refractory Syndic for a fortnight in the prison of La Force; on his liberation he was discharged, and a new Syndic appointed in his stead. Thereupon the Syndic appealed to the parlement. I have not been able to find the conclusion of the proceedings, but the parlement took occasion to declare that the imprisonment of the Syndic and the nullification of his election could not but be considered "arbitrary and despotic acts". The courts were sometimes badly muzzled in those days.

## 50 (page 142)

The educated and wealthy classes, the *bourgeoisie* included,

were far from being oppressed or enslaved under the old régime,
On the contrary, they had generally too much freedom; for the
Crown could not prevent them from securing their own position
at the sacrifice of the people's, and, indeed, almost always felt
bound to purchase their good will or soothe their animosity by
abandoning the people to their mercy. It may be said that a
Frenchman belonging to this class in the eighteenth century
was better able to resist government and protect himself than
an Englishman of the same period would have been in the like
case. The Crown felt bound to use more tenderness and deal
more gently with him than the English government would
have done to a man of the same standing. So wrong it is to
confound independence with liberty. No one is less independent
than a citizen of a free state.

### 51 (page 142)   *A reason which often compelled the government of the old order to use moderation*

In ordinary times, the most perilous acts for governments
are the augmentation of old or the creation of new taxes. In
olden times, when a King had expensive tastes, when he rushed
into wild political schemes, when he let his finances fall into
disorder, or when he needed large sums of money to sustain
himself by gaining over his opponents, by paying heavy salaries
that were not earned, by keeping numerous armies on foot, by
undertaking extensive works, etc., he was obliged to have recourse to taxation, and this at once aroused all classes, especially
that one which achieves violent revolutions—the people. Nowadays, in the same circumstances, loans are effected which are
not immediately felt, and whose burden falls on the next generation.

### 52 (page 144)

One of the many examples of this is to be found in the
*election* of Mayence. The chief domains of that *election* were
farmed out to farmers-general, who hired as sub-farmers small
wretched peasants, who had nothing in the world, and to whom
the most necessary farm tools had to be furnished. It is easy
to understand how creditors of this stamp would deal harshly

with the farmers or debtors of the feudal seigneur whom they represented, and would render the feudal tenure more oppressive than it had been in the Middle Ages.

### 53 (page 144)  *Another example*

The inhabitants of Montbazon had entered on the *taille*-roll the stewards of a duchy owned by the Prince of Rohan, in whose name it was worked. The Prince, who was no doubt very rich, not noly has "this abuse", as he calls it, corrected, but recovers a sum of 5344 *livres* 15 *sous*, which he had been wrongfully made to pay, and has the same charged to the inhabitants.

### 54 (page 147)  *Example of the effect of the pecuniary rights of the clergy in alienating the affections of those whose isolation should have made them friends of the Church*

The curé of Noisai declares that the people are bound to repair his barn and wine-press, and proposes that a local tax be imposed for the purpose. The Intendant replies that the people are only bound to repair the parson's house; the curé, who seems more attentive to his farm than to his flock, must himself repair his barn and wine-press. (1767.)

### 55 (page 149)

The following passage is taken from a clear and moderate memorial presented in 1788 by the peasantry to a provincial assembly: "To the other grievances incident to the collection of the *taille* must be added that of the bailiff's followers. They usually appear five times during the levy. They are, in general, invalid soldiers or Swiss. At each visit they remain four or five days in the parish, and for each of them 36 *sous* a day are added to the tax-levy. As for the distribution of the tax, we will not expose the well-known abuses of authority, or the bad effects of a distribution made by persons who are often incapable, and almost invariably partial and vindictive. These causes have, however, been a source of trouble and strife. They have led to lawsuits which have been very costly to litigants, and very advantageous to the places where the courts sit."

56 (page 150)   *Superiority of the methods used in the* pays d'états *admitted by officials of the central government itself*

In a confidential letter dated 3rd June, 1772, and addressed by the Director of Taxes to the Intendant, it is stated, "In the *pays d'états* the imposition is a fixed percentage, which is exacted and really paid by the taxable. This percentage is raised in the levy in proportion to the increase in the total required by the King (a million, for instance, instead of 900,000 *livres*). This is a very simple matter. In our districts, on the contrary, the tax is personal, and, to a certain degree, arbitrary. Some pay what they owe, others only half, others a third, others a quarter, and some nothing at all. How is it possible to increase such a tax one ninth, for instance?"

57 (page 152)   *Arbitrary imprisonment for* corvées

Example—It is stated in a letter to the High Provost in 1768, "I ordered three men to be arrested yesterday on the requisition of M. C., the assistant engineer, for not having performed their *corvée*. The affair made quite a stir among the women of the village, who cried, 'Nobody thinks of the poor people when the *corvée* is in question; nobody cares how they live—do you see?' "

58 (page 153)   *Of the manner in which the privileged classes originally understood the progress of civilisation in reference to roads*

The Count of K., in a letter to the Intendant, complains of the want of zeal with which a road that is to pass near his place is prosecuted. He says it is the fault of the sub-delegate, who is not energetic enough, and does not force the peasantry to perform their *corvées*.

59 (page 153)

There were two means of making roads. One was by *corvées* for all heavy work requiring mere manual labour; the other—and the least valuable resource—was by imposing a general tax, whose proceeds were placed at the disposal of the Department of Bridges and Roads for the construction of scientific works. The privileged classes, that is to say the principal land-holders, who were of course the parties most interested in the roads, had nothing to do with *corvées*; and as the general tax in favour of the Bridge and Road Department was always joined with the *taille*, and levied on those who paid it, they escaped that too.

60 (page 153)  *Instance of* corvées *for the removal of convicts*

A letter dated 1761, and addressed to the Intendant by the commissioner of the chain-service, states that the peasants were forced to transport the convicts in carts; that they did so very reluctantly; that they were often maltreated by the keepers of the convicts, "who," says the letter, "are coarse, brutal men, while the peasants, who dislike this duty, are often insolent."

61 (page 153)

Turgot's sketches of the inconveniences and annoyances of *corvées* for the transportation of military baggage do not seem to me exaggerated now that I have read the documents bearing on the subject. He says, among other things, that the first inconvenience of the system is the extreme inequality with which this heavy burden is borne. It falls wholly on a small number of parishes, who are exposed to it by the misfortune of their position. The distance to be traversed is often five, six, and sometimes ten or fifteen leagues; three days are consumed in the journey and the return. The sum allowed is not one fifth the value of the labour. These *corvées* are almost invariably required in summer during harvest time. The oxen are almost always overdriven, and often come home sick, so that many farmers prefer paying fifteen or twenty *livres* to furnishing a cart and four oxen. The work is done in a most disorderly manner; the peasantry are constantly prey to the violence of the soldiery. Officers almost always exact more than the law allows: they sometimes compel the farmers to yoke saddle horses to carts, whereby the animals are often lamed. Soldiers will insist on riding on carts that are already heavily laden; in their impatience at the slow gait of the oxen, they will prick them with their swords, and if the farmer objects he is very roughly handled.

62 (page 153)   *Example of the use of* corvées *for every need*

The marine Intendant of Rochefort complains that the peasants are indisposed to perform their *corvées* by carting the timber that has been purchased by the naval purveyors in the various provinces. (This correspondence shows that the peasants were, in fact, still—1755—bound to *corvées* of this kind, for which the Intendant fixed their remuneration.) The Minister of Marine sends the letter to the Intendant of Tours, and says that the carts required must be supplied. The Intendant, M. Ducluzel, refuses to sanction *corvées* of this nature. The Minister of Marine writes him a threatening letter, in which he notifies him that he will apprize the King of his resistance. The Intendant replies directly (11th December, 1775), and states firmly that during the whole ten years of his service as Intendant at Tours he has always refused to authorise these *corvées* in consequence of the abuses they involve—abuses which the rates of wages do not compensate; "for," says he, "the cattle are often lamed by drawing heavy logs over roads as bad as the weather in which this service is usually required of them." The secret of this Intendant's firmness seems to have been a letter of M. Turgot's, filed with the correspondence, and dated 30th July, 1774, when Turgot entered the ministry; the letter states that Turgot never sanctioned these *corvées* at Limoges, and approves M. Ducluzel for refusing to sanction them at Tours.

Other portions of this correspondence show that purveyors of timber frequently exacted these *corvées* without being authorised to do so by a bargain with the State. They saved at least a third in freight. A sub-delegate gives the following instance of this profit: "Distance to draw the logs from the place where they are cut to the river, over roads almost impassable, six leagues; time consumed, two days. The *corvéables* are paid at the rate of six *liards* a league per cubic foot; they will thus receive 13 *fs*. 10 *s*. for the journey, which will barely cover the expenses of the farmer, his assistant, and the cattle yoked to his cart. He loses his own time, his trouble, and the labour of his cattle."

On 17th May, 1776, a positive order of the King to insist

on this *corvée* is intimated to the Intendant by the Minister. M. Ducluzel having died, his successor, M. L'Escalopier, hastens to obey, and to promulgate an ordinance stating that "the sub-delegate is empowered to distribute the duty among the parishes; and all persons liable to *corvées* in the said parishes are hereby ordered to be present, at the hour directed by the Syndics, at the place where the timber lies, and to cart it at the rate that shall fixed by the sub-delegate."

63 (page 155) *Instance of the manner in which the peasantry were often treated*

1768. The King remits two thousand francs of the *taille* to the parish of Chapelle Blanche, near Saumur. The curé claims a portion of this sum to build a steeple, and so rid himself of the noise of the bells, which disturbs him in his parsonage. The inhabitants object and resist. The sub-delegate takes the side of the curé, and has three of the principal inhabitants arrested at night, and locked up in jail.

Another example: Order of the King to imprison for two days a woman who has insulted two troopers of the horse police. Another to imprison for a fortnight a stocking-maker who has spoken ill of the horse police. In this case the Intendant replies that he has already had the fellow arrested, for which he is warmly praised by the Minister. The police, it seems, had been insulted in consequence of the arrests of beggars, which had shocked people. When the Intendant arrested the stocking-maker, he gave out that any person thereafter insulting the police would be still more severely punished.

The correspondence between Intendant and sub-delegates (1760-1770) shows that the former ordered the arrest of mischievous persons, not to bring them to trial, but to get them out of the way. The sub-delegate asks permission to keep two dangerous beggars he has arrested in perpetual confinement. A father protests against the imprisonment of his son, who has been arrested as a vagabond because he travelled without papers. A landowner of X. demands that a neighbour of his, who has lately come to settle in his parish, whom he aided, but who is conducting himself badly towards him and annoying him, be forthwith arrested. The Intendant of Paris begs his colleague of Rouen to oblige him in this matter, as the petitioner is his friend.

To someone who desired to have some beggars set at liberty, the Intendant replied that "poorhouses must not be considered prisons, but mere establishments intended for the detention of beggars and vagabonds by way of *administrative correction*." This idea found its way into the Penal Code. So well preserved have been the notions of the old régime in this matter.

## 64 (page 162)

It has been said that the character of the philosophy of the eighteenth century was a sort of adoration of human intellect, an unlimited confidence in its power to transform at will laws, institutions, customs. To be accurate, it must be said that the human intellect which some of these philosophers adored was simply their own. They showed, in fact, an uncommon want of faith in the wisdom of the masses. I could mention several who despised the public almost as heartily as they despised the Deity. Towards the latter they evinced the pride of rivals— the former they treated with the pride of parvenus. They were as far from real and respectful submission to the will of the majority as from submission to the will of God. Nearly all subsequent revolutionaries have borne the same character. Very different from this is the respect shown by Englishmen and Americans for the sentiments of the majority of their fellow citizens. Their intellect is proud and self-reliant, but never insolent; and it has led to liberty, while ours has done little but invent new forms of servitude.

## 65 (page 173)

Frederick the Great says in his *Memoirs*, "The Fontenelles, the Voltaires, the Hobbeses, the Collinses, the Shaftesburys, the Bolingbrokes—all these great men dealt a deadly blow to religion. Men began to examine what they had stupidly adored. Intellect overthrew superstition. Fables that had long been believed fell into disgust. Deism made many converts. If Epicureanism was fatal to the idolatrous worship of the pagans, Deism was equally fatal to the Judicial visions of our ancestry. The

liberty of thought which reigned in England was very favourable to the progress of philosophy."

It may be here seen that Frederick the Great, at the time he
wrote these lines, that is to say, in the middle of the eighteenth
century, regarded England as the centre of irreligious doctrines.
A still more striking fact is the total ignorance displayed by one
of the most enlightened and experienced sovereigns of history
of the political utility of religion. The faults of his masters had
injured the natural qualities of his mind.

66 (page 193)

A similar spirit of progress manifested itself at the same time
in Germany, and there, as in France, was accompanied by a
desire for a change of institutions. See the picture which a
German historian draws of the state of his country at that time:

"During the second half of the eighteenth century," says he,
"the new spirit of the age has been introduced even into ecclesiastical territory, on which reforms are commenced. Industry
and tolerance penetrate into every corner of it; it is reached by
the enlightened absolutism which has already mastered the
greater states. And it must be acknowledged that at no period
during the century has the territory of the Church been ruled
by sovereigns as worthy of esteem and respect as those who
figured during the ten years which preceded the French Revolution."

Note how this sketch resembles France, where progress and
reform took a start at the same moment, and the men who
were most worthy of governing appeared just when the
Revolution was about to devour them all.

Note, also, how visibly this part of Germany was drawn into
the French movement of civilisation and politics.

67 (page 194) *How the organisation of the English courts
proves that institutions may have made secondary faults without
failing in their original object*

Nations have a faculty of prospering in spite of imperfections
in the secondary parts of their institutions, so long as the general principles and spirit of these institutions are imbued with
vitality. This phenomenon is well illustrated by the judicial

organisation of England during the last century, as we find it in Blackstone.

Two anomalies at once meet the eye: 1st. The laws differ; 2nd. They are carried into effect by different tribunals.

1st. As to the laws:

1. One set of laws is in force for England proper, another for Scotland, another for Ireland, another for certain European possessions of Great Britain, such as the Isle of Man and the Channel Islands, others for the colonies.

2. In England alone four systems of law are in use: customary law, statute law, Roman law, equity. Customary law, again, is subdivided into general customs which apply to the whole kingdom, customs which apply to certain manors or towns, and customs which apply to certain classes—such, for instance, as the customs of merchants. Some of these customs differ widely from the others, as, for instance, those which, in opposition to the general spirit of the English laws, direct the equal division of property among children (*gavelkind*), and those more singular customs still which award a right of primogeniture to the youngest child.

2nd. As to the courts:

The law, says Blackstone, has established an infinite variety of courts. Some idea may be formed of their number from the following very brief analysis:

1. One meets first with the courts established out of England proper, such as the courts of Scotland and Ireland, which were not subordinate to the superior courts of England, though they were all, I fancy, subject to appeal to the House of Lords.

2. As to England proper, if my memory serves me, Blackstone counts, 1st. eleven kinds of courts existing at common law, of which four seem, indeed, to have fallen into disuse in his time. 2nd. Three kinds of courts exercising jurisdiction over certain cases throughout the country. 3rd. Ten kinds of special courts: one of these is local courts, created by special acts of Parliament or existing by custom, either at London or in the towns or boroughs of the provinces. These are so numerous and so varied in their systems and rules that Blackstone abandons the attempt to describe them in detail.

Thus, in England proper, if Blackstone is to be believed,

there existed at the time he wrote, that is to say, during the second half of the eighteenth century, twenty-four kinds of courts, of which several were subdivided into various species, each having a particular physiognomy. Setting aside those which seem to have fallen into disuse, there yet remain eighteen or twenty.

Now the least examination of this judicial system brings to light ever so many imperfections.

Notwithstanding the immense number of courts, there are none, it seems, close at hand, which can hear petty cases promptly and at small expense, and hence the administration of justice is embarrassing and costly. Several courts exercise jurisdiction over the same class of cases, whence troublesome doubts are thrown upon the validity of judgments. Nearly all the courts of appeal exercise original jurisdiction of one kind or another, either at common law or as equity courts. There are a variety of courts of appeal. The only point where all business centres is the House of Lords. Suits against the Crown are not distinguished from other suits, which would seem a great deformity in the eyes of most of our lawyers. Finally, all these courts judge according to four different systems of laws, one of which consists wholly of precedents, and another—equity—has no settled basis, being designed, for the most part, to contradict the customs or statutes, and to correct the obsolete or overharsh provisions of these by giving play to the discretion of the judge.

Here are astounding defects. Compare this old-fashioned and monstrous machine with our modern judiciary system, and the contrast between the simplicity, the coherence, and the logical organisation of the one will place in still bolder relief the complicated and incoherent plan of the other. Yet there does not exist a country in which, even in Blackstone's time, the great ends of justice were more fully attained than in England; not one where every man, of whatever rank, and whether his suit was against a private individual or the sovereign, was more certain of being heard, and more assured of finding in the court ample guarantees for the defence of his fortune, his liberty, and his life.

This does not indicate that the faults of the judiciary system of England served the ends of justice. It only shows that there

may exist in every judiciary system secondary faults which are
but a slight impediment to the proper transaction of business,
while there are radical faults which, though they coexist with
many secondary excellences, may not only interfere with, but
absolutely defeat the ends of justice. The former are the easiest
to detect; they are instantly noticed by common minds. One
can see them at a glance. The others are more difficult to discover, and lawyers are not always the people who perceive or
point them out.

Note, also, that the same qualities may be secondary or principal, according to the times and the political organisation
of society. In aristocratic times, all inequalities, or other contrivances to diminish the privileges of certain individuals before
the courts, to guarantee the protection of the weak against the
strong, or to give predominance to the action of the government, which naturally views disputes between its subjects with
impartiality, are leading and important features. They lose
their importance when society and political institutions point
towards democracy.

Studying the judiciary system of England by the light of this
principle, it will be discovered that while defects were allowed
to exist which rendered the administration of justice among our
neighbours obscure, complicated, slow, costly, and inconvenient,
infinite pains had been taken to protect the weak against the
strong, the subject against the monarch; and the closer the
details of the system are examined, the better will it be seen that
every citizen had been amply provided with arms for his
defence, and that matters had been so arranged as to give to
everyone the greatest possible number of guarantees against the
partiality and venality of the courts, and, above all, against
that form of venality which is both the commonest and the
most dangerous in democratic times—subserviency to the
supreme power.

In all these points of view, the English system, notwithstanding its secondary faults, appears to me superior to our own.
Ours has none of its vices, it is true, but it is not endowed with
the same excellences. It is admirable in respect of the guarantees
it offers to the citizen in suits against his neighbour, but it
fails in the particular that is most essential in a democratic

society like ours, namely, the guarantees of the individual against the State.

## 68 (page 195)  *Advantages enjoyed by the district of Paris*

This district (*généralité*) enjoyed as large advantages in respect of government charities as of taxes. For example, the Controller-General writes, on 22nd May, 1787, to the Intendant of the district of Paris, to say that the King has fixed the sum to be spent in charitable works, in the district of Paris, during the year, at 172,800 *livres*. Besides this, 100,000 *livres* are to be spent in cows to be given to farmers. This letter shows that this sum of 172,800 *livres* was to be distributed by the Intendant alone, in conformity with the general rules laid down by the government, and subject to the general approval of the Controller-General.

## 69 (page 196)

The administration of the old order comprised a multitude of different powers, which had been created—rather to help the treasury than the government—at various times, and often entrusted with the same sphere of action. Confusion and conflicts of authority could only be avoided on condition that each power should agree to do little or nothing. The moment they shook off inertia, they clashed and incommoded each other. Hence it happened that complaints of the complications of the administrative system and of the confusion of powers were much more pressing just before the Revolution than they had been thirty or forty years previous. Political institutions had grown better, not worse; but political life was more active.

## 70 (page 202)  *Arbitrary increase of the taxes*

What the King here says of the *taille* might have been said with equal truth of the *vingtièmes*, as is shown by the following correspondence. In 1772, Controller-General Terray had decided upon a considerable increase—100,000 *livres*—in the *vingtièmes* in the district of Tours. M. Ducluzel, an able administrator and a good man, shows all the grief and annoyance he feels at the step in a confidential letter, in which he says, "It is the facility with which the 250,000 *livres* were obtained by the last increase

which has doubtless suggested the cruel step, and the letter of
the month of June."

In a very confidential letter from the Director of Taxes to the
Intendant, in reference to the same matter, he says, "If you
still think the increase as aggravating and revolting, in view of
the public distress, as you were good enough to say it was, it
would be desirable that you should contrive to spare the province—which has no other defender or protector but yourself—
the supplementary tolls, which, being retroactive in their effect,
are always odious."

This correspondence likewise shows how sadly some standard rule of action was needed, and how arbitrarily matters
were managed even with honest views. Intendant and Minister
both throw the surplus tax sometimes on agriculture rather than
labour, sometimes on one branch of agriculture (vines, for instance) rather than another, according to their own ideas as to
which interest requires gentle treatment.

71 (page 203)  *Style in which Turgot speaks of the people of
the country parts in the preamble of a royal declaration*

"The country commonalties," says he, "in most parts of the
kingdom, are composed of poor, ignorant, and brutal peasants,
incapable of self-government."

72 (page 207)  *How revolutionary ideas were spontaneously ger-
minating in the men's minds under the old order*

In 1779 a lawyer begs the Council to pass an order establishing a maximum price for straw throughout the kingdom.

73 (page 208)

The chief engineer wrote to the Intendant, in 1781, on the
subject of a demand for increased indemnity: "The applicant
forgets that these indemnities are a special favour granted to
the district of Tours, and that he is fortunate in obtaining
partial repayment for his loss. If all the parties in interest were
reimbursed on the scale he proposes, four millions would not
suffice."

74 (page 214)  *Conflict of the several administrative powers in 1787*

Example—The intermediate commission of the Provincial Assembly of Ile-de-France claims the administration of the poorhouse. The Intendant insists on retaining control of it, as "it is not kept up out of the provincial funds." During the discussion, the commission applies to the intermediate commissions of other provinces for their opinion. That of Champagne, among others, replies that the same difficulty has been raised there, and that it has, in like manner, resisted the pretensions of the Intendant.


75 (page 217)

I find in the reports of the First Provincial Assembly of Ile-de-France this assertion, made by the reporter of a committee: "Hitherto the functions of Syndic have been moré onerous than honourable, and persons who possessed both means and information suitable to their rank were thus deterred from accepting the office."

# GENERAL NOTES

### Feudal rights existing at the time of the Revolution, according to the feudal lawyers of the day

I do not design to write a treatise on feudal rights, or to inquire into their origin. My object is merely to state which of them were still exercised in the eighteenth century. They have played so important a part in subsequent history, and filled so large a place in the imagination of those who have been freed from them, that I have thought it would be curious to ascertain what they really were at the time the Revolution destroyed them. With this view I have studied, first, the *terriers,* or registers of a large number of *seigneuries*, choosing those which were most recent in date in preference to the older ones. Finding that this plan led to no satisfactory results, as the feudal rights, though regulated by the same general system of laws throughout Europe, varied infinitely in matters of detail in the different provinces and cantons, I resolved to pursue a different method, which was this. The feudal rights gave rise to countless law-suits. These suits involved such questions as, How were these rights acquired? How were they lost? In what did they con-sist? Which of them required to be based on a royal patent? Which on a private contract? Which on the local custom or long-established practice? How were they valued in case of sale? What sum of money was each class supposed to represent in proportion to the others? All these had been and still were litigated questions, and a school of lawyers had devoted their whole attention to their study. Of these, several wrote during the second half of the eighteenth century, some shortly before the Revolution. They were not jurisconsults, properly so called; they were legal practitioners, whose sole aim was to furnish the profession with rules of practice for a special and unattrac-tive branch of the law. A careful study of these writers throws light on the intricate and confused details of the subject. I give below the most succinct analysis that I have been able to make of my work. It is mainly derived from the work of Edme de

Freminville, who wrote about 1750, and that of Renauldon, written in 1765, and entitled *Traité Historique et Pratique des Droits Seigneuriaux.*

The *cens* (that is to say, the perpetual rent, in money or produce, which the feudal laws impose on certain possessions) still continues, in the eighteenth century, to modify the condition of many landholders. It is still indivisible; that is to say when the property which owes the *cens* has been divided, it may be exacted from any one of the owners. It is not subject to prescription. According to some customs, the owner of a property burdened with *cens* cannot sell it without exposing himself to the *retrait censuel*; that is to say, the creditor of the *cens* may take the property by paying the same price as the other purchaser. The custom of Paris ignores this right.

*Lods et ventes* (mutation-fine)—The general rule, in those parts of France where customary law obtains, is that a mutation-fine is due on every sale of land subject to *cens*: it is a due on the sale which accrues to the seigneur. These dues differ in different customs, but they are considerable in all. They exist also in those parts of the country where written law obtains; there they amount to a sixth of the price, and are called *lods*; but the seigneur, in these districts, must prove his right. Throughout the country the *cens* creates a privilege for the seigneur, in virtue of which he is preferred to all other creditors.

*Terrage* or *champart, agrier, tasque*—These are dues in produce which the debtor of the *cens* pays to the seigneur; the quantity varies according to custom and private agreement. These dues were often met with during the eighteenth century I believe that, even where customary law obtained, *terrage* required to be founded on a contract. It was either seigneurial, or connected with the land (*foncier*). It would be superfluous to explain here the signs by which these two kinds were distinguished; suffice it to say that the latter, like ground rents, was subject to a prescription of thirty years, while the former could never be lost by prescription. Land subject to *terrage* could not be hypothecated without the consent of the seigneur.

*Bordelage*—This was a due which existed only in Nivernais and Bourbonnais, and consisted in an annual rent payable by all land subject to *cens,* in the shape of money, grain, and poultry. This due entailed very rigorous consequences: the non-payment of it for three years involved the *commise*, or confiscation of the property to the seigneur. The rights of property of debtors of *bordelage* were, moreover, inchoate: in certain cases the seigneur was entitled to their inheritance, to the exclusion of the rightful heirs. This was the most rigorous of all the dues of the feudal tenure, and its exercise had gradually been restricted to the rural districts; for, as the author says, "peasants are mules ready to carry any load."

*Marciage* was a peculiar right, only exercised in certain places. It consisted in a certain return which was paid by the possessors of property liable to *cens* on the natural death of the seigneur.

*Enfeoffed tithes*—A large portion of the tithes were still enfeoffed during the eighteenth century. In general, they could only be claimed in virtue of a contract, and did not result from the mere fact of the land being seigneurial.

*Parcières* were dues levied on the harvest. They bore some resemblance to the *champart* and enfeoffed tithes, and were chiefly in use in Bourbonnais and Auvergne.

*Carpot*, a due peculiar to Bourbonnais, was to vines what *champart* was to arable land—a right to a portion of the produce. It was one quarter of the vintage.

*Serfdom*—Those customs which retain traces of serfdom are called serf customs; they are few in number. In the provinces where they obtain, no lands, or very few indeed, are wholly free from traces of serfdom. (This was written in 1765.) Serfdom, or, as the author terms it, servitude, was either personal or real.

Personal servitude was inherent in the person, and clung to him wherever he went. Wherever he removed his household, the seigneur could pursue and seize him. The authors contain several judgments of the courts based on this right. Among them, one, dated 17th June, 1760, rejects the claim of a seigneur of Nivernais upon the succession of one Pierre Truchet. Truchet was the son of a serf under the custom of Nivernais, who had married a free woman of Paris, and died there. The court rejected the seigneur's demand on the ground that Paris was a place of refuge from which serfs could not be recovered. The ground of this judgment shows that the seigneurs were entitled to claim the property of their serfs when they died in the *seigneurie*.

Real servitude flowed from the possession of certain land, and could not be got rid of except by removing from the land and residing elsewhere.

*Corvées* were a right by which the seigneur employed his vassals or their cattle for so many days for his benefit. *Corvées* at will, that is to say at the discretion of the seigneur, are wholly abolished. They were long since reduced to so many days' work in the year.

*Corvées* were either personal or real. Personal *corvées* were due by every labourer living on the *seigneurie*, each working at his own trade. Real *corvées* were attached to the possession of certain lands. Noblemen, ecclesiastics, clergymen, officials of justice, advocates, physicians, notaries, bankers, notables were exempt from *corvées*. The author quotes a judgment of 13th August, 1735, rendered in favour of a notary whose seigneur wished to compel him to work for three days in the year in drawing up deeds for the seigneur. Also another judgment of 1750, deciding that when the *corvée* is to be paid either in money or in labour, the choice rests with the debtor. *Corvées* must be substantiated by a written document. Seigneurial *corvées* had become very rare in the eighteenth century.

*Banality*—There are no banal rights in the provinces of Artois, Flanders, and Hainault. The custom of Paris strictly forbids the exercise of this right when it is not founded on a proper title. All who are domiciled in the *seigneurie* are subject to it—men of rank and ecclesiastics even oftener than others.

Independently of the banality of mills and ovens, there are many others:

1st. *Banality of Factory-mills,* such as cloth-mills, cork-mills, hemp-mills. Several customs, among others those of Anjou, Maine, and Touraine, establish this banality.

2nd. *Banality of Wine-presses*—Very few customs speak of it. That of Lorraine establishes it, as also does that of Maine.

3rd. *Banal Bull*—No custom alludes to it, but it is established by certain deeds. The same is true of banal butcheries.

Generally speaking, this second class of banalities are rarer and less favourably viewed than the others. They can only be established in virtue of a clear provision of the custom, or, in default of this, by a special agreement.

*Ban of the Vintage*—This was a police authority, which high justiciary seigneurs exercised, without special title, throughout the kingdom during the eighteenth century. It was binding on everyone. The custom of Burgundy gave to the seigneur the right of gathering his crop of grapes one day before any other vine-grower.

*Right of Banvin*—This right, which, according to the authors, a host of seigneurs exercised either in virtue of the custom or under private contracts, entitled them to sell the wine made on their own estates a certain time—usually a month or forty days—before any other vine-grower could send his wine to market. Of the greater customs, those of Tours, Anjou, Maine, and Marche are the only ones which recognise and regulate this right. A judgment of the Court of Aides, bearing date 28th August, 1751, permits innkeepers to sell wine during the *banvin*; but this was an exceptional case; they were only allowed to sell to strangers, and the wine sold must have come from the seigneur's vineyard. The customs which mention and regulate the right of *banvin* usually require that it be founded on written titles.

*Right of Blaire*—This is the right in virtue of which high justiciary seigneurs grant permission to the inhabitants of the *seigneurie* to pasture their cattle upon the lands within their jurisdiction, or waste lands. This right does not exist in those districts which are governed by written law; but it is well known within the limits of the various customs. It is found under different names in Bourbonnais, Nivernais, Auvergne, and Burgundy. It rests on the assumption that the property of all the land was originally in the seigneur, and that, after having distributed the best portions in feuds, copyholds (*censives*), and other concessions, for specific rents, he is still at liberty to grant the temporary use of those lands which are only fit for pasture. *Blairie* is established by several customs; but no one can claim it but a high justiciary, and he must be able to show either a positive title to it, or old acknowledgments of its existence, fortified by long usage.

*Tolls*—Originally, say the authors, there existed a vast num-, ber of seigneurial tolls on bridges, rivers, and roads. Louis XIV abolished many of them. In 1724, a commission appointed to inquire into the subject abolished twelve hundred of them; and in 1765 they were still being reduced. The first principle in this matter, says Renauldon, is that a toll, being a tax, must not only be established in virtue of a title, but that title must emanate from the Crown. The toll is mentioned as being *de par le roi*. One of the conditions of tolls is that there must be attached to them a tariff of the rates which all merchandise must pay. This tariff must always be approved by an Order in Council. The title, says the author, must be confirmed by uninterrupted possession. Notwithstanding the precautions taken by the legislator, the value of some tolls has largely increased of late years. I know a toll, he adds, which was farmed out for one hundred *livres* a century since, and which now brings in fourteen hundred; another, farmed out for thirty-nine thousand *livres*, now produces ninety thousand. The chief ordinances and edicts regulating tolls are the 29th title of the ordinance of 1669, and the edicts of 1683, 1693, 1724, and 1775.

The authors whom I quote, though rather prepossessed, in general, in favour of feudal rights, acknowledge that great abuses are practised in the collection of tolls.

*Ferries*—The right of ferry differs sensibly from the right of tolls. The latter is levied on merchandise only; the former on persons, cattle, and vehicles. This right cannot be exercised without the King's sanction, and the tariff of rates charged must be included in the Order in Council authorising or establishing the ferry.

*The Right of Leyde* (its name varies in different places) is an impost on merchandise sent to fairs or markets. The lawyers I am quoting say that many seigneurs erroneously consider this a right appurtenant to high justice, and purely seigneurial; whereas it is a tax which requires the sanction of the King. At any rate, the right can only be exercised by a high justiciary, who receives the fines levied in virtue thereof. And it appears that though theoretically the right of *leyde* could not be exercised except by grant from the King, it was often in part exercised in virtue of a feudal title and long usage.

It is certain that fairs could only be established by authorisation of the King.

Seigneurs need no specific title or royal grant to regulate the weights and measures that are to be used in the *seigneurie*. It suffices that the right is founded on the custom or long continued usage. The authors say that all the attempts that have been made by the Kings to introduce a uniform standard of weights and measures have been failures. No progress has been made in this matter since the customs were drawn up.

*Roads*—Rights exercised by the seigneurs over the roads.

The highways, which are called the King's roads, belong wholly to the Crown. Their establishment, their repairs, crimes committed upon them, are not within the jurisdiction of the seigneurs or their judges; but all private roads within the limits of a *seigneurie* belong, without doubt, to the high justiciary. They have entire control over them, and all crimes committed thereon, except cases reserved to the King, are within the jurisdiction of the seigneurial judges. Formerly the seigneurs were expected to keep in repair the high roads which traversed their *seigneurie*, and rights of toll, boundary, and *traverse* were granted them by way of indemnity; but the King has since taken the direction of all highways.

*Rivers*—All rivers navigable for boats or rafts belong to the King, though they traverse *seigneuries,* any title to the contrary notwithstanding (ordinance of 1669). Any rights which the seigneurs may exercise on these rivers—rights of fishing, establishing mills or bridges, or levying tolls—must have been acquired by grant from the King. Some seigneurs claim civil or police jurisdiction over these rivers; but any such rights have been usurped or obtained by fraudulent grants.

Small rivers undoubtedly belong to the seigneurs whose domain they traverse. They have the same rights of property, jurisdiction, and police, as the King has over navigable rivers. All high justiciaries are universal seigneurs of non-navigable rivers flowing through their territory. They need no better title to establish their right of property than the fact of their existence as high justiciaries. Some customs, such as that of Berri, authorise individuals to erect mills on seigneurial rivers flowing through their property without permission from the seigneur. The custom of Bretagne granted this right to noblemen. Generally, the law restricts to the high justiciary the right of granting permission to build mills within his jurisdiction. Even traverses cannot be made upon a seigneurial river, for the protection of a farm, without permission from the seigneurial judges.

*Fountains, Pumps, Retting-tanks, Ponds*—Rain falling upon the highway belongs exclusively to the high justiciary, who alone can make use of it. He can make a pond in any part of his jurisdiction, even on the property of his tenants, by paying them for the land that is submerged. This rule is distinctly laid down by several customs; among others, by those of Troyes and Nivernais. Private individuals can only have ponds on their own land; and even for this, according to several customs, they must obtain leave from the seigneur. The customs which require leave to be asked of the seigneur forbid his selling permission.

*Fishery*—The right of fishery in rivers navigable for boats or rafts belongs to the King. He alone can grant it. His judges have sole cognisance of infractions of the fishery laws. Many seigneurs, however, enjoy rights of fishery on these rivers, but they have either usurped them, or hold them by special grant from the King. As for non-navigable rivers, it is forbidden to fish therein, even with line, without the leave of the high justiciary in whose domain they flow. A judgment of 30th April, 1749, condemned a fisherman on this rule. Seigneurs themselves must obey the general regulations regarding fisheries in fishing in these rivers. The high justiciary may grant the right of fishing in his river, either as a feud, or for a yearly *cens*.

*Hunting*—The right of hunting cannot be farmed out like the right of fishery. It is a personal right. It is held to be a royal right, which even men of rank cannot exercise within their own jurisdiction, or on their own feud, without the King's permission. This doctrine is laid down in the 30th title of the ordinance of 1669. The seigneurial judges are competent to sit in all cases relative to hunting, except those which refer to the chase of *red* beasts (these are, I imagine, large game, such as stags and deer), which must be left to the royal courts.

The right of hunting is, of all seigneurial rights, the one

most carefully withheld from commoners; even the *francaleu roturier* does not carry it. The King does not grant it in his pleasures. So strict is the principle that a seigneur cannot grant leave to hunt. That is the law. But in practice seigneurs constantly grant permission to hunt, not only to men of rank but to commoners. High justiciaries may hunt throughout the limits of their jurisdiction, but they must be alone. Within these limits they are entitled to make all regulations, prohibitions, and ordinances regulating hunting. All feudal seigneurs, even without justiciary rights, may hunt within their feud. Men of rank, who have neither feud nor justiciary rights, may hunt upon the lands adjoining their residences. It has been held that a commoner who owns a park within the limits of a high justice must keep it open for the pleasures of the seigneur; but the judgment is old; it dates from 1668.

*Warrens*—None can now be established without a title. Commoners can establish warrens as well as noblemen, but none but men of rank can have forests.

*Pigeon-houses*—Certain customs restrict the right of having pigeon-houses to high justiciaries; others grant it to all owners of feuds. In Dauphiné, Brittany, and Normandy, no commoner can own a pigeon-house; no one but a noble can keep pigeons. Most severe punishments, often corporal, were inflicted on those who killed pigeons.

Such are, according to the authors quoted, the chief feudal rights, exacted during the latter half of the eighteenth century. They add that "these rights are generally established. There are a host of others, less known and less extended, which exist only in certain customs or in certain *seigneuries* in virtue of special titles." These rare or restricted rights which the authors enumerate number ninety-nine. Most of them weigh upon agriculture, being dues to the seigneur on harvests, or on the sale or transport of produce. The authors say that many of these rights were disused in their time. I fancy, however, that several of them must have been enforced in some places as late as 1789.

Having ascertained from the feudal lawyers of the eighteenth century what feudal rights were still enforced, I wished to ascertain what pecuniary value was set upon them by the men of that day.

One of the authors I have quoted, Renauldon, furnishes the requisite information. He gives a set of rules for legal functionaries to follow in appraising in inventories the various feudal rights which existed in 1765, that is to say twenty-four years before the Revolution. They are as follows:

*Rights of Jurisdiction*—He says, "Some of our customs value the right of jurisdiction, high, low, and middle (*justice haute, basse, et moyenne*), at one tenth the revenue of the land. Seigneurial jurisdictions were then highly important. Edme de Freminville thinks that, in our day, jurisdiction should not be valued higher than a twentieth of the income of the land. I think even this valuation too high."

*Honorary Rights*—Though these rights are not easily appreciated in money, our author, who is a practical man, and not easily imposed upon by appearances, advises the appraisers to value them at a very small sum.

*Seigneurial Corvées*—The author supplies rules for the valuation of *corvées*, which shows that they were still occasionally enforced. He values the day's work of an ox at twenty *sous*, and that of a man at five *sous*, besides his food. This is a fair indication of the wages paid at the time.

*Tolls*—With regard to the valuation of tolls, the author says: "No seignurial rights should be valued at a lower rate than these tolls. They are very fluctuating; and now that the King and the provinces have taken charge of the roads and bridges which are of most use to trade, many tolls have become useless, and they are being abolished daily."

*Right of Fishing and Hunting*—The right of fishery may be farmed out and regularly appraised. The right of hunting cannot be farmed out, being a personal right. It is, therefore, an honorary, not a productive right, and cannot be estimated in money.

The author then proceeds to speak of the rights of banality, *banvin, leyde, blairie,* and the space he devotes to them shows that they were the most frequently exercised and the most important of the surviving feudal rights. He adds: "There are, besides, a number of other seigneurial rights, which are met with from time to time, but it would be tedious and even impossible to enumerate them here. In the examples we have given, appraisers will find rules to guide them in estimating the rights which we have not specially valued."

*Valuation of the Cens*—Most of the customs say that the *cens* must be valued at rather more than three and three-tenths per cent. This high valuation is due to the fact that the *cens* carries with it various casual benefits, such as mutation-fines.

*Enfeoffed Tithes, Terrage*—Enfeoffed tithes cannot be valued at less than four per cent, as they involve no care, labour, or expense. When the *terrage* or *champart* carries with it mutation-fines to the seigneur, this casualty must settle the value at three and three-tenths per cent, otherwise it must be valued like the tithes.

Ground rents, bearing no mutation-fines or right of redemption—that is to say, which are not seigneurial—must be valued at five per cent.

ESTIMATE OF THE VARIOUS TENURES USED IN FRANCE BEFORE THE REVOLUTION:

We only know in France, says the author, three kinds of real estate:

1st. The *franc-aleu*, which is a freehold, exempt from all burdens, and subject to no seigneurial dues or rights, either beneficial or honorary.

*Francs-aleux* are either noble or common (*roturiers*). Noble *francs-aleux* carry with them a right of jurisdiction, or they have feuds or lands held by *cens* depending on them. They are divided according to feudal law. Common *francs-aleux* have no jurisdiction, or feuds, or lands held by *cens*. They are divided according to the ordinary rules (*roturièrement*). The author considers that the holders of *francs-aleux* are the only landholders who enjoy a complete right of property.

The *franc-aleu* was valued higher than any other kind of tenure. The customs of Auvergne and Burgundy valued it two and one-half per cent. The author thinks that three and one-third per cent would be a better valuation.

It must be noticed that common *francs-aleux*, existing within the limits of a seigneurial jurisdiction, were dependent thereon. It was not a sign of subjection to the seigneur, but an acknowledgment of the jurisdiction of courts which took the place of the royal tribunals.

2nd. Lands held by feudal tenure (*à fief*).

3rd. Lands paying *cens*, or, as they are here called in law, *rotures*.

The valuation of lands held by feudal tenure was the lower in proportion to the feudal burdens laid upon them. In some customs, and in that part of the country which was governed by written law, feuds paid nothing but "*la bouche et les main*", that is to say, feudal homage. In other customs, such as Burgundy, feuds not only owed homage, but were what was called *de danger*; that is to say, they were liable to *commise*, or feudal confiscation, when the owner took possession of them without having rendered "fealty and homage". Other customs, such as that of Paris, for instance, and many more, declared feuds subject not only to fealty and homage, but likewise to re-emption, *quint* and *requint*. Others again, such as that of Poitou and some others, burdened them with a fine on the oath of fealty (*chambellage*), and service on horseback, etc.

The first class of feuds must be valued higher than the others. The custom of Paris set them down at five per cent, which the author thinks very reasonable.

To arrive at a valuation of lands held *en roture* and those subject to *cens*, they must be divided into three classes:

1st. Lands paying the mere *cens*.

2nd. Lands liable not only to *cens,* but to other burdens.

3rd. Lands mainmortable, subject to real *taille,* to *bordelage*.

The first two classes of lands *en roture* were common enough in the eighteenth century. The third was rare. The first, says the author, must be valued higher than the second, the second than the third. Indeed, landholders of the third class can hardly be called owners, in the strict sense of the word, as they cannot alienate their property without leave from the seigneur.

*Terriers*—The feudal lawyers I have quoted furnish the following rules for drawing up or renewing the seigneurial registers called *terriers*, which I have mentioned in the text. The *terrier*, as is known, was a great register, in which all the deeds establishing rights belonging to the *seigneurie*, whether beneficial or honorary, real, personal, or mixed, were entered at length. It contained all the declarations of the copyholders, the customs of the *seigneurie*, quit-rent leases, etc. In the custom of

Paris, the authors say that seigneurs may renew their *terriers* every thirty years at the expense of the copyholders. They add, however, that "one is fortunate to find a fresh one every century". The *terrier* could not be renewed (it was a troublesome formality for all those who held under the seigneur) without obtaining an authorisation which was called *lettres à terrier*. When the *seigneurie* was within the jurisdiction of several parlements, this was obtained from the high chancellor; in other cases it was procured from the parlement. The court named the notary, before whom all vassals, noblemen and commoners, copyholders, emphyteutic lessees, and persons amenable to the seigneurial jurisdiction, were bound to appear. A plan of the *seigneurie* was required to be attached to the *terrier*.

Besides the *terriers*, there were kept in each *seigneurie* other registers called *liéves*, in which the seigneurs or their stewards entered the sums they had received from their copyholders, with their names, and the dates of the payments.

# SOME SUGGESTIONS FOR FURTHER READING

The literature of the French Revolution is of course enormous; and that on Tocqueville, though tiny by comparison, is not small. The following titles are only offered as first steps along some of the many avenues that a reading of *The Ancien Régime* opens up.

A. COBBAN. *The Social Interpretation of the French Revolution.*

D. DAKIN. *Turgot and the Ancien Régime.*

FRANKLIN L. FORD. *Robe and Sword. The Regrouping of the French Aristocracy after Louis XIV.*

P. GEYL. "French Historians For and Against the Revolution" in *Encounters In History.*

R. HERR. *Tocqueville and the Old Régime.*

G. LEFEBVRE. *The Coming of the French Revolution.* (Translated by R. R. Palmer.)
  *The French Revolution.* (Translated by E. M. Evanson, J. H. Stewart, and J. Friguglietti.)

J. LIVELEY. *The Social and Political Thought of Alexis de Tocqueville.*

K. MARTIN. *French Liberal Thought in the Eighteenth Century* (edited by J. P. Mayer).

J. P. MAYER. *Alexis de Tocqueville: A Biographical Study In Political Science.*

R. R. PALMER. *The Age of the Democratic Revolution: A Political History of Europe and America, 1760–1800.*

G. W. PIERSON. *Tocqueville and Beaumont in America.*

A. DE TOCQUEVILLE. *L' Ancien Régime et la Révolution.* (Edited by J. P. Mayer. Introduction by G. Lefebvre.)
  *The European Revolution* and *Correspondence with Gobineau.* (Edited and Translated by John Lukacs.)

*Democracy in America*. (Translated by Henry Reeve; Revised and Edited by Phillips Bradley.)

*Recollections*. (Translated by A. T. de Mattos. Edited and introduced by J. P. Mayer.)

A. YOUNG. Travels in France in 1787, 1788 and 1789.